LINGUISTIC EVIDENCE IN DATING

EARLY HEBREW POETRY

LINGUISTIC EVIDENCE IN DATING EARLY HEBREW POETRY

by

David A. Robertson

Published by

SOCIETY OF BIBLICAL LITERATURE

for

The Seminar on Form Criticism

DISSERTATION SERIES, NUMBER THREE

1972

LINGUISTIC EVIDENCE IN DATING EARLY HEBREW POETRY

by

David A. Robertson
University of California, Davis
Davis, California 95616

Ph.D., 1966
Yale University

Advisor:
Marvin H. Pope

ISBN: 978-1-628-37245-8

Library of Congress Catalog Card Number: 72-87886

TABLE OF CONTENTS

	Page
ABBREVIATIONS	vii
ABSTRACT	ix
CHAPTER ONE - INTRODUCTION	1
CHAPTER TWO - SYNTAX	7
CHAPTER THREE - MORPHOLOGY	57
CHAPTER FOUR - THE CUMULATIVE EVIDENCE	135
CHAPTER FIVE - EVALUATION	147
BIBLIOGRAPHY	157

ABBREVIATIONS

1. Publications

BH^3	Biblica Hebraica, 3rd ed., ed. Kittel-Kahle
CBQ	Catholic Biblical Quarterly
FF	Forschungen and Fortschritte
G-K-C	W. Gesenius, *Hebrew Grammar*, ed. E. Kautzsch, trans. A. E. Cowley
HUCA	Hebrew Union College Annual
JAOS	Journal of the American Oriental Society
JBL	Journal of Biblical Literature
JCS	Journal of Cuneiform Studies
JJS	Journal of Jewish Studies
JNES	Journal of Near Eastern Languages
JQR	Jewish Quarterly Review
JRAS	Journal of the Royal Asiatic Society
JTS	Journal of Theological Studies
SAYP	F. M. Cross, Jr., *Studies in Ancient Yahwistic Poetry*
VT	Vetus Testamentum
ZAW	Zeitschrift für die alttestamentliche Wissenschaft
ZDMG	Zeitschrift der deutschen morgenländischen Gesellschaft

2. Miscellaneous

f	feminine
G	The Septuagint
Hie	Hieronymus
K	Kethibh
m	masculine
MT	The Massoretic Text
Q	Qere
s	singular
S	The Peshitta
Sam	The Samaritan Pentateuch
V	The Vulgate

ABSTRACT

The purpose of this study is to determine whether any biblical poetry can be dated to the early period of Israelite historical development, the period from the thirteenth to the tenth century. Sound methodology requires that first we write a linguistic history of poetic Hebrew on the basis of poetry datable by other than linguistic evidence, and then compare with this poetry of known date poetry of unknown date. But there is a major obstacle to the application of this methodology to the dating of early Hebrew poetry: while there is an abundance of poetry datable by non-linguistic evidence by which to establish the nature of poetic Hebrew during and after the eighth century, labelled in this study "standard" poetic Hebrew, there are no poems that can with any real confidence be dated by non-linguistic evidence to the early period. Therefore, the nature of "early" poetic Hebrew must be reconstructed by a correlation of rare grammatical features of biblical poetry as a whole with Ugaritic poetry and the Amarna glosses.

After early poetic Hebrew has been thus reconstructed, the morphological and syntactic differences between it and standard poetic Hebrew are delineated. The two poetic dialects differ in the distribution of the two finite verbal conjugations in past narrative, in the preservation of the y/w of a final y/w root when it opens a syllable, and in the use of *ze/zō/zū* as relative pronouns, of the affixes *-anhū* and *-annū*, of the 3mpl pronominal suffix *-mw*, of the affixes *-y* and *-w*, and of enclitic *-m*.

Then a survey of all poetry of unknown date is made to determine which poems resemble early poetry and which standard poetry. When the syntactical and morphological differences are considered one by one, Ex 15, Jud 5, Hab 3, 2 S 22 = Ps 18, Dt 32 and Job resemble early poetry in the distribution of the prefix and suffix conjugations in past narrative, and Ex 15 resembles early poetry in the use of the 3mpl suffix *-mw*. When these same differences are considered cumulatively, Ex 15, Dt 32, and Job resemble early poetry. All of these poems except Ex 15, however, contain significant evidence of archaizing (that is, grammatical forms characteristic of standard poetic Hebrew but thought not to exist in early poetic Hebrew are found in them). Therefore, Ex 15 is the only poem which unambiguously resembles early poetry.

Two methodological problems are given special attention. One is raised by the possibility that forms characteristic of standard poetic Hebrew were already present in early poetic Hebrew. If they were, then the tests used to detect archaizing are invalid, and the evidence against an early date for Jud 5, Hab 3, 2 S 22 = Ps 18, Dt 32 and Job must be ruled out of court. The other arises because most of the poetry by which the nature of standard poetic Hebrew is established is prophetic in form, while all of the poetry significantly resembling early poetry is composed in hymnic (or a close imitation of hymnic) style. As a result, it may be that the linguistic differences between these two groups is a function not of date but of style. Therefore, an attempt is made to show that hymnic did not significantly differ from prophetic poetry during the eighth century or thereafter.

CHAPTER ONE
INTRODUCTION

The purpose of this study is to determine if any of the poetry in the Old Testament can be dated by linguistic evidence to the early phase of Israelite political, cultural and literary development, the period beginning in the thirteenth century[1] with the exodus and conquest and ending in the tenth century with the establishment of the monarchy. In dating by linguistic evidence considerations of method are of decisive significance. At the outset, then, it is best to state explicitly the methodology which is used in this study and its rationale, and to explain how it can be applied to the dating of early Hebrew poetry.

Methodology

What follows is a general statement of method, applicable to any language. The growth of a language has two aspects: addition and subtraction. Simultaneously with the accretion of new forms by internal development and by borrowing, old forms atrophy, either disappearing entirely or continuing in limited use as archaisms. Before linguistic evidence can be utilized for dating, one must chart this process of growth. As precisely as possible it is necessary to know when new forms are added and when old forms disappear. In other words, a history of the language is needed. Given the availability of documents datable on other than linguistic grounds for each of the stages of its growth, such a history can be written.

One begins by making a series of synchronic linguistic analyses of the language at periodic intervals in its development. Each synchronic description presents the dialectal form of the language at a particular historical moment. Then a diachronic analysis is made by comparing and contrasting the successive synchronic descriptions. The results of the diachronic analysis constitute a history of the language, that is, a catalogue of the consecutive dialectal forms it assumes. This history reveals its structure in the earliest written documents and its metamorphosis with the passage of time.

Given such a history it is possible to date literary documents of unknown date. First, the document to be dated is subjected to linguistic analysis. This analysis presents the dialectal form of the language written by the author of the document. Then his dialect is compared with the successive dialectal forms which the language assumes throughout its history.

1. All dates in this study are B.C.

An approximate date of the document in question can be fixed by the date of the dialectal form of the language that the dialect of the document's author most closely resembles. To take an example from English poetry, suppose one had the poetry of Shakespeare, Milton, Pope, Keats, Browning and Eliot, the date of all of which is known, and a poem of unknown date. By comparing the dialect of the poem in question with that of these poets, an approximate date could be assigned to it. If the poem resembles the poetry of Eliot, a date in the twentieth century would be probable; if Shakespeare, then a date around 1600 would be likely.

One problem involved in this type of dating demands comment, for it is such an important factor in this study. It is the problem of archaizing. Succinctly put, the problem is this: while the *terminus a quo* of a document can be determined by the presence of newly developed or borrowed forms, its *terminus ad quem* cannot necessarily be determined by the absence of such forms. The reason is that, though an author's own dialect may contain newly developed or borrowed forms, he may choose for some reason to utilize older forms. Sometimes it is possible to detect archaizing. An author may be inconsistent in using archaic forms. He may use them in ways foreign to the time when they were living. Or he may slip occasionally and employ the forms proper to his own dialect. But if he is consistent, detection is impossible.

Application to Dating Early Hebrew Poetry

In applying this methodology to the dating of early Hebrew poetry, the first task is to determine what biblical poetry can be dated on non-linguistic evidence.[2] Practically all of it comes from the prophetic books. Thus, the genuine oracles of Amos date from around 750, those of Hosea around 730, those of Micah and Isaiah around 730-700, those of Nahum, Zephaniah, Habakkuk, Obadiah, and Jeremiah from the period immediately preceding the exile, and those of Second Isaiah and Ezekiel from the exile or perhaps slightly earlier. The oracles collected in Joel, Isa 56-66, and Zech 9-14 almost certainly date to the post-exilic period. The non-genuine oracles in these prophetic books may, for the most part, be dated sometime after the genuine ones, ranging from possibly as early as c. 700 to the late post-exilic period. Since the concern here is with early poetry, it is not necessary to date these non-genuine oracles more precisely. To say that they are post-eighth century is sufficient. To this catalogue of prophetic material can be added from psalmodic types Ps 137 and the laments collected in the book of Lamentations, all of which are exilic or post-exilic.

The dating of the remainder of biblical poetry sparks fierce debate.

2. The magnitude of the linguistic differences between biblical prose and poetry prevent our utilizing the former in dating the latter.

To be sure, some areas of general agreement are discernible. Most concur in dating certain psalms (e.g. 105, 106 and 136) as well as Prv 1-9 and Ecclesiastes to the post-exilic period. But opinions on the dating of psalmodic and proverbial literature are so mobile at present that to base a linguistic analysis even on apparent scholarly consensus in these areas is like laying foundations on quicksand.

Also, there is near unanimity that a few poems are early, e.g. Gen 49, Jud 5 and 2 S 1:19-27. The main argument in favor of an early date is historical verisimilitude, and it must be admitted that this argument is cogent. But there are several uncertainties in the dating of these poems. For one thing, we know that the Hebrews habitually composed narrative poems celebrating past historical events long after those events transpired. Ps 78 rehearses the exodus but cannot be earlier than the Israelite hostilities with the Philistines, and if vv. 67-72 are not spurious, cannot be pre-davidic. To judge from Ben Sira's paean in praise of the fathers, this habit persisted until his time. In light of this propensity we must reckon with the possibility that a poet had access to early traditions, and so his poem seems to be more or less historically accurate, but wrote his poem in his own dialect. For another thing, we have no reliable estimate of how long these poems were transmitted orally before they were written down. Possibly they were first recited in an early dialect but written down centuries afterward in a later one.

Because of uncertainties like these it is circumspect to proceed on the assumption that not a single poem can be dated on non-linguistic evidence to the early period. The method outlined above requires documents datable by such evidence. But if doubt attaches to their dating, then doubt must also attach to the results obtained by the method. A rigid adherence to methodological principles is called for.

On the dating of the remainder of biblical poetry, Job, Song of Songs, Prv 10-31, and most of the psalms, including those embedded in the prophetic corpus, not even a semblance of concord has been arrived at.

In summary, abundant datable poetry is available from the middle of the eighth century until late in the post-exilic period. From it the nature of poetic Hebrew during this extended era can be reliably determined. For convenience this poetic Hebrew is labelled in this study "standard" poetic Hebrew, since it is exemplary of the poetic dialect commonly used in the Old Testament. Poetry written in this dialect is termed standard poetry and grammatical forms characteristic of it are called standard poetic forms, or simply standard forms. The term standard is not intended to convey a value judgment. It is merely a shorthand designation of the poetic Hebrew found in poetry datable by non-linguistic evidence to the eighth century and after. To be sure, the poetic Hebrew of this period manifests certain internal differences; since, however, our concern is with dating early poetry, they are irrelevant here.

But no datable poetry exists from the thirteenth to the tenth century from which to establish the nature of early poetic Hebrew. Clearly a project proposing to determine by linguistic evidence if any biblical poetry can be dated to this early period is faced with an impasse. Sound method requires that material of unknown date be compared with material of known date. To utilize such a method, then, the nature of early poetic Hebrew must be known, and poems datable to the early period on other than linguistic grounds provide the only direct access to it. But the impasse can be skirted by a flanking maneuver. Though denied direct access to a knowledge of early poetic Hebrew, an oblique route is available. Involved in this route is a reconstruction of early poetic Hebrew via a correlation of Ugaritic poetry and the Amarna glosses, on the one hand, with rare grammatical features of biblical poetry as a whole, on the other.

None of these sources is sufficient in itself. It is true that many of the rare linguistic features of biblical poetry as a whole are probably archaic. But a reconstruction of early poetic Hebrew solely on the basis of these is haphazard. That a form is rare does not necessarily mean that it is old. Only a relatively small amount of poetry has been preserved; thus, it is quite likely that a form may have been in common use throughout the biblical period and occur only a few times in the preserved corpus. Or possibly it developed late in the biblical period, or was borrowed from Aramaic or another language contiguous to Hebrew and never assimilated into the standard poetic diction. Or it may have been peculiar to a dialect not extensively represented in the canon. In short, innumerable possibilities are available for accounting for a rare form other than postulating its antiquity.

Occasionally it is possible to establish that a rare form is archaic by reference to comparative Semitic philology. But too often our knowledge of how Hebrew developed from Proto-Semitic is conjectural. What we need is some reliable means of determining which rare features are survivals from early poetic Hebrew and which are not. Because Ugaritic poetry and the Amarna glosses delineate the linguistic situation in Syria-Palestine in the period just prior to the Israelite settlement, they provide us with this means. One may confidently assume that a form rare in biblical poetry and at the same time present in one or both of these sources was once common in early poetic Hebrew.

Nor can early poetic Hebrew be convincingly reconstructed solely on the basis of Ugaritic poetry or the Amarna glosses. The value of Ugaritic is in direct proportion to the closeness of its relationship to Hebrew. The closer the relationship the more valuable it is. And, at best, it is a quite distant relative. Whether it can even be called a Canaanite dialect is debatable. Furthermore, it was written in northern Syria, not Palestine, some one to three hundred years before the Israelites appeared as a cohesive political and cultural group in Palestine. By the same reasoning the value of the Amarna glosses is enhanced, as they were written in Palestine just prior to the Israelite entry. Thus, in location and date they are far closer to early poetic Hebrew than is Ugaritic. But their value is depreciated because they are in prose. We have no justification for assuming that poetic and prose dialects were at all close at this time.[3]

The value of Ugaritic and the Amarna glosses is increased when they corroborate one another, but still confirmation is needed that a linguistic form in one or both of them was actually present in early poetic Hebrew. Rare forms of biblical poetry as a whole supply this confirmation. Therefore, by correlating Ugaritic and the Amarna glosses with rare forms of biblical poetry, early poetic Hebrew can be at least partially reconstructed. Forms characteristic of this dialect are called early poetic forms and poetry written in it early poetry. Since early poetic Hebrew is reconstructed, all of these forms refer to hypothetical entities and are used for the sake of convenience.

We have, then, as the material of known date, a reconstructed early poetic Hebrew and standard poetic Hebrew. They are alike with regard to the vast majority of linguistic phenomena. They disagree with regard to only a few, a score more or less. Only the latter are relevant for dating. Hence, the method of dating early Hebrew poetry by linguistic analysis involves a comparison of the language of poetry of unknown date with early poetic Hebrew and standard poetic Hebrew with respect to the grammatical forms which differentiate them.

Similarity between a poem of unknown date and early poetry constitutes evidence in favor of an early date; similarity between a poem of unknown date and standard poetry constitutes evidence in favor of a date in the eighth century or thereafter. Since the material of known date comes from such widely separated periods, precision in dating any given poem is not possible. It is best to think of the thirteenth and eighth centuries as poles, with the poetry of unknown date attracted to one or the other.

Granting the lack of precision in dating any given poem, the results obtained by an application of this method ought to be fairly reliable. But the possibility of archaizing must also be reckoned with, especially when forms peculiar both to early and to standard poetic Hebrew are present within the same poem.

3. We can assess to what extent they differed by reference to Num 21:14b-15, the famous quote from the Book of the Wars of Yahweh, which I, contrary to most, believe to be prose and which virtually all agree to be early. It contains the particle *'t*, the article, and the relative pronoun *'šr*, all of which are rare in the greater portion of biblical poetry of whatever date.

Definition of Linguistic

Theoretically, the term linguistic can apply to almost any aspect of the study of languages, from grammar (which includes phonology, morphology, and syntax) to lexicography, orthography and even style. This study is con-cerned with grammar only. All of the other areas must be investigated before the total effect of linguistic evidence can be assessed, but the methodologi-cal problems peculiar to each area and the enormous bulk of available material bar their consideration here. And within the area of grammar phonology must be disqualified. On the one hand, with two exceptions only, the vocalization of the pertinent texts is not open to direct observation, since the texts are written in a consonantal script. The exceptions are the Amarna glosses, written in the Akkadian syllabary, and the vowels accompanying the consonant ' in Ugaritic. In certain other cases one can make intelligent guesses about vocalization, but the margin of error is far too great for variations in vowel articulation to be of value in dating. On the other hand, although some con-sonantal changes can be charted, a preliminary investigation revealed no con-sistent differences between early and standard poetic Hebrew. Thus the term linguistic in this study refers to morphology and syntax only. Accordingly, chapter two discusses the major syntactical feature that significantly dis-tinguishes early from standard poetic Hebrew: the use of the two finite ver-bal forms in past narrative; chapter three deals with various morphological features.

Previous Studies

The debt that this study owes to W. F. Albright and many of his students is great indeed. F. M. Cross, Jr. and D. N. Freedman under his tutelage pioneered in the use of the Ugaritic and Amarna materials for dat-ing Hebrew poetry. Other of his students, especially M. Dahood, helped ini-tiate the search within Biblical Hebrew for morphemes present in Ugaritic and the Amarna glosses but not recognized by the Massoretes.[4] This study leans heavily upon all this prior research. All too often, however, the explicit formulation and rigorous execution of a methodology for testing the validity of using linguistic evidence in dating early Hebrew poetry have been neglected. As a result, many studies can be criticized for failing to provide proper con-trols. For example, if a form rare in biblical poetry as a whole occurs in Ugaritic and the Amarna glosses but also in standard poetry, it cannot with-out qualification serve as evidence of an early date. Furthermore, all too frequently the possibility of archaizing has been left unexplored. In light of these deficiencies, the principal aim of this study is to formulate and apply a methodology that will provide proper controls.

4. For the publications of these scholars consult the bibliography and see further in chapters two and three.

CHAPTER TWO
SYNTAX

Problems of Procedure

This chapter is concerned with the syntax of the verb in past narrative. Any study of the verb in Northwest Semitic, and in Hebrew in particular, is faced with several procedural problems. Some stem from the nature of the Massoretic Text.[1] In its final form it consists of three dialects, each superimposed upon the other. First, there is the dialect of the original autograph. Second, there is the dialect represented by any vowel letters which may have been added to the autograph. Third, there is the dialect represented by the vowel pointings which have been added by the Massoretes to the consonantal text.

Linguistically speaking, one dialect must be studied at a time, and the dialect we are interested in is that of the original autograph. The problem is to arrive at the text which is most nearly identical with it. Omitting the vowel points raises no problems, because it is known that they were added in the Christian era. The elimination of vowel letters, however, is a tricky business. The reason is that the practice of indicating pronunciation by vowel letters underwent several radical changes during the course of Israelite history. According to the work of Cross and Freedman, who employ Hebrew inscriptional material as their guide, the use of vowel letters went through three distinct stages:[2] before c. 900 no vowel letters were employed; from c. 900 to the exile only final vowel letters were used; during the exile and after the system developed whereby all final vowels and most internal vowels are indicated. The system in use in the MT is a compromise between stages two and three, in that virtually all final vowels but only certain types of internal vowels are as a rule indicated.

Since, however, the evidence that Hebrew manuscripts were written without final vowel letters in the period before c. 900 is very slim, resting solely on an interpretation of the Gezer Calendar, it seems unwise to make any modifications in the final vowel letters of the MT. But, on the other hand, since the use of medial vowel letters was an exilic and post-exilic development in the main, it seems best to regard them as accretions to any text possibly written before the exile. Therefore, in this study all medial vowel letters both of poems dating to the pre-exilic period on non-

---

1. Hereafter, abbreviated MT.

2. F. M. Cross, Jr. and D. N. Freedman, *Early Hebrew Orthography: a Study of the Epigraphic Evidence*, American Oriental Series, vol. 36 (New Haven, 1952).

linguistic grounds and of poems of unknown date are disregarded. In quoting from these texts, however, the consonantal MT will be reproduced.

The elimination of vowel points and certain vowel letters radically affects our analysis of the morphology of the verb. In a consonantal text with only final vowels indicated, many forms appear as identical. For example, one can no longer distinguish on the basis of orthography all verbal forms which are represented by the three, two, or four radicals of the root. To take only the B[3] stem for illustration, the 3ms suffix conjugation, the ms participle, the ms imperative, and the absolute infinitive and the bound[4] infinitive are all identical. According to strict linguistic method these forms can be distinguished one from another only after a painstaking analysis of the syntax of each, and, then, identification in any individual case may be problematical.

Such a thorough linguistic analysis is beyond the scope of this study, so certain compromises must be made. Since the two finite verbal forms only are under investigation, the designation of participles, infinitives and imperatives in the MT will be followed. In any exhaustive study the possibility that some of these might be finite forms and vice versa would have to be considered. Taking into account only finite forms, there is a problem with initial y/w verbs in the B stem. Here the 3ms and pl suffix conjugation forms cannot be distinguished from the corresponding forms of the prefix conjugation. In this paper, therefore, they are omitted from consideration.

The next problem concerns the terminology used to describe the morphology of the Northwest Semitic finite verb. It may take two forms, one with the pronominal element prefixed to the root and one with the pronominal element suffixed to the root. The terms in general use to describe these two forms, imperfect and perfect, respectively, are not descriptive but grammatical, that is, they describe not physical appearance but usage. In view of the main structural feature which distinguishes them, here they are labelled, respectively, the prefix conjugation (abbreviated pref conj) and the suffix conjugation (abbreviated suff conj).

To each of these two forms it is possible to prefix the conjunction *w*- "and." Since in certain periods of Hebrew literature the presence or absence of *w*- affects the syntactical meaning of the verb, in any grammatical

---

3. In this study the seven major stems of the Hebrew verb are labelled B, N, D, Dpass, H, Hpass, and HtD. In addition, the poel is labelled L, the poal Lpass.

4. For the use of the term bound for the traditional term construct, see J. W. Wevers, "Semitic Bound Structures," *Canadian Journal of Linguistics* 7 (1961) 9-14.

analysis involving Hebrew there are four forms which must be morphologically distinguished, namely, the two conjugations with and the two conjugations without prefixed *w*-. They are abbreviated pref, w-pref, suff and w-suff.

In describing the use of these four forms in past narrative the following steps are followed. First, that the passages in question actually narrate events which begin and end in past time is demonstrated. Only passages which beyond reasonable doubt refer to past time are eligible for consideration. Generally speaking, it is the nature of the events narrated which removes such doubt (e.g., when Yahweh's activity at creation or in delivering Israel from Egypt is recited). But, also, form criticism can perform the same function (e.g., when narrative poetry is found in a victory hymn like Jud 5 or in a thanksgiving hymn like 2 S 22). Many passages which are customarily translated by the English past tense are excluded from this study. In every case an argument of no little cogency can be mounted against such a translation. Before these passages were omitted, however, it was determined that even if included, they would not qualify the conclusions here arrived at. But even with passages which unambiguously refer to past time, no claim is made for completeness. It is only hoped that the overwhelming majority have been detected, so that the patterns described below are in no danger of modification by the inclusion of passages formerly overlooked.

Second, a list is compiled of all verbs that, though they are within passages of past narrative, must be disqualified. All B stem 3ms and pl forms of initial y/w verbs must be excluded because it is impossible to distinguish on the basis of the consonantal text the suff from the pref conjugation. Some verbs must be eliminated because they do not refer to past time, even though other verbs in the same context may. How this may be so will be discussed where such deletions are made. Also, all verbs in subordinate clauses are omitted for the sake of consistent linguistic method. Before verbs in subordinate clauses can be considered with verbs in independent clauses, one must demonstrate that the particle, preposition or pronoun, expressed or unexpressed, which introduces the clause does not affect the syntax of the verb. Such a demonstration is beyond the scope of this study.

Third, the distribution and patterning of the verbal forms which remain are described.

Early Poetic Hebrew

Following these steps the first task is to reconstruct the verbal forms which were in all probability used in early poetic Hebrew to narrate past events. In this task Ugaritic poetry constitutes the primary source. The isolation of narrative sections in it is a simple matter. One needs only to prune away all passages in which speech is quoted directly. The remainder is descriptive narration. It is theoretically possible, however, that the

Ugaritians considered the events in the narrative sections of the mythological poems as happening not in the past but in the present. For at any one recitation the listener may have pictured the events as happening simultaneously with the recitation according to the canons of cultic re-presentation.

There are two weighty arguments against this theory. First, the Babylonian myths, which most likely played the same role in the cult as the Ugaritic ones, are told almost exclusively by the preterit tense. Second, at this point in our evolving understanding of the Ugaritic epics Keret and Danel, it seems very unlikely that they were used in any re-presentation rite. Hence, an excuse to doubt the past reference of the verbs in them is absent. Yet the choice of verbal forms in these epics is identical with that in the myths. The logical conclusion is that the verbs in the myths have the same force as those in the epics.

As typical of the mythological texts the following well-preserved and fairly lengthy narrative passages have been chosen:

4 (51,IIAB)[5] iv-v 8-30, 82-88 + 97-112; vi 16-36 + 38-59
3 (ʿnt, VAB) ii

Of the verbs in these passages the following must be excluded: *yblnn* in 1.100 and 1.102 and *wyṯṯb* in 1.109 of column iv-v because they are 3m forms of initial y/w verbs; *wtr* in 1.83 of column iv-v, *td* in 1.32, *šql* in 1.41 and *wpq* in 1.56 of column vi because all are inadequately understood. The remaining verbs in independent clauses are the following:

4 iv-v 8-30

pref (12)	w-pref (6)	suff (6)
'ḫd - yuhdm 16		
		'ṯr - aṯr 18
	bw' - wtbu 23	
gly - tgly 23		
hbr - thbr 25		
ḥbq - yḥbq 13		
ḥwy - tšṭḥwy 26		
	kbd - wtkbdh 26	
	krr? - wykrkr 29	
		mdl - mdl 9
nš' - yšu 30		
ntn - lttn 20		
		ʿdb - ʿdb 12
ph - kyphnh 27		
prq - yprq 28		
	ṣḥq - wyṣḥq 28	
	ṣyḥ - wy[ṣḥ] 30	

5. The primary designation of the Ugaritic texts follows the classification in *Corpus des Tablettes en Cuneiformes Alphabetiques Decouvertes a Ras Shamra-Ugarit de 1929 a 1939*, par Andrée Herdner, Mission de Ras Shamra Tome X, Paris, 1963, with the classifications of Gordon and Virolleaud given in parentheses.

šyt - yštn 14
šmʿ - yšmʿ 8

ṯpd - yṯpd 29

qll - wtql 25

ṣmd - ṣmd 9

šyt - št 10

tbʿ - tbʿ 19

4 iv-v 82-88 + 97-112

pref (5)
'kl - yakl 103
dʿṣ - tdʿṣ 82

nš' - tšu 87
ntn - lttn 84
ʿdb - tʿdb 108

w-pref (2)

ʿny - w[y]ʿn 111

ṣyḥ - wtṣḥ 88

suff (8)

lḥm - lḥm 110
mġy - mġy 106

ṣḥq - ṣḥq 87
ṣyḥ - ṣḥ 98
šyt - št 107
šmḫ - šmḫ 82.97
šty - št[y] 110

4 vi 16-36 + 38-59

pref (8)
'kl - tikl 24.27.29
bny - tbnn 16

ʿdb - yʿdb 39

rwm - trmm 17
šyt - tšt 22

šty - tšty 58

suff (17)

ṭbḫ - ṭbḫ 40
lḥm - lḥm 55
sbb - sb 34
- nsb 35
ʿdb - ʿdb 39
pyq - špq 47.48.49.50.
51.52.53.54
ṣyḥ - ṣḥ 44.45

šmḫ - šmḫ 35
šty - šty 55

3 ii

pref (14)
grš - tgrš 15

ḥsp - [t]ḥspn 38
ḫṣb - tḫtṣb 6.24
mḫṣ - tmtḫṣ 5-6
- tmḫṣ 7
- tmtḫṣn 23
ml' - ymlu 25
mġy - tmġyn 17

ġdd - tġdd 25
ġll - tġll 27
śmt - tśmt 8

w-pref (4)

ḥdy - wtḥdy 24

ʿyn - wtʿn 23

qry - wtqry 4

suff (2)

ʿtk - ʿtkt 11

rḥṣ - trḥṣ 32	rḥṣ wtrḥṣ 38	šns - šnst 12
šql - tštql 18		
ṯᶜr - tṯᶜr 20		

Lines 156-211 of 14 (Krt, IK) iii-iv have been selected as typical of the narrative sections of the epic poems. In lines 59-153 of this same text El in a dream details what Keret must do to get Lady Ḥurriya for his wife. Lines 156ff narrate Keret's execution of El's instructions. Lines 156-211 form the best preserved and best understood part of this latter section. The following verbs are omitted: *yṣq* in 1.164, *yrd* in 1.171, and *wybl* in 1.189 because they are 3m forms of initial y/w verbs; *tškn* in 1.192 because it occurs in a relative clause.

14 iii 156-211

pref (12)	w-pref (1)	suff (10)	w-suff (1)
	'dm - wyadm 156		
bᶜr - ybᶜr 190			
		dbḥ - dbḥ 168	
hlk - ylk 207		hlk - hlk 180.182	
		yrd - šrd 169	
lkn - tlkn 194			
		lqḥ - lqḥ 159.163	
mzl - ymzl 188			
mġy - ym [ġy] 197			
- ymġy 210			
ndr - yd[r] 200			
nš' - yšu 187		nš' - nša 167	
sgr - ysgr 184			
		ᶜdb - ᶜdb 172	
			ᶜly - wᶜly 165
		ᶜrb - ᶜrb 159	
rḥṣ - yrtḥṣ 156			
- yrḥṣ 157			
		rkb - rkb 166	
škr - tškr 186			

It is apparent from the above lists that, of the four morphologically distinct forms with which we are concerned, the pref and suff are the ones predominantly used in past narrative. Naturally the question arises whether they are grammatically equivalent. Or does each impart its own peculiar quality to the verbal idea? At least two options for distinguishing them are available. One, using the verbal syntax of Hebrew prose as an analogy, is to interpret the suff conj as indicating complete action and, therefore, as equivalent to a past narrative tense, and the pref conj as indicating incomplete action in past time. The other, using the Akkadian verbal system as the model, is to interpret the suff conj as stative and the pref as preterit.

Each theory is on track in one of its points but has derailed in the other. On the one hand, the Ugaritic suff conj is much more like the Hebrew suff conj than the Akkadian. Like the Hebrew, in addition to expressing a state, it also expresses motion and transitivity. The Akkadian suff conj with rare exception is limited to designating states and passives. Albrecht Goetze, the principal proponent of the theory that the Ugaritic and the Akkadian suff conjugations are correlative has to resort to a questionable stratagem to obviate this dissimilarity between the two forms.[6] He says that with verbs of motion the Ugaritic suff conj denotes either a state of continuous motion (e.g. *hlk* "he went" means that he is in a state of going from one place to another) or a state of rest after motion has ceased (e.g. *mġy* "he arrived" means that he is in the state of having already arrived). And he says that with transitive verbs the suff conj denotes a state which one has effected vis-a-vis an object or another person (e.g. *ḏbḥ* "he sacrificed" means that he has produced the state in which something has been sacrificed).

There are some compelling arguments against Goetze. Most decisive are the following two: first, with transitive verbs it is most difficult to discern the difference between suff and pref forms when both are used in the same context. Take, for example, 4 iv-v 8-14:

8 yšmᶜ qdš wamr[r]
9 mdl ᶜr ṣmd pḥl
10 št gpnm dt ksp
11 dt yrq nqbnm
12 ᶜdb gpn atnth
13 yḥbq qdš wamrr
14 yštn aṯrt lbmt ᶜr

Goetze is forced to conclude that in lines 8-12 where all the forms are suff *Qdš wamrr* effects a series of states. For example, in 1.9 he translates *mdl ᶜr* as "He had the ass yoked." But in lines 13-14 where the forms are pref he takes *Qdš wamrr* as performing a series of actions. So he translates "*Qdš wamrr* embraced (and) placed Atherah on the back of the ass." But that the activity of yoking is of a different quality from placing is not at all apparent from the context. The second telling argument against Goetze is the use of suff forms to express a series of actions which rapidly follow one upon the other. What is emphasized is the sequence of actions not a sequence of states. Take, for example, 14 iii-iv 159-169

159 ᶜrb bẓl ḫmt lqḥ
160 imr dbḥ bydh
161 lla klatnm
162 klt lḥmh dnzl
163 lqḥ msrr ᶜṣr db[ḥ]
164 yṣq bgl ḥtṯ yn
165 bgl ḫrṣ nbt wᶜly
166 lzr mgdl rkb

6. A. Goetze, "The Tenses of Ugaritic," JAOS 58 (1939) 266-309.

167 ṯkmm ḫmt nša
168 [y]dh šmmh dbḥ
169 lṯr abh il

To describe Keret's "entering, taking, pouring, going up, riding, lifting up, and sacrificing" as a series of states is forced, to say the least. The sequence is much more easily thought of as one of actions.

But, on the other hand, although the Ugaritic suff conj resembles the Hebrew suff conj and not the Akkadian, its pref conj is much more like the Akkadian than the Hebrew. For in Hebrew the pref conj in past narrative is scarce and usually the context or accompanying adverbs show that the force is frequentative. In Ugaritic the pref conj is, by a slight margin, the predominant form in narrative passages, and is employed in contexts where it cannot indicate actions which occurred repeatedly. Take lines 13-14 of 4 iv-v quoted above. *Qdš wamrr* does not lift Atherah on to the ass over and over again.

In summary, Ugaritic seems to have a past narrative suff conj resembling the Hebrew suff conj and a past narrative pref conj resembling the Akkadian preterit tense, and to all appearances there is no syntactical difference between them. Reinforcing this impression of syntactical equivalence is that a narrative can be related with the pref conj predominant (as in 3 ii) or with the suff conj predominant (as in 4 vi 38-59) or with neither predominant (as in 14 iii 156-211). The parallelism of suff and pref conjugations provides further reinforcement. From the five narrative passages listed above we find:[7]

4 iv-v	82-83	šmḫ btlt ʿnt	//	tdʿṣ pʿnm wtr arṣ
	87-88	ṣḥq btlt ʿnt	//	tšu gh wtṣḥ
vi	38-40	ʿdbt bht[h bʿ]l yʿdb	//	hdʿdb [ʿd]bt hklh

If, therefore, the pref and suff conjugations are syntactically equivalent, what about the status of the w-pref conj? Is it equivalent syntactically to the pref and, thereby, to the suff conj? All the evidence points to an affirmative answer. The positioning of the w-pref conj within a line of poetry follows a very stereotyped pattern.[8] It very rarely is initial;

7. Cf. Moshe Held, "The YQTL - QTL (QTL - YQTL) Sequence of Identical Verbs in Biblical Hebrew and in Ugaritic," *Studies and Essays in Honor of Abraham A. Neuman*, ed. by Meir ben-Horin *et al* (Brill, Leiden for Dropsie College, Philadelphia, 1962) pp. 281-290.

8. Because the positioning of the w-pref conj in the poetic line plays an important part in the analysis which follows, it is necessary to explain the terminology which is used in describing it. The basic unit of Ugaritic and Hebrew poetry is termed a line. A line is composed of two or three parallel members, which are termed *stichoi*. If a w-pref conj begins the line itself, it is said to be initial. If it occurs anywhere within the line, either at the beginning of the second or third stichos, or within any of the stichoi, it is said to be medial. For the purpose of this study there is no need to distinguish between the two types of medial position.

rather, it habitually is medial. Below is an exhaustive list of w-pref forms in past narrative in texts 2 iv (68, IIIAB A), 3, 4, and 5 (67 I*AB), a representative sample of the mythological texts, arranged according to their position in the poetic line. A survey of the epic texts KRT and AQHT disclosed no deviation from the pattern found in the mythological texts.

Initial

2 iv 6-7	wttn gh yġr tḥt ksi zbl ym
23-4	wyrtqṣ ṣmd bd bʿl // [km] nšr busbʿth
30-1	wyṣa b[.....] // ybṯ nn aliyn bʿl
4 iii 27	wtʿn rbt aṯrt ym
32-3	wtʿn btlt ʿnt
iv-v 40	wtʿn rbt aṯrt ym
58	wyʿn lṭpn il dpid
64	wtʿn rbt aṯrt ym
120	wyʿn kṯr wḫss
125	wyʿn aliyn bʿl
vi 1	wyʿn k[ṯr wḫs]s
14-5	wyʿn kṯr [wḫss]
vii 37-8	wyʿn aliyn bʿl
5 i 11-2	wyʿn gpn wugr
v 22	w[th]rn wtldn mṯ

Medial (at the beginning of the second or third stichos)

2 iv 11.18	kṯr ṣmdm ynḥt // wypʿr šmthm
26	tngṣn pnth // wydlp tmnh
3 ii 3-5	klat tġrt bht ʿnt // wtqry ġlmm bšt ġr
4 iv-v 23-4	tgly ḏd[9]il // wtbu qrš mlk ab šnm
29-30	pʿnh lhdm yṯpd // wykrkr usb th
108-9	tʿdb ksu // wyṯṯb lymn aliyn bʿl

Medial (within any one of the parallel stichoi)

2 iv 27	yqṯ bʿl wyšt ym
3 i 4-5	qm ytʿr w yšlḥmnh
8-9	ndd yʿsr wyšqnyh
18	qm ybd wyšr
ii 23-4	mid tmtḫṣn wtʿn // tḫtṣb wtḥdy ʿnt
38	[t]ḥspn mh wtrḥṣ
iii 32-3	tšu gh wtṣḥ
iv 86	tḥspn mh wtrḥṣ
4 ii 21	tšu gh wtṣḥ
iii 12	ydd wyqlṣn
13	yqm wywptn
iv-v 25-6	lpʿn il thbr wtql // tštḥwy wtkbdh
28	yprq lṣb wyṣḥq
30	yšu gh wy[ṣḥ]
87-8	tšu gh wtṣḥ
vii 22	yšu gh wyṣḥ
5 i 9	tbʿ wl ytb ilm
ii 13	tbʿ wl ytb ilm
16-7	tša ghm wtṣḥ
v 22	w[th]rn wtldn mṯ
vi 22	yšu gh wyṣḥ
25-6	ap ʿnt ttlk wtṣd

9. Possibly šd. On the polyphony of 𐎏, cf. M. Dahood, *Ugaritic-Hebrew Philology* (Rome, 1965) p. 7.

Eleven times in these texts a w-pref form beginning a line occurs in the conventional formula for introducing a speech "and so-and-so answered." Only four times otherwise does it occur initially in narrative, whereas it is found 32 times in medial position (although seven of these should perhaps be omitted, since they concern another conventional introduction for direct speech "so-and-so lifted his voice and cried"). In contrast to this inflexibility the pref and suff conjugations are very mobile, occurring initially or medially with equal frequency.

The reason for the circumscribed position patterning of the w-pref conj is obvious. Its position is determined not by any peculiar syntactical meaning it has, but by the appropriateness of its *w*- component. Generally speaking, the connection between clauses within a stichos or line is much closer than the connection of clauses in separate lines. So, the w-pref conj generally occurs within lines, not at their beginning. If, therefore, the position of the w-pref conj is not determined by any syntactical meaning of its own, we are justified in concluding that it and the pref conj are syntactically equivalent, but are in complimentary distribution. Where a *w*- is not appropriate, the pref conj is used; where a *w*- is appropriate, the w-pref conj is used. That the w-pref conj is invariably paralleled by the pref conj supports this conclusion. For an exhaustive list of examples in texts 2, 3, 4 and 5, see the examples of w-pref forms in medial and initial position listed above. Again, a survey of KRT and AQHT yielded no exceptions to this rule.

Without doubt the easiest interpretation of this data is that the pref and w-pref conjugations are syntactically equivalent. But there is strong evidence that the pref components of the two conjugations are not identical morphologically. It appears that the w-pref ends in zero vowel, whereas the pref ends in a short vowel, presumably -*u* on the basis of Arabic. The evidence is as follows: diphthongs seem never to be represented in the consonantal script. Hence when a pref form of a final y/w verb is written *yᶜny*, it was probably pronounced with a final vowel, something like *yaᶜnayu*. When, on the other hand, a w-pref form is written *wyᶜn*, presumably it was pronounced something like *wayaᶜnay wayaᶜnē*. These conclusions must be held tentatively, for there are isolated examples of pref forms of final y/w verbs written without the *yodh* and of w-pref forms written with the *yodh*. To date there has been no satisfactory explanation of these deviations from the norm.

The occurrence of only one w-suff form in the texts selected for illustration (wᶜly in 14 iii 165) makes it impossible to say anything definite about it. Since this one example is parallel with a suff form, probably the w-suff should be understood on the analogy of the w-pref conj. That is, as the latter is in complimentary distribution with the pref conj, likewise is the former with the suff conj.

That the pattern of finite verbal forms in past narrative in early poetic Hebrew closely resembles the Ugaritic pattern is made eminently likely by the occasional presence of what is certainly a vestige of this pattern (the pref conj referring to simple past events) in all genres of biblical poetry. Its presence there has been recognized by innumerable scholars ever since the discovery of the cuneiform literature of Mesopotamia.

Standard Poetic Hebrew

The next task is to describe the pattern of verbal forms in past narrative in the Hebrew characterized by the poetry datable on non-linguistic grounds to the eighth century or thereafter.

A. *The Pre-exilic Prophets*

1. *Amos*

Two passages of undoubted past narration in Amos are 2:9-12 and 9:7.[1] The first deals with the exodus and conquest and the second with the exodus only. None of the verbs needs to be omitted.

w-pref (4)	suff (4)
hlk - w'wlk 2:10	
	ᶜlh - hᶜlyty 2:10, 9:7
	ṣwh - ṣwytm 2:12
qwm - w'qym 2:11	
šmd - w'šmyd 2:9	šmd - hšmdty 2:9
šqh - wtšqw 2:12	

2. *Hosea*

In Hosea, there are at least five passages narrating some event in Israel's history, either one of the events in Israel's salvation history or some event in the life of one of the patriarchs: 9:10, 11:1-4, 12:4-5, 12:13-14, and 13:5-6. Three of the verbs in these passages must be eliminated: *ydᶜw* in 11:3 and *wykl* in 12:5 because they are 3m forms of initial y/w verbs, and *rp'tym* in 11:3 because it is in a *ky* clause.

Pref (6)	w-pref (11)	suff (16)
	'hb - w'hbhw 11:1	
'kl - 'wkyl 11:4		
		bw' - b'w 9:10
		bkh - bkh 12:5
	brh - wybrḥ 12:13	
dbr - ydbr 12:5		

---

1. The reader is reminded that I make no claim to have spotted every passage of past narrative. Rather I hope only to have included every passage that unambiguously refers to past action and to have omitted discussion of no ambiguous passage that would qualify my results.

	hyh - wyhyw 9:10	
	- w'hyh 11:4	
		hlk - hlkw 11:2
zbḥ - yzbḥw 11:2		
	ḥnn - wytḥnn 12:5	
		ydᶜ - ydᶜtyk 13:5
mṣ' - ymṣ'nw 12:5		mṣ' - mṣ'ty 9:10
mšk - 'mškm 11:4	nzr - wynzrw 9:10	
	nṭh - w'ṭ 11:4	
	ᶜbd - wyᶜbd 12:13	
		ᶜlh - hᶜlh 12:14
		ᶜqb - ᶜqb 12:4
qṭr - yqṭrwn 11:2		
		qr' - qr'ty 11:1
		- qr'w 11:2
		r'h - r'yty 9:10
	rwm - wyrm 13:6	
	śbᶜ - wyśbᶜw 13:6	śbᶜ - śbᶜw 13:6
	śrh - wyśr 12:5	śrh - śrh 12:4
		škḥ - škḥwnw 13:6
		šmr - šmr 12:13
		- nšmr 12:14
		trgl - trglty 11:3

3. *Isaiah*

In Isaiah there are no passages which refer straightforwardly to past time. But there is the parable in 5:1b-2 in which the founding of Israel by Yahweh is likened to his planting a vineyard. Since it is clear from the indictment lodged against Israel that the planting has already occurred, it seems legitimate to include this passage here. None of the verbs must be omitted.

w-pref (6)	suff (2)
bnh - wybn 5:2	
	hyh - hyh 5:1
	ḥṣb - ḥṣb 5:2
ntᶜ - wyṭᶜhw 5:2	
sql - wysqlhw 5:2	
ᶜzq - wyᶜzqhw 5:2	
ᶜśh - wyᶜś 5:2	
qwh - wyqw 5:2	

4. *Jeremiah*

Two parts of the long oracle against Israel in chapter two of Jeremiah refer to Yahweh's past grapplings with his people, verses 5-8 and 20-21. The following verbs must be eliminated: *ydᶜwny* in 2:8 because it is a 3pl of an initial y/w verb; *ᶜbr* and *yšb* in 2:6 and *ywᶜlw* in 2:8 because they occur in relative clauses; *rḥqw* in 2:5 and *šbrty* and *ntqty* in 2:20 because they occur in *ky* clauses; and finally, *'ᶜbd* in 2:20 because it is in direct speech.

w-pref (6)	suff (9)
'mr - wt'mry 2:20	'mr - 'mrw 2:6.8
bw' - w'by' 2:7	
- wtb'w 2:7	
hbl - wyhblw 2:5	
hlk - wylkw 2:5	hlk - hlkw 2:8
	hpk - nhpkt 2:21
ṭm' - wtṭm'w 2:7	
	mṣ' - mṣ'w 2:5
	nb' - nb'w 2:8
	nṭ^{c} - nṭ^{c}tyk 2:21
	pš^{c} - pš^{c}w 2:8
	śym - śmtm 2:7

B. *The Exilic Prophets*

1. *Second Isaiah*

Second Isaiah, like the pre-exilic prophets, lacks an abundance of passages that refer unequivocally to past time. Those which do chronicle either an event in Israel's history or Yahweh's activity at creation. For convenience, the former group can be divided into two parts, those passages which concern the exile and those which do not.

The passages that recount the exile are 42:24-25, 43:27-28, 47:6-7a, 50:1b and 54:7a.8aα. It is apparent at practically every point in the writings of Second Isaiah that he is addressing people already in exile. Therefore, the actual fall of Jerusalem and deportation, referred to in the above verses, must be events in the past. Of the verbs in these passages, only the the following two need to be omitted: *ht'mw* in 42:24 because it is in a relative clause and *yd^{c}* in 42:25 because it is a 3m form of an initial y/w verb.

pref (1)	w-pref (7)	suff (13)
		'bh - 'bw 42:24
	'mr - wt'mry 47:4	
	b^{c}r - wtb^{c}r 42:25	
		ḥṭ' - ḥṭ' 43:27
	ḥll - w'ḥll 43:28	ḥll - ḥllty 47:6
		kbd - hkbdt 47:6
	lhṭ - wtlhṭhw 42:25	
		mkr - nmkrtm 50:1
	ntn - w'tnh 43:28	ntn - ntn 42:24
	- w'tnm 47:6	
		str - hstrty 54:8
		^{c}zb - ^{c}zbtyk 54:7
		pš^{c} - pš^{c}w 43:27
		qṣp - qṣpty 47:6
śym - yśym 42:25		śym - śmt 47:6
		šlḥ - šlḥh 50:1
		šm^{c} - šm^{c}w 42:24
	špk - wyšpk 42:25	

Those passages which concern Yahweh's past dealings with his people other than the punishment he meted out at the exile are 48:3-5a, 51:2b, and

55:4. The last recites Yahweh's installation of David as leader of Israel, the next to last his election of Abraham. The first seems to refer to no specific event, unless it be the foretelling of the exile by the prophets, but to the fact that Yahweh always tipped his hand in advance. All doubt about the past reference of the verbs is removed by the adverbs *m'z* in verses 3 and 5 and *bṭrm* also in verse 5. From these three passages *yṣ'w* in 48:3 because it is a 3mpl form of an initial y/w verb and *tbw'* in 48:5 because it follows *bṭrm* must be omitted.

pref (5)	suff (5)
bw' - wtb'nh 48:3	
brk - w'brkhw 51:2	
ngd - w'gyd 48:5	ngd - hgdty 48:3
	ntn - nttyw 55:4
	ᶜśh - ᶜśyty 48:3
	qr' - qr'tyw 51:2
ṛbh - w'rbhw 51:2	
šmᶜ - w'šmyᶜm 48:3	šmᶜ - hšmᶜtyk 48:5

Verbs which refer to the creation are found in 45:12.18 and 48:13a. Only *yṣrh* in 45:18, a 3ms of an initial y/w verb, needs to be omitted.

suff (8)
br' - br'ty 45:12
- br'h 45:18
ṭpḥ - ṭpḥh 48:13
ysd - ysdh 48:13
kwn - kwnnh 45:18
nṭh - nṭw 45:12
ᶜśh - ᶜśyty 45:12
ṣwh - ṣwyty 45:12

Besides these passages that unequivocally rehearse past events, a group narrating the call of the servant also most likely refers to past time: 41:8-9, 42:6, 49:1b-3a and 49:8. There can be no doubt that 49:1b-3a refers to a past call, for verse 1b reads, "Yahweh called me from the womb // from the bowels of my mother he named me." But decisive evidence that the other three recount a past commission is not forthcoming. Of the verbs in these passages three in chapter 41 must be eliminated: *bḥrtyk* in verse 8, *hḥzqtyk* and *qr'tyk* in verse 9 because they are in relative clauses.

w-pref (9)	suff (7)
'mr - w'mr 41:9	
- wy'mr 49:3	
	zkr - hzkyr 49:1
	ḥb' - hḥby'ny 49:2
ḥzq - w'ḥzq 42:6	
nṣr - w'ṣrk 42:6.49:8	
ntn - w'tnk 42:6.49:8	
	str - hstyrny 49:2
	ᶜnh - ᶜnytyk 49:8

		^{c}zr - ^{c}zrtyk 49:8
		qr' - qr'tyk 42:6
		- qr'ny 49:1
	śym - wyśm 49:2	
	- wyśymny 49:2	

2. *Ezekiel*

In Ezekiel two passages contain verbs unambiguously referring to past time: 19:2-12 and 28:12b-19. The past reference of the verbs in the first passage is demonstrated by the adverb *'th* "now" in verse 13. What has gone before describes Israel's past behavior, what follows this adverb describes her present state. In verse 7 *wyd^{c}* and in verse 12 *wybšw* because they are 3m forms of initial y/w verbs and *yšm^{c}* in verse 9 because it follows *lm^{c}n* must be ignored.

pref (1)	w-pref (17)	suff (16)
		'bd - 'bdh 5
		'kl - 'kl 3.6
		- 'klthw 12
bw' - yb'hw 9	bw' - wyb'hw 4.9	
	gbh - wtgbh 11	
	hyh - wyhyw 11	hyh - hyh 3.6
		- hyth 10
	hlk - wythlk 6	
		ḥrb - hḥryb 7
		ybš - hwbyš 12
	lmd - wylmd 3.6	
	lqḥ - wtqḥ 5	
	ntn - wytnw 8	
	- wytnhw 9	
	ntš - wttš 12	
	^{c}lh - wt^{c}l 3	
		prq - htprqw 12
	prś - wyprśw 8	
	r'h - wtr' 5	
	- wyr' 11	
		rbh - rbth 2
		rbṣ - rbṣh 2
		śym - śmthw 5
		šlk - hšlkh 12
	šmm - wtšm 7	
	šm - wyšm^{c}w 4	
		tpś - ntpś 4.8

The reference to the creation of Tyre in 28:13 and the use of the Garden of Eden motif as a symbol of her original bounty show that Tyre's past, not her present or future, is described in the second passage. In verse 15 *nmṣ'* because it follows *^{c}d* and *wnttyk* in verse 14 and *w'bdk* in verse 16 because they are probably corrupt must be omitted.

w-pref (4)	suff (12)
	'kl - 'kltk 18
	hyh - hyyt 13.14.19
	hlk - hthlkt 14
ḥṭ' - wtḥṭ' 16	
ḥll - w'ḥllk 16	ḥll - ḥllt 18
yṣ' - w'wṣ' 18	
	kwn - kwnnw 13
	ml' - mlw 16
ntn - w'tnk 18	ntn - nttyk 17
	šḥt - šḥt 17
	šlk - hšlktyk 17
	šmm - šmmw 19

C. *The Post-exilic Prophets*

1. *Third Isaiah*

No passages whose verbs unambiguously refer to past time are found in Joel and Zc 9:14. In Third Isaiah there is one, 63:8-14. The past reference of its verbs is proved beyond doubt by the introduction in verse 7, "I will recount the loyal acts of Yahweh...", by the unmistakable allusion to the deliverance from Egypt under Moses, and by the phrase in verse 9 "all the days of old." Two verbs, *yšgrw* in verse 8 and *trd* in v. 14, both in asyndetic relative clauses, must be omitted.

pref (2)	w-pref (6)	suff (6)	suff (1)
	'mr - wy'mr 8		
		g'l - g'lm 9	
	hyh - wyhy 8		
	hpk - wyhpk 10		
	zkr - wyzkr 11		
		yš^{c} - hwšy^{c}m 9	
kšl - ykšlw 13			
		lḥm - nlḥm 10	
		mrh - mrw 10	
		nhg - nhgt 14	
nwḥ - tnyḥnw 14			
	nṭl - wynṭlm 9		
	nś' - wynś'm 9		
			^{c}ṣb - w^{c}ṣbw 10
		ṣrr - ṣr 9	

D. *The Psalmodic Types*

1. *Lamentations*

Whether there are verbs which refer to simple events in the past in Lamentations is difficult to decide. Form critically speaking, the poems in this book are petition psalms. Generally, in this type the psalmist describes his present state. He complains of indignities suffered in the past which are still being endured at the moment he recites the psalm. But the situation in Lamentations could conceivably be different. For what led to the state being lamented was one specific event in the past, the fall of Jerusalem. Hence it is possible that some of the verbs, especially those which describe Yahweh venting his anger on his people, refer not to repeated atrocities by the enemy but to this one event. Good examples of such verbs are found in 2:2-8. Only *'klh* in verse 3 must be omitted, being in an asyndetic relative clause.

w-pref (6)	suff (24)
'bl - wy'bl 8	
	'mll - 'mllw 8
	bl^c - bl^{c}2.5.5
b^{c}r - wyb^{c}r 3	
	gd^c - gd^c 3
	drk - drk 4
	hyh - hyh 5
hrg - wyhrg 4	
	hrs - hrs 2
	znḥ - znḥ 7
	ḥll - ḥll 2
	ḥml - ḥml 2
ḥms - wyḥms 6	
	ḥšb - ḥšb 8
n'ṣ - wyn'ṣ 6	
	n'r - n'r 7
	ng^c - hgy^c 2
	nṭh - nṭh 8
	nṣb - nṣb 4
	ntn - ntnw 7
	sgr - hsgyr 7
rbh - wyrb 5	
	šwb - hšyb 3.8
	šḥt - šḥt 5.6
	škḥ - škḥ 6
	špk - špk 4

2. *Psalm 137*

Verses 1-3 of Ps 137 also seem to refer to past events. In verse 3 *š'lwnw* because it follows *ky* must be omitted.

suff (3)
bkh - bkynw 1
yšb - yšbnw 1
tlh - tlynw 2

From the foregoing lists it is clear that in standard poetry the suff and the w-pref conjugations are the ones habitually used in narrating past events. There is not the slightest hint that the two differ syntactically. In some poems the suff conj predominates (as in Ezk 28:12b-19), in others the w-pref (as in Isa 5:1b-2). Usually, the two occur in equal proportion with a constant alternation between them (as in Ezk 19:2-12). Furthermore, as the following list shows, the two are repeatedly in parallelism or are found together within the same stichos.

Amos 2:12	wtšqw // ṣwytm
Hosea 9:10	b'w // wyṅzrw // wyhyw
11:1	w'hbhw // qr'ty
12:5	wyśr &[2] (wykl)[3] // bkh & wytḥnn
12:13	wybrḥ // wyʿbd // šmr
13:6	wyśbʿw // śbʿw & wyrm // škḥwny
Isa 5:2	wybn // ḥṣb
42:6	qr'tyk // w'ḥzq
48:3	hgdty // (ys'w) & w'smy m // śyty & wtb'nh
48:5	w'gyd // hšmʿtyk
49:2	wyśm // hḥby'ny
49:2	wyśymny // hstyrny
51:2	qr'tyw // w'brkhw // w'rbhw
63:10	wyhpk // nlḥm
Jer 2:7	wtb'w & wtṭm'w // śmtm
Ezk 19:3	wtʿl // hyh
19:3.6	wylmd // 'kl
19:4	wyšmʿw // ntpś
19:5	wtr' // 'bdh
19:5	wtqḥ // śmthw
19:6	wythlk // hyh
19:8	wyprśw // ntpś
19:12	wttš // hšlkh
28:16	mlw // wtḥṭ'
28:18	w'wṣ' // 'kltk
Lam 2:8	wy'bl // 'mllw

The exceptions to this pattern are scarce indeed, the w-pref paralleling a pref form three times (Hos 11:4, Isa 42:25, and Ezk 19:9) and the suff form paralleling a w-suff form once (Isa 63:10).

The w-pref conj often occurs medially, as one would expect because of the conjunction. But even more frequently it is initial. The examples of it in each of these positions are given in the list below.

Medial		*Initial*	
Hosea 9:10	wynzrw	Amos 2:9	w'šmyd
11:1	w'hbhw	2:10	w'wlk
11:4	w'ṭ	2:11	w'qym
12:5	wytḥnn	2:12	wtšqw
12:13	wyʿbd	Hos 9:10	wyhyw
13:6	wyrm	11:4	w'hyh
13:6	wyśbʿw	12:5	wyśr
Isa 5:2	wyṭʿhw	12:13	wybrḥ
5:2	wysqlhw	Isa 5:2	wybn
5:2	wyʿś	5:2	wyʿzqhw
42:6	w'ḥzq	5:2	wyqw
42:6	w'ṣrk	42:25	wyšpk
42:6	w'tnk	41:9	w'mr
42:25	wtbʿr	42:25	wtlhṭhw
43:28	w'tnh	43:28	w'ḥll
48:3	wtb'nh	47:6	w'tnm
48:3	w'šmyʿm	47:7	wt'mry

2. The & sign indicates that the forms on either side of it occur within the same stichos.

3. Parentheses enclose forms which have been omitted from consideration.

	49:8	w'ṣrk
	49:8	w'ṭnk
	51:2	w'brkhw
	51:2	w'rbhw
	63:9	wynś'm
Jer	2:5	wyhblw
	2:7	wtṭm'w
Ezk	19:9	wyḃ'hw
	28:16	wtḥṭ'
Lam	2:4	wyhrg

	48:5	w'gyd
	49:2	wyśm
	49:2	wyśymny
	49:3	wy'mr
	63:8	wy'mr
	63:8	wyhy
	63:9	wynṭlm
	63:10	wyhṗk
	63:11	wyzkr
Jer	2:5	wylkw
	2:7	w'by'
	2:7	wtb'w
	2:20	wt'mry
Ezk	19:3	wylmd
	19:3	wtʿl
	19:4	wyb'hw
	19:4	wyšmʿw
	19:5	wtqḥ
	19:5	wtr'
	19:6	wythlk
	19:6	wylmd
	19:7	wtšm
	19:8	wytnw
	19:8	wyprśw
	19:9	wytnhw
	19:11	wtgbh
	19:11	wyhyw
	19:11	wyr'
	19:12	wttš
	28:16	w'ḥllk
	28:18	w'wṣ'
	28:18	w'ṭnk
Lam	2:3	wybʿr
	2:5	wyrb
	2:6	wyḥms
	2:6	wyn'ṣ
	2:8	wy'bl

As the above list shows, the use of the w-pref conj in initial position is characteristic of every poem or group of poems except Ps 137, where no w-pref forms occur.

The only exceptions to the otherwise exclusive use of suff and w-pref forms are a few scattered pref and one w-suff form. There are six pref forms in Hosea, one in Second Isaiah, two in Third Isaiah, and one in Ezekiel. Very likely the one in Ezekiel should be excluded from consideration because the G, followed by the V, reads the conjunction before it. In the overwhelmingly predominant use of the suff and w-pref conjugations in past narrative, standard poetic Hebrew is identical with Hebrew Prose. In the latter the pref conj is almost exclusively a past frequentative.[4] The question is whether the pref forms in the former are also to be considered as past frequentatives or whether they are to be taken as syntactically

4. Good examples of this use of the pref conj in prose may be found in 1 S 1:3-7 and Job 1:4-5.

equivalent to the w-pref conj.

Two factors support the latter alternative. One is that in three of the ten examples a pref form is paralleled by a w-pref form. These are:

Hosea 11:4	w'ṭ // 'wkyl
Isa 42:25	wtlhṭhw & (yd^{c}) // wtb^{c}r & yśym
Ezk 19:9	wytnhw // wyb'hw // yb'hw

The other is that in several of the examples interpreting the pref forms as past frequentatives is strained. They are much more easily taken as referring to simple events in the past. The best example is Hosea 12:5, "At Bethel he found him // there he spoke with him." From the context, which mentions Jacob's bout with the angel, it is obvious that Hosea is referring to the specific encounter between Yahweh and Jacob narrated in Gen 28. Likewise, the pref forms in Isa 42:25 and Ezk 19:9, if the MT is correct, are most naturally taken as preterits.

But, on the other hand, the pref forms in Hos 11:2 and Isa 63:13-14 are better taken as frequentatives, the two passages being translated, respectively, "The more they called (suff) to them the more they went (suff) to them; to baals they kept sacrificing (pref), and to idols they continually burned incense (pref),"[5] and "Like horses in the desert they would never stumble, like cattle which go down into the valley Yahweh's spirit would give them rest." In the second case, the similes stating what horses and cattle habitually do provide the clue to the proper interpretation of the pref forms. Because of the obscure context, it is difficult to determine what the force of the two pref forms in Hos 11:4 is.

It has often been claimed that Second Isaiah frequently uses the pref conj as an equivalent of the w-pref and suff conjugations. Since this opinion is contradicted here, it is well to discuss at some length the instances alleged as examples of this use. Saydon[6] in his article on the tenses in Second Isaiah has the most complete list. Of the passages he cites only five merit serious attention. One is 42:25, already dealt with above. Another is 51:2, "Look to Abraham your father and to Sarah who bore you (*ṯḥwllkm*)." There can be no doubt that *ṯḥwllkm* is a pref form referring to a simple, not a frequently recurring event in the past, and probably *yśym* in 42:25 should be similarly understood, though one would have to admit the possibility of taking it as a past frequentative, translating, "And it seared him (w-pref) on all sides, but he would not understand (*yd*^{c}, pointed by the

5. For the presence of suff or w-pref forms in the same context with pref forms that are definitely frequentative, see 1 S 1:7 and Job 1:5.

6. P. O. Saydon, "The Use of Tenses in Deutero-Isaiah," *Biblica* 40 (1959), 290-301.

Massoretes as a suff form) // it burned him up (w-pref), but he would not take it to heart (*yśym*)."

It is not clear, however, whether the pref forms in the remaining three passages refer to past or present time. In two of them the call of Cyrus is narrated. In 41:2-3.5 the beginning suff form certainly implies that Cyrus has already been aroused, but the following pref forms most likely relate to the victories which Cyrus was in the process of accomplishing at the time Second Isaiah composed the lines. Likewise, in 45:4-5 the problem is whether the betitling and the girding recount what Yahweh did once upon a time or has done in the past and is continuing to do. Because the w-pref form can be used to describe action beginning at a point in the past and still continuing in the present,[7] the parallelism of *'knk* with *w'gr'* is irrelevant. Factors other than the presence of a w-pref form must be used to establish that the passage relates to past actions.

The third ambiguous passage is 40:12-14. In the first place, it is not at all clear that verse 12 refers to creation, for the activities of Yahweh mentioned in it could be ones he performs in his role as sustainer rather than as creator. But, supposing that verse 12 does refer to creation, it is still problematical whether verses 13-14 refer to counsel proffered at the time of creation or to advice given for the right government of the universe once created. The phrase *'rḥ mšpṭ* implies the latter. Certainly, if the word *'yš* refers to human rather than divine counselors, then the passage cannot refer to advice given at creation.

In conclusion, there is in Second Isaiah one incontrovertible example of a pref form as a preterit (*ṭḥwllkm* in 51:2) and one more which is probable (*yśym* in 42:25). The examples in 41:2-3.5, 45:4-5 and 40:12-14 are dubious. But, even if one were to allow them, the grand total hardly justifies the generalization that the use of the pref conj as a preterit is habitual with Second Isaiah.

Thus, it appears that the pref conj in datable poetry is both a past frequentative and the equivalent of a preterit. Which it is in any individual case the context must determine.

Comparison of Early with Standard Poetic Hebrew

The differences between early and standard poetic Hebrew are profound and clear cut. Regarding overall patterns, in the former the suff and pref conjugations are predominantly used to narrate past events, whereas in the latter the suff and the w-pref conjugations are used. In the former the w-pref conj seldom occurs conditioned by the appropriateness of its *w*-

7. For example, see the use of suff and w-pref forms in the statement of the complaint in petition psalms.

component. In the latter the pref conj occurs occasionally, sometimes as a frequentative, sometimes as a preterit.

Regarding individual forms, the suff conjugations of both appear to be identical. But the w-pref conj in early poetic Hebrew is merely a conditioned variant of the pref conj, whereas in standard poetic Hebrew it cannot be described vis-a-vis the pref conj. It is a fully independent verbal form, whose position in the poetic line is not determined by the appropriateness of its *w*- component. Thus, in early poetic Hebrew it almost always is medial; in standard poetic Hebrew it is more often initial than medial. And, finally, the pref conj in early poetic Hebrew is on a par with the suff conj as a narrative conjugation. In standard poetic Hebrew mere vestiges of this earlier use are found, and, in addition, it also functions as a past frequentative.

The presence of the pattern typical of early poetic Hebrew in a poem of unknown date constitutes evidence of an early date. It is important to emphasize the stipulation that a definite pattern be discernible. For, since two outstanding features of early poetic Hebrew (the pref conj to narrate simple past events and the parallelism of pref with w-pref forms) are found vestigially in standard poetic Hebrew, a random appearance of either in an undatable poem cannot be utilized as evidence of an early date.

The presence of the pattern typical of standard poetic Hebrew in a poem of unknown date constitutes evidence of a date in the eighth century or thereafter. The presence of both patterns constitutes evidence of archaizing. For example, in the three examples in standard poetry of the parallelism pref // w-pref (Hosea 11:4, Isa 42:25, and Ezk 19:9) the pref conj is used as it is in early poetic Hebrew. But that the w-pref forms are initial and the pref ones medial is reminiscent of standard poetic Hebrew. Therefore, we have good reason to suspect that the pref forms are archaistic.

Undatable Poetry

With the radical difference between early and standard poetic Hebrew regarding the verbal forms employed in past narrative clearly delineated, we can compare with them the poems which cannot be dated by non-linguistic evidence.

A. Poems That Resemble Early Poetry

1. *Exodus 15*

The nature of the events narrated in Ex 15 show clearly that they took place in past time. The first and second verses are introduction to the historical narrative and verse 18 is a concluding cultic affirmation which refers to the future, so both of these sections are omitted. Also, in the body of the poem the poet speaks at least once, and perhaps more often, of Yahweh in general terms, describing what he habitually is and does, not simply what he did in the past at the Red Sea. The one certain instance of this is v. 11 "Who is like you exalted in holiness, awesome in praiseworthy acts, doer of wonders." The comparisons and the participles are clues that reveal that the poet is interrupting his narration to praise Yahweh's present status among the gods, a status gained and secured by the fact that he has done, does, and will do marvelous deeds worthy of praise.

Such statements of general truths may also occur in v. 3 and vv. 6-7. Since v. 3 contains no verb, it is irrelevant. The same cannot be said of vv. 6-7, for they contain four verbs, all pref forms. On the one hand, they may speak of how Yahweh is wont to dispose of his enemies, "Thy right hand, O Yahweh, who art mightily exalted[8] // thy right hand, O Yahweh shatters the enemy", etc. On the other hand, the poet may be reciting Yahweh's particular action at the Red Sea, "Thy right hand, O Yahweh, who art mightily exalted // thy right hand, O Yahweh, shattered the enemy", etc.

The best argument for the former alternative is that the metaphor used in v. 7 (that of anger likened to a consuming fire) does not reflect the means Yahweh uses to defeat the Egyptians as described in the remainder of the poem. He drowns rather than incinerates them. But the motif of a consuming fire is a conventional one used throughout Israelite poetry to describe Yahweh's devastating attack. Hence, it should not be taken too literally. Besides that, Israelite poets frequently mix metaphors. Nevertheless, taking only verbs which unambiguously refer to past time, the four pref forms of verses 6-7 must be eliminated. They are enclosed in parentheses in the list given below.

Besides the verbs in verses 1-2, 6-7 and 18, the following are omitted: first, all the pref forms in v. 9 because they occur in direct speech, and in context obviously refer to the future; second, four forms in relative clauses, *g'lt* in v. 13, *qnyt* in v. 16, and *p*^{c}*lt* and *kwnnw* in v. 17; third, both instances of *y*^{c}*br* in v. 16 because they occur in noun clauses after the preposition ^{c}*d*; fourth, *yrh* in v. 4 and *yrdw* in v. 5 because they are 3m forms of initial y/w verbs.

pref (7) or (11)	w-pref (1)	suff (15)
'ḥz - y'ḥzmw 15		'ḥz - 'ḥz 14
('kl - y'klmw 7)		
		'mr - 'mr 9
		bhl - nbhlw 15
bw' - tb'mw 17		
bl^{c} - tbl^{c}mw 12		
dmm - ydmw 16		

8. For a discussion of the syntax of this verse, see p. 70 n. 1.

(hrs - thrs 7)		ṭbʿ - ṭbʿw 4
ksh - yksymw 5		ksh - ksmw 10
		mwg - nmgw 15
		nhl - nhlt 13
		nḥh - nḥyt 13
		nṭh - nṭyt 12
	nṭʿ - wtṭʿmw 17	
npl - tpl 16		
		nṣb - nṣbw 8
		nšp - nšpt 10
		ʿrm - nʿrmw 8
		ṣll - ṣllw 10
		qp' - qp'w 8
rgz - yrgzwn 14(MT)[9]	rgz - wyrgzw14 (Sam)[9]	
(rʿṣ - trʿṣ 6)		
(šlḥ - tšlḥ 7)		
		šmʿ - šmʿw 14

It is clear that the distribution of verbs in Ex 15 is similar to that in those Ugaritic poems where both the pref and suff conjugations occur abundantly but the suff predominates. The only way to substantiate a claim that the verbal pattern here is similar to that of standard poetic Hebrew is to demonstrate that the pref forms are past frequentatives. This cannot be done with any credibility.

Of the seven pref forms two definitely refer to non-repeated events, *yksymw* in v. 5 and *tblʿmw* in v. 12. The deeps covered, the earth swallowed the Egyptians not several times, nor habitually, but once. On the other hand, at first glance it might be argued that *yrgzwn* in v. 14, *y'ḥzmw* in v. 15, and *tpl* and *ydmw* in v. 16 describe a state which was characteristic of Israel's enemies over an extended period of time, namely, that they were in perpetual fear. But such an argument is highly artificial. To begin with, vv. 14-16 describe in a series of clauses, none of which is subordinate to another, the fear which gripped the inhabitants of Canaan and Trans-Jordan at the approach of the Israelites. The succession of verbal forms is: suff-pref-suff-suff-pref-suff-pref-pref. If the suff and pref forms describe qualitatively different types of action or states, the poet went from one to another in a bewildering fashion. It is easier to take all the verbs as syntactically equivalent. And, furthermore, an analysis of the specific verbal roots confirms the impression given by the apparently haphazard sequence of the conjugations. Most impressive is the fact that in v. 14 trembling (*ḥyl*) is said to have seized the peoples. The verbal root is *'ḥz* and it is in the suff conj. In v. 15 trembling (*rʿd*) is said to have seized Moab's mighty men. The verbal root is again *'ḥz* but it is in the pref conj. Not much less impressive is the fact that in vv. 14-15 three verbs are used to describe the

9. Read MT against Sam and G.

condition brought on by fear, *yrgzwn* "they were agitated," *nbhlw* "they were dismayed," and *nmgw* "they melted." Two of them are suff and one pref.

The above arguments make clear that any attempt to understand the pref forms in Ex 15 as past frequentatives is extremely forced. It is better to understand them as syntactically equivalent to suff forms, as in Ugaritic. The validity of this interpretation is corroborated by the fact that the two occur in parallelism three times:

v. 12 nṭyt // tbl^{c}mw
v. 14 šm^{c}w // yrgzwn // 'ḥz
v. 15 nbhlw // y'ḥzmw // nmgw

Finally, the one w-pref form functions as do w-pref forms in Ugaritic: it is in medial position and follows a pref form: v. 17 *tb'mw* // *wtṭ^{c}mw*.

2. *Judges 5*

The nature of the events narrated in Judges 5, a victory of Israel over her enemies, shows that they happened in past time. The form critical consideration that it is a victory hymn substantiates this conclusion. The following verbs are not considered: one, the verbs in vv. 2-3 because they are imperatives or precative in meaning; two, *bšš* and *'ḥrw* in v. 28 and *ymṣ'w* and *yḥlqw* in v. 30 because they are in direct speech; three, *qmty* (two times) in v. 7 because they follow *^{c}d š-*, *b'w* in v. 23 because it follows *ky* and *kr^{c}* in v. 27 because it follows *b'šr*, all of which are in subordinate clauses; four, *ybḥr* in v. 8, *ytnw* in v. 11, *yrd* (two times) in v. 13 and *tdrky* in v. 21 because they occur in contexts whose interpretation is difficult; five, *yr'h* in v. 8 because it follows the particle *'m*, here probably the oath formula; six, *tbrk* (two times) in v. 24 because they are jussives; and seven, *yrdw* in v. 11 and v. 14 and *yšb* in v. 17 because they are 3m forms of initial y/w verbs.

pref (6)	w-pref (1)	suff (31)	w-suff (3)
		'mr - 'mr 23	
		bw' - b'w 19	
gwr - ygwr 17			
		grp - grpm 21	
hlk - ylkw 6			
		hlm - hlmw 22	hlm - whlmh 26
		zll - nzlw 5	
		ḥdl - ḥdlw 6.7.7	
			ḥlp - wḥlph 26
		ḥrp - ḥrp 18	
	ybb - wtybb 28		
		yšb - yšbt 16	
		kr^{c} - kr^{c} 27.27	
		lḥm - nlḥmw 19.19.20.20	
		lqḥ - lqḥw 19	
			mḥṣ - wmḥṣh 26
		mḥq - mḥqh 26	
		nṭp - nṭpw 4.4	
		npl - npl 27.27.27	
		ntn - ntnh 25	

ᶜnh - tᶜnynh 29	
	qrb - hqrybh 25
	rᶜš - rᶜšh 4
	š'l - š'l 25
šwb - tšwb 29	
	škb - škb 27
škn - yškwn 17	škn - škn 17
šlḥ - tšlḥnh 26	šlḥ - šlḥ 15
	šqp - nšqph 28

Like Ex 15, Judges 5 strongly resembles those Ugaritic poems in which both the pref and suff conjugations occur, but the latter predominates. Any attempt to show that the pref forms are frequentatives is abortive. In v. 6 *ylkw* is theoretically capable of being so interpreted, although its being in parallelism with *ḥdlw* militates against it. The two in v. 17 might be so interpreted if the suff forms in the same verse could be taken as statives, so that the translation would read "Gilead was dwelling beyond the Jordan // and Dan, why was he staying where the ships are? Asher was living at the sea coast // and at the wharfs he was dwelling." Such a translation, however, is not permissible. Verses 13-15a and v. 18 catalogue the tribes who came to fight against Sisera. They "went down," they "dared to die." Hence, vv. 15b-17 must refer to the tribes who got cold feet and refused to help out. Instead of coming down, they "stayed" in their own territory. Therefore, the verbal forms in v. 17 must refer to their concrete act of staying home, yielding the translation "Gilead remained beyond the Jordan // and Dan, why did he stay with the ships? Asher sat down at the sea coast // and at the wharfs he remained." None of the remaining three pref forms can be interpreted as past frequentatives.

Therefore, the pref and suff conjugations should be considered syntactically equivalent. Here again the pattern of verbal parallelism supports this conclusion. The two forms are parallel twice:

v. 6 ḥdlw // ylkw
v. 17 škn // ygwr

The three w-suff forms are parallel with a suff form in the Ugaritic fashion. Also two of them are medial. And in the case of the exception it should be noted how closely the action described by *whlmh* "she hammered" follows upon the action of *tšlḥnh* "she stretched out (her hand)" in the preceding line. Thus, the conjunction on *hlmh* at the beginning of the line is understandable in terms of the rapid sequence of actions: v. 26 *whlmh // mḥqh // wmḥṣh* & *wḥlph*.

The one w-pref form occurs medially as in Ugaritic, but follows a suff form: v. 28 *nšqph // wtybb*. This is the only resemblance between Judges 5 and the verbal pattern of standard poetic Hebrew.

3. *Habakkuk 3*

It is the introduction which is decisive in showing that vv. 3-15 of this poem refer to past time. In v. 2 the psalmist says that he has heard (suff) the report of Yahweh and has seen (suff, reading *r'ty* for *yr'ty*) his work. In vv. 3-15 he gives an account of that work. The following verbs are not considered: ^{c}*br* in v. 10 and *ys*^{c}*rw* in v. 14 because our understanding of these verses is defective; *trkb* in v. 8 because it occurs in a subordinate clause introduced by *ky*; *yhlkw* in v. 11 because it is in a relative clause; and *wyṣ'* in v. 5 because it is a 3m form of an initial y/w verb.

pref (9)	w-pref (3)	suff (15)
bw' - ybw' 3		
bq^c - tbq^c 9		
dwš - tdwš 12		
		drk - drkt 15
hyh - thyh 4		
hlk - ylk 5		
ḥyl - yḥylw 10		
		ḥrh - ḥrh 8
		yṣ' - yṣ't 13
		ksh - ksh 3
	mdd - wymdd 6	
		mḥṣ - mḥṣt 13
		ml' - ml'h 3
		nqb - nqbt 14
		nś' - nś' 10
		ntn - ntn 10
	ntr - wytr 6	
^{c}wr - t^{c}wr 9		
		^{c}md - ^{c}md 6.11
	pṣṣ - wytpṣṣw 6	
ṣ^{c}d - tṣ^{c}d 12		
		r'h - r'h 6
		- r'yty 7
		- r'wk 10
rgz - yrgzwn 7		
		šḥḥ - šḥw 6

Here, again, the resemblance is to the pattern which we have reconstructed for early poetic Hebrew. Both pref and suff forms are numerous. While it is theoretically possible for each one of the pref forms to be taken as past frequentatives, the large number of pref forms and the alternation between them and suff forms makes such an interpretation an unviable option. The syntactical equivalence of the two conjugations is shown also by the two instances in which they are parallel:

v. 7	r'yty // yrgzwn
v. 9b-10aa	tbq^c // r'wk & yḥylw

As in Judges 5 only the presence of w-pref forms parallel with suff forms fails to harmonize with the pattern found in Ugaritic poetry. There are two examples of suff // w-pref and one example of w-pref // suff, with the w-pref initial:

v. 6 ^{c}md & wymdd // r'h & wytr
v. 6 wytpṣṣw // šḥw

4. *2 Samuel 22 = Psalm 18*

A form critical analysis of this poem reveals that it is an individual thanksgiving psalm. Therefore, the deliverance wrought by Yahweh described in vv. 5-25 must have necessarily taken place in the past. The psalmist stands before Yahweh and an assembly of his people to give thanks for the deliverance which Yahweh has already effected. Evidence, apart from form critical considerations, that this is a thanksgiving psalm comes from the superscription, the authors of which certainly understood it as such and understood the events narrated as having already happened, "Belonging to David, the servant of Yahweh, who recited the words of this song to Yahweh on the day Yahweh delivered him from the power of all his enemies and from the power of Saul."

The following verbs are omitted: *'mṣw* in v. 18, *ḥpṣ* in v. 20, and *šmrty*, *rš^{c}ty* and *'swr* in vv. 22-23 because they occur in subordinate clauses introduced by *ky*; *wyṣ'* (Ps. *wywṣy'ny*) in v. 20 and *wyrd* in v. 10 because they are 3m forms of initial y/w verbs.

pref (18)	w-pref (15)	suff (6)
'kl - t'kl 9		
		'pp - 'ppny 5
bw' - tbw' Ps 7 (2S omits)		
		b^{c}r - b^{c}rw 9
		- b^{c}rw 2S 13 (Ps ^{c}brw)[1]
b^{c}t - yb^{c}tny 5		
glh - yglw 2S 16 (Ps wy-)	glh - wyglw Ps 16 (2S y-)	
gml - ygmlny 21		
	g^{c}š - wtg^{c}š 8	
	- wytg^{c}šw 8	
	d'h - wyd' Ps 11 (2S wyr')	
	hyh - wyhy 19	
	- w'hyh 2S 24 (Ps w'hy)	
	hmm - wyhmm 15	
ḥlṣ - yḥlṣny 20		
lqḥ - yqḥny 17		
mšh - ymšny 17		
	nṭh - wyṭ 10	
nṣl - yṣylny 18		
ntn - ytn 14		sbb - sbny 6
		^{c}br - ^{c}brw Ps 13 (2S b^{c}rw)
	^{c}wp - wy^{c}p 11	
		^{c}lh - ^{c}lh 9
	pwṣ - wypyṣm 15	
qdm - yqdmny 19		qdm - qdmny 6
qr' - 'qr' 7		

1. Omit from totals, reading Ps *^{c}brw* as the correct text.

- 'qr' 2S 7 (Ps 'šw^c)[2]	
	r'h - wyr' 2S 11 (Ps wyd')[3]
	- wyr'w 16
rgz - yrgzw 8	
	rkb - wyrkb 11
r^{c}m - yr^{c}m 2S 14 (Ps wy-)	r^{c}m - wyr^{c}m Ps 14 (2S y-)
	r^{c}š - wyr^{c}š 8
	šwb - wyšb 25
šw^c - 'šw^c Ps 7 (2S 'qr')	
šyt - yšt Ps 12 (2S wy-)	šyt - wyšt 2S 12 (Ps y-)
šlḥ - yšlḥ 17	šlḥ - wyšlḥ 15
šm^c - yšm^c Ps 7 (2S wy-)	šm^c - wyšm^c 2S 7 (Ps y-)
	šmr - w'štmrh 2S 24 (Ps w'štmr)

Cross and Freedman have demonstrated rather convincingly that in this poem the text with the pref form more likely represents the original autograph than the text with the w-pref form.[4] Ps 18 and 2 S 22 agree in reading a pref form 13 times. A pref form is found in 2 S alone two times and in Ps 18 alone three times. Taking the text with the pref form this means that there are eighteen in the oldest textual tradition to which we have access. By the same reasoning, reading a w-pref form only where 2 S and Ps 18 agree, there are fifteen.

This psalm is like those Ugaritic poems where the pref is the predominant conjugation, but the suff and the w-pref also occur. The pref forms are surely not past frequentatives, for the narration of an entire story with frequentatives would be bizarre, to say the least. They are better understood in terms of the Ugaritic pref conj. The two cases of parallelism between pref and suff forms verify this conclusion:

v. 5 'ppny // yb^{c}tny
v. 9 ^{c}lh // t'kl // b^{c}rw

How the w-pref forms should be understood is, however, debatable. Its positioning in the poetic line is as follows:

	Medial		*Initial*
v. 8	wytg^{c}šw	v. 8	wtg^{c}š
8	wtr^{c}š	10	wyṭ
11	wyd' (2S wyr')	11	wyrkb
11	wy^{c}p	15	wyšlḥ
15	wyhmm	16	wyr'w

2. Omit from totals, reading Ps *'šw^c* as the correct text.

3. Omit from totals, reading Ps *wyd'* as the correct text.

4. F. M. Cross, Jr., *Studies in Ancient Yahwistic Poetry*, Dissertation, John Hopkins University (Baltimore, 1950), pp. 321ff. Cf. F. M. Cross, Jr., and D. N. Freedman, "A Royal Song of Thanksgiving - II Samuel 22 = Psalm 18," JBL 72 (1953), 15-34.

15	wypyṣm	24	w'hyh (Ps w'hy)
19	wyhy	25	wyšb
24	w'štmrh (Ps w'štmr)		

In the eight cases where it is medial there is no deviation from the Ugaritic pattern. But not only do the seven cases where it is initial diverge from it, but, when added to the eight cases where it is medial, make the proportionate number of w-pref forms greater than is generally the case in Ugaritic. It is very unlikely, in spite of this, that any of them should be understood in terms of the w-pref conj of standard poetic Hebrew. In the first place, three times in this poem a w-pref is paralleled by a pref form according to the Ugaritic pattern, and not once is it paralleled by a suff form according to the pattern found in standard poetic Hebrew. In two of these the w-pref form is initial (vv. 8, 16) and in one it is medial (v. 19):

v. 8 wtgᶜš & wtrᶜš // yrgzw // wytgᶜšw
16 wyr'w // yglw (Ps wyglw)
19 yqdmny // wyhy

In the second place, the discrepancy in the number of conjunctions between 2 S 22 and Ps 18 makes one strongly suspect that Cross and Freedman are right in stating that the autograph of this psalm had far fewer w-pref forms than either of the two preserved copies. If their theory is correct, and it is certainly plausible, then the sole way in which this poem differs from Ugaritic poems is eliminated.

5. *Deuteronomy 32*

In this poem all the verbs in independent clauses referring unambiguously to past time are contained in vv. 8-20. The nature of the events narrated show their past reference. There are six verbs which must be omitted. Five of them are in relative clauses: in v. 15 *ᶜśhw*, in v. 17 *ydᶜwm*, *b'w*, and *śᶜrwm*, and in v. 18 *yldk*. The sixth is *wynqhw* in v. 13, a 3m form of an initial y/w verb.

pref (19)	w-pref (7)	suff (3)
'kl - y'kylhw 13 (Sam)[5]	'kl - wy'kl 13 (MT)[5]	
	'mr - wy'mr 20	
	bᶜṭ - wybᶜṭ 15	
byn - ybwnnhw 10(MT)[6]	byn - wybnnhw 10 (Sam)[6]	
zbḥ - yzbḥw 17		
kᶜs - ykᶜyshw 16		
		kśh - kśyt 15
lqḥ - yqḥhw 11 (MT)[7]	lqḥ - wyqḥhw 11 (Sam)[7]	

---

5. Read Sam with G against MT.

6. Read MT against Sam and G.

7. Read MT with G against Sam.

mṣ' - ymṣ'hw 10		
	n'ṣ - wyn'ṣ 19	
	nbl̇ - wynbl̇ 15	
nḥh - ynḥnw 12		
	nṭš - wyṭš 15	
nṣb - yṣb 8		
nṣr - yṣrnhw 10(MT)[8]	nṣr - wyṣrnhw 10 (Sam)[8]	
nś' - yś'hw 11		
sbb - ysbbnhw 10		
		ᶜbh - ᶜbyt 15
ᶜwr - yᶜyr 11		
prś - yprś 11		
qn' - yqn'hw 16 (MT)[9]	qn' - wyqny'hw 16 (Sam)[9]	
	r'h - wyr' 19	
rḥp - yrḥp 11		
rkb - yrkbhw 13		
šyh - tšy 18		
	škḥ - wtškḥ 18	
šmn - yšmn 15 (Sam)[1]	šmn - wyšmn 15 (MT)[1]	šmn - šmnt 15
šth - tšth 14		

Following the MT there are seventeen pref and nine w-pref forms. Following the text without the conjunction, there are nineteen pref and seven w-pref. As in 2 S 22 = Ps 18 the latter of these alternatives is probably the one which most nearly represents the autograph. In either case, the picture presented by Dt 32:8-20 is identical in every respect with that in 2 S 22 = Ps 18. The pref conj is the one predominantly used, and so cannot easily have frequentative force. But the total number of w-pref forms and the percentage of them which are initial are slightly greater than one would expect according to the Ugaritic pattern. Of the nine w-pref forms according to the MT, four are initial; of the seven according to the text without the conjunction, three are initial:

Medial		*Initial*	
v. 13	wy'kl (Sam y'kylhw)	v. 15	wyṭš
15	wybᶜṭ	15	wyšmn (Sam yšmn)
15	wynbl̇	19	wyr'
18	wtškḥ	20	wy'mr
19	wyn'ṣ		

But also as in 2 S 22 = Ps 18, the parallelism corresponds to the Ugaritic pattern. According to the text without the conjunction, there is one example of pref // w-pref; according to the MT, there are three:

v. 13 yrkbhw // wy'kl (Sam y'kylhw)
v. 15 wyšmn (Sam yšmn) & wybᶜṭ
v. 18 tšy // wtškḥ

---

8. Read MT against Sam and G.

9. Read MT with G against Sam.

1. Read Sam against MT. G omits the verb.

And, finally, the fact that the Massoretic and Samaritan recensions manifest six discrepancies regarding the conjunction *w-* strongly suggests that the autograph of this poem had even less than seven w-pref forms.

At the beginning of this chapter it was stated as a methodological principle that finite verbs in subordinate clauses would not be examined. Up to now there has been no need to consider them, for they present the same pattern as is found in the independent clauses of the poems in question. At this point, however, the consecution of verbs in the relative clause in Dt 32:6 must be mentioned because it resembles the pattern of standard poetry. In this verse two suff forms are continued by a w-pref form: v. 6 qnk // ᶜśk and wyknnk.

6. *Job*

There is one passage of extensive past narrative in Job plus several more modest in length and a few which are quite brief. Each of these will be considered separately. In chapter 29, the first part of Job's peroration, he depicts at great length his former weal. He begins "O that I were as in the months of old // as in the days God protected me, when his lamp shone over my head // when I walked by his light through darkness." He then proceeds to elaborate on the blessedness of his past life under God's nurture. All the verbs in vv. 18aβ-20 must be omitted because in them Job relates his former thoughts on how he would die. The verbs refer to the future, not the past. In addition, the following must also be eliminated: one, after *ky*, *šmᶜh* and *r'th* in v. 11 and *'mlṭ* in v. 12; two, after *k'šr*, *hyyty* in v. 4 and *ynḥm* in v. 25; three, after *my* expressing a wish, *ytnny* in v. 2; four, in a noun clause, *yšmrny* in v. 2; and, five, in a relative clause, *ydᶜty* in v. 16.

Job 29

pref (14)	w-pref (8)	suff (10)	w-suff (3)
'mn - y'mynw 24			
	'mr - w'mr 18		
	'šr - wt'šrny 11		
bw' - tb' 13			
bḥr - 'bḥr 25			
		dbq - dbqh 10	
	dmm - wydmw 21		
		hyh - hyyty 15	
hlk - 'lk 3			
		ḥb' - nḥb'w 10	ḥb' - wnḥb'w 8
ḥqr - 'ḥqrhw 16			
	yšb - w'šb 25		
			yḥl - wyḥlw 21.23
kwn - 'kyn 7			
	lbš - wylbšny 14	lbš - lbšty 14	
nṭp - tṭp 22			
npl - ypylwn 24			
	ᶜwd - wtᶜydny 11		
		ᶜmd - ᶜmdw 8	
		ᶜṣr - ᶜṣrw 9	
		pᶜr - pᶜrw 23	
ṣwq - yṣwq 6			

qwm - qmw 8
r'h - r'wny 8
rnn - 'rnn 13
śḥq - 'śḥq 24
śym - yśymw 9
šbr - w'šbrh 17
škn - w'škwn 25
šlk - 'šlyk 17
šmᶜ - šmᶜw 21
šnh - yšnw 22

The resemblance between Job 29 and Ugaritic poems can hardly be gainsaid: pref and suff forms are predominant, the two being in parallelism once: v. 9 *ᶜṣrw // yśymw*. Six of the w-pref forms are medial:

Medial		*Initial*	
v. 11	wt'šrny	v. 17	w'šbrh
11	wtᶜydny	18	w'mr
14	wylbšny		
21	wydmw		
25	w'šb		
25	w'škwn		

Three of them, two medial and one initial, are parallel with pref forms:

v. 17 w'šbrh // 'šlyk
v. 25 'bḥr & w'šb // w'škwn

Two of the w-suff forms are medial:

Medial		*Initial*	
v. 8	wnḥb'w		
21	wyḥlw	v. 23	wyḥlw

And all three are parallel with suff forms:

v. 8 r'wny & wnḥb'w // qmw & ᶜmdw
21 šmᶜw & wyḥlw // wydmw
23 wyḥlw // pᶜrw

In only two respects is there any resemblance with standard poetic Hebrew: the initial position of one w-suff and two w-pref forms and the parallelism of two of the w-pref with suff forms:

v. 14 lbšty // wylbšny
21 šmᶜw & wyḥlw // wydmw

But the effect of this resemblance is vitiated by the fact that one of the initial w-pref forms (*w'šbrh*) is parallel with a pref not a suff form, that the one initial w-suff form is parallel with a suff not a pref form; and that in one of the cases where a suff is paralleled by a w-pref form, it is also paralleled by a w-suff form (v. 21).

In spite of all this resemblance between Job 29 and the Ugaritic poems, the interpretation of the pref and w-suff forms as frequentatives must be considered more of a live option in this chapter than in any of the preceding five poems. There a specific sequence of events is narrated, but not so here. Job is describing what he habitually did for others and what God habitually did for him. The past frequentatives are designed precisely for this type of past narration. The patterns of parallelism listed above, however, do not support this interpretation. The pref and w-suff forms are never parallel with one another, as would be expected if they are frequentatives. Rather, the former is parallel with suff and w-pref forms and the latter with suff forms.

Most of the other passages of past narrative in Job likewise resemble the verbal pattern found in the Ugaritic poems. In 4:12-16 Eliphaz relates to Job what was said to him one night by a mysterious apparition. None of the verbs must be omitted.

Job 4:12-16

pref (6)	w-pref (1)	suff (2)
gnb - ygnb 12		
ḥlp - yḥlp 15		
	lqḥ - wtqḥ 12	
nkr - 'kyr 16		
smr - tsmr 15		
ʿmd - yʿmd 16		
		pḥd - hpḥyd 14
		qr' - qr'ny 14
šmʿ - 'šmʿ 16		

The pref conj is predominant. The one w-pref form is medial and parallel with a pref form: v. 12 *ygnb // wtqḥ*.

In 10:10-11 Job describes how he was formed in the womb by God. Again no omissions are necessary.

Job 10:10-11

pref (4)
lbs - tlbyšny 11
ntk - ttykny 10
skk - tskkny 11
qp' - tqpy'ny 10

And in 15:7 Eliphaz asks Job if he was the first man born.

Job 15:7

pref (1)	suff (1)
	ḥll - ḥwllt 7
yld - twld 7	

In 38:4-11aα and 10:8a, however, the verbal pattern resembles that of standard poetic Hebrew. In the first Yahweh asks Job if he was present when he formed the world. *Yd^{c}t* after *'m* in v. 4, *td^c* after *ky* in v. 5, and *yrh* in v. 6 and *yṣ'* in v. 8 because they are 3ms forms of initial y/w verbs must be disregarded.

Job 38:4-11a

w-pref (5)	suff (4)
'mr - w'mr 11	
	hyh - hyyt 4
	ṭb^c - hṭb^{c}w 6
	nṭh - nṭh 5
swk - wysk 8	
rw^c - wyry^{c}w 7	
śym - w'śym 10	śym - śm 5
šbr - w'šbr 10	

There are no parallels. Three of the w-pref forms are initial and two medial:

Medial		*Initial*	
v. 7	wyry^{c}w	v. 8	wysk
10	w'śym	10	w'šbr
		11	w'mr

In the second of these two passages Job refers to the fact that God is the one who made him.

Job 10:8a

w-pref (1)	suff (1)
	^{c}ṣb - ^{c}ṣbwny 8
^{c}śh - wy^{c}śwny 8	

The two are coordinated within the same stichos, with the w-pref medial.

In the final passage of unambiguous past narrative in Job, chapter 26:12-13, where Job describes the battle between God and the sea dragon preliminary to creation, only suff forms are used. Since they are employed in both early and standard poetic Hebrew, it is impossible to tell which system is being used.

Job 26:12-13

suff (4)
ḥll - ḥllh 13
mḥṣ - mḥṣ 12
rg^c - rg^c 12
špr - šprh 13

7. *Miscellaneous Shorter Passages*

It was stated above that, since features characteristic of early poetic Hebrew do occur here and there in standard poetic Hebrew, one cannot conclude from the presence of a few of them that a poem is early. A definite pattern must be observable, and this usually requires a passage of some length. The following two passages appear to contain the pattern of early poetry, but their brevity prohibits any firm assurance on the matter.

a. *Psalm 81*

In verses 7-8 and 12-13 of this poem Yahweh speaks of his deliverance of Israel and of their consequent rebellion. None of the verbs must be excluded.

pref (4)	w-pref (2)	suff (4)
		'bh - 'bh 12
bḥn - 'bḥnk 8		
hlk - ylkw 13		
	ḥlṣ - w'ḥlṣk 8	
		swr - hsyrwty 7
ᶜbr - tᶜbrnh 7		
ᶜnh - 'ᶜnk 8		
		qr' - qr't 8
	šlḥ - w'šlḥhw 13	
		šmᶜ - šmᶜ 12

As with several of the poems already discussed, an attempt to prove that the pattern here is that of standard poetry hinges on demonstrating that the pref forms are frequentatives. Any such attempt fails. First of all, the patterns of parallelism do not favor such an interpretation. Once a pref is parallel with a suff form (v. 7), once with a w-pref form (v. 13), and once with both (v. 8):

v. 7 hsyrwty // tᶜbrnh
8 qr't & w'ḥlṣk // 'ᶜnk
13 w'šlḥhw // ylkw

Second, one of the pref forms (*'bḥnk* in v. 8) refers to a single historical event.

The occurrence of *qr't* and *w'ḥlṣk* in the same stichos and the initial position of one of the w-pref forms (*w'šlḥhw*) resemble the pattern of standard poetry. It is questionable, however, how much value should be attached to these resemblances, for *qr't* and *w'ḥlṣk* are paralleled by *'ᶜnk*, and *w'šlḥhw* is paralleled by *ylkw*, both pref forms.

b. *Psalm 104*

In verses 5-8 of this psalm the process of creation is described. In v. 5 *ysd* and in v. 8 *yrdw* because they are 3m forms of initial y/w verbs, *tmwṭ* in v. 5 because it refers to the future, and *ysdt* in v. 8 because it is a relative clause must be excluded.

pref (4)	suff (1)
ḥpz - yḥpzwn 7	
	ksh - ksytw 6
nws - ynwswn 7	
ᶜlh - yᶜlw 8	
ᶜmd - yᶜmdw 6	

As with 2 S 22 = Ps 18, it is doubtful that a historical narrative would be told almost exclusively with frequentatives. It is better to take the pref forms as having preterit force, the one example of parallelism (*ksytw // y^cmdw* in v. 6) supporting this interpretation.

In all the above six poems the use of the finite verbal conjugations in past narrative impressively corresponds to their use in early poetic Hebrew. Only in Ex 15 and Ps 104, however, is this correspondence total. In the remaining five certain aspects of the use of the w-pref conj show a resemblance to its use in standard poetic Hebrew. In Jud 5, Hab 3, and Ps 81 there are w-pref parallel with suff forms. In 2 S 22 = Ps 18 there is a greater number of w-pref forms and a greater percentage of them occur initially than would be expected according to the pattern of early poetry. This same phenomenon reappears in Dt 32, and, in addition, in a relative clause a w-pref parallels two suff forms. Both parallelism of w-pref with suff forms and initial w-pref forms are found in Job.

With the possible exception of Job, it is very questionable whether these isolated deviations result from the influence of standard poetic Hebrew. The examples of w-pref parallel with suff forms in Jud 5 and Hab 3 can easily be considered the result of chance variation. Where it is common to parallel pref with suff forms it is almost inevitable that some of these forms will occasionally have the conjunction prefixed to them. As for 2 S 22 = Ps 18 and Dt 32, textual evidence supports the hypothesis that the autographs of these two poems had fewer conjunctions than any extant copy. The verbal patterns in parts of Job (especially 38:4-11aα) make one more hesitant to claim the absence of any influence of standard poetic Hebrew.

B. *Poems that Resemble Standard Poetry*

1. *Psalm 78*

The nature of the events narrated in Ps 78:9-72 show that the verbs refer to past time. The following are omitted: *hrgm*, *wdršwhw*, *wšbw* and *wšḥrw* in v. 34 because they are in the protasis and apodosis of a conditional sentence introduced by *'m*; *hr'm* in v. 11, *yšwb* in v. 39, *pdm* in v. 42, *śm* in v. 43, *qnth* in v. 54, *škn* in v. 60, *'hb* in v. 68, and *ysdh* in v. 69 because they occur in relative clauses.

pref (18)	w-pref (56)	suff (39)	w-suff (1)
	'kl - wy'klw 29	'kl - 'kl 25	
	- wy'klm 45	- 'klh 63	
		'mn - h'mynw 22.32	
		- n'mnw 37	
		'mr - 'mrw 19	
	bgd - wybgdw 57		
bw' - yb' 29	bw' - wyby'm 54	bw' - hby'w 71	
	bḥr - wybḥr 68	bḥr - bḥr 67	

		bṭḥ - bṭḥw 22	
bkh - tbkynh 64			
	bnh - wybn 69		
bq^{c} - ybq^{c} 15		bq^{c} - bq^{c} 13	
	grš - wygrš 55		
	dbr - wydbrw 19		
		hll - hwllw 63	
	hpk - wyhpk 44	hpk - hpkw 9	
		- nhpkw 57	
hrg - yhrg 47	hrg - wyhrg 31		
	zwb - wyzwbw 20		
		zwr - zrw 30	
	zkr - wyzkrw 35	zkr - zkrw 42	
	- wyzkr 39	ḥṭ' - ḥṭ'w 32	
		ḥśk - ḥśk 50	
	ysp - wywsypw 17		
	yṣ' - wywṣ' 16		
	yrd - wywrd 16		
		kwn - nkwn 37	
kzb - ykzbw 36			
	klh - wykl 33		
		ksh - ksh 53	
	k^{c}s - wyk^{c}yswhw 58		
kpr - ykpr 38			
		kr^{c} - hkry^{c} 31	
	lqḥ - wyqḥhw 70		
		m'n - m'nw 10	
	m's - wym's 59.67		
	mṭr - wymṭr 24.27		
mrh - ymrwhw 40	mrh - wymrw 56		
	nhg - wynhg 26		
	- wynhgm 52		
nḥh - ynḥm 72	nḥh - wynḥm 14.53		
	nṭš - wyṭš 60		
	nkh - wyk 51.66	nkh - hkh 20	
	nsg - wysgw 57		
	nsh - wynsw 18.41.56		
ns^{c} - ys^{c} 26	ns^{c} - wys^{c} 52		
	npl - wypl 28	npl - nplw 64	
	- wypylm 55		
	nṣb - wyṣb 13		
	ntn - wytn 46.61	ntn - ntn 24.66	
	sgr - wysgr 48.62	sgr - hsgyr 50	
	^{c}br - wy^{c}byrm 13	^{c}br - ht^{c}br 62	
	- wyt^{c}br 21.59		
^{c}wr - y^{c}yr 38			
		^{c}lh - ^{c}lh 21.31	
^{c}ṣb - y^{c}ṣybwhw 40			
		^{c}śh - ^{c}śh 12	
		pḥd - pḥdw 53	
pls - ypls 50			
	pth - wyptwhw 36		
		ptḥ - ptḥ 23	
	ṣwh - wyṣw 23		
	qyṣ - wyqṣ 65		
qn' - yqny'whw 58			
			rbh - whrbh 38
	r^{c}m - wyr^{c}m 72		
	śb^{c} - wyśb^{c}w 29		
		ślq - nśqh 21	
	šwb - wyšwbw 41		
šḥt - yšḥyt 38	šḥt - wtšḥytm 45		
šṭp - yšṭpw 20			

	škḥ - wyškḥw 11	
	škn - wyškn 55	
šlḥ - yšlḥ 45.49		šlḥ - šlḥ 25
		šmʿ - šmʿ 21.59
		šmr - šmrw 10.56
	šqh - wyšq 15	
šth - yštywn 44		
		twh - htww 41

That the pattern found in this poem is that of standard poetic Hebrew is readily apparent. The suff and w-pref conjugations are predominant and very often parallel:

v. 13	bqʿ & wyʿbyrm // wyṣb
19	wydbrw & 'mrw
20	hkh // wyzwbw // yšṭpw
21	šmʿ & wytʿbr // nśqh // ʿlh
23	wyṣw // ptḥ
24	wymṭr // ntn
31	wyhrg // hkryʿ
41	wyšwbw // wynsw // htww
53	wynḥm // pḥdw // ksh
56	wynsw // wymrw // šmrw
57	wysgw & wybgdw // nhpkw
59	šmʿ & wytʿbr // wym's
62	wysgr // htʿbr
66	wyk // ntn
67	wym's // bḥr

Furthermore, the w-pref conj is initial almost twice as often as it is medial, 38 to 19 respectively:

	Medial				*Initial*		
v. 13	wyʿbyrm	v. 45	wyšḥytm	v. 11	wyškḥw	v. 31	wyhrg
13	wyṣb	52	wynhgm	14	wynḥm	33	wykl
15	wyšq	55	wypylm	16	wywṣ'	35	wyzkrw
16	wywrd	55	wyškn	17	wywsypw	36	wyptwhw
20	wyzwbw	56	wymrw	18	wynsw	39	wyzkr
21	wytʿbr	57	wybgdw	19	wydbrw	41	wyšwbw
26	wynhg	59	wym's	23	wyṣw	44	wyhpk
29	wyśbʿw	59	wytʿbr	24	wymṭr	46	wytn
41	wynsw	70	wyqḥhw	27	wymṭr	48	wysgr
45	wy'klm			28	wypl	51	wyk
				29	wy'klw	52	wysʿ
				53	wynḥm	62	wysgr
				54	wyby'm	65	wyqṣ
				55	wygrš	66	wyk
				56	wynsw	67	wym's
				57	wysgw	68	wybḥr
				58	wykʿyswhw	69	wybn
				60	wytṣ	70	ywbḥr
				61	wytn	72	wyrʿm

If the resemblance to standard poetry is to be total, however, the pref forms must be explained as frequentatives. Such as explanation is probable for five of them. Verse 38 contains a summary statement of God's dealings with

Israel's forebearers, "He was compassionate, he would forgive iniquity, he would not destroy, he time and again stayed his anger, and did not arouse his full fury." What is said in this verse is enough to demonstrate that the three pref forms in it have frequentative force. That they are paralleled by a w-suff form offers striking confirmation: *ykpr // yšḥyt // whrbh // yʿyr*. This is precisely the parallelism expected if the pattern of standard poetic Hebrew is operative in this poem. The presence of *kmh* "how often" in v. 40 shows that its two pref forms (*ymrwhw // yʿṣybwhw*) also are frequentative.

All of the remaining twelve pref forms, however, are better understood as referring to simple events in the past, though in several cases one might quibble over the precise interpretation. The patterns of parallelism decisively support the understanding of them as having preterit force. One is paralleled by a suff and a w-pref form and two more by suff forms only:

v. 20 hkh // wyzwbw // yšṭpw
50 ypls // ḥśk // hsgyr
64 nplw // ṭbkynh

Eight more are parallel with w-pref forms:

v. 15 ybqʿ // wyšq
26 ysʿ // wynhg
29 wy'klw // wyśbʿw // yb'
36 wyptwhw // ykzbw
44 wyhpk // yštywn
45 yšlh // wy'klm // wtšḥytm
58 wykʿyswhw // yqny'whw
72 wyrʿm // ynḥm

2. *Psalm 105*

The nature of the events narrated clearly demonstrates that the verbs in Ps 105:12-45 refer to past action. The following are excepted from consideration: *tgʿw* and *trʿw* in v. 15 because they are precatives after the negative particle *'l*; *yḥkm* in v. 22 and *ynṣrw* in v. 45 because they express purpose, the former in parallelism with *l'sr* and the latter after the particle *bʿbwr*; *bḥr* in v. 26 because it is in a relative clause; *npl* in v. 38 and *zkr* in v. 42 because they are in *ky* clauses; *mrw* in v. 28 because of the uncertainty of the text; and, finally, *yyršw* in v. 44 because it is a 3m form of an initial y/w verb.

pref (1)	w-pref (22)	suff (22)
	'kl - wy'kl 35.35	
		'mr - 'mr 31.34
	bw' - wyb' 23.31 34.40	bw' - b'h 18
	hlk - wythlkw 13	hlk - hlkw 41
		hpk - hpk 25.29
	zwb - wyzwbw 41	
	ḥšk - wyḥšk 28	
	ykḥ - wywkḥ 14	
	yṣ' - wywṣy'm 37	
	- wywṣ' 43	

	mwt - wymt 29	
		mkr - nmkr 17
		nwḥ - hnyḥ 14
	nkh - wyk 33.36	
	ntn - wytn 44	ntn - ntn 32
	ntr - wytyrhw 20	
		ᶜnh - ᶜnw 18
	ᶜsm - wyᶜsmhw 24	
	prh - wypr 24	
	ptḥ - wyptḥhw 20	ptḥ - ptḥ 41
		ṣrp - ṣrpthw 19
	qr' - wyqr' 16	
śbᶜ - ysbyᶜm 40		
		śwm - śmw 21.27
		śmḥ - śmḥ 38
		š'l - š'l 40
	šbr - wyšbr 33	šbr - šbr 16
		šlḥ - šlḥ 17.20.26.28
		šrṣ - šrṣ 30

Quite obviously the verbal pattern here is that of standard poetic Hebrew. The suff and w-pref conjugations are in equal proportion, and occasionally are parallel:

v. 14	hnyḥ // wywkḥ
16	wyqr' // šbr
20	šlḥ & wytyrhw // wyptḥhw
29	hpk // wymt

Twelve of the 22 w-pref forms are medial, ten initial:

Medial				*Initial*			
v. 14	wywkḥ	v. 31	wyb'	v. 13	wythlkw	v. 35	wy'kl
20	wytyrhw	33	wyšbr	16	wyqr'	36	wyk
20	wyptḥhw	34	wyb'	23	wyb'	37	wywṣy'm
24	wyᶜṣmhw	35	wy'kl	24	wypr	43	wywṣ'
28	wyḥšk	40	wyb'	33	wyk	44	wytn
29	wymt	41	wyzwbw				

The one pref form is parallel with a w-pref form (v. 40 *š'l & wyb' // yśbyᶜm*) and, hence, is best taken as referring to a single event.

3. *Psalm 106*

As in Pss 78 and 105 the nature of the events narrated in Ps 106:7-46 prove that they happened in past time. *ᶜmd* in v. 23 because it is in the protasis of a conditional sentence after *lwly*, *hmrw* in v. 33 after *ky*, and *'mr* in v. 34 and *zbḥw* in v. 38 because they are in relative clauses must be disregarded.

pref (6)	w-pref (54)	suff (10)
	'wh - wyt'ww 14	
	'kl - wy'klw 28	
	'mn - wy'mynw 12	'mn - h'mynw 24
	'mr - wy'mr 23	
	bṭ' - wybṭ' 33	
	blʿ - wtblʿ 17	
	bʿr - wtbʿr 18	
	g'l - wyg'lm 10	
	gʿr - wygʿr 9	
	hyh - wyhyw 36	
	hlk - wywlykm 9	
	zbḥ - wyzbḥw 37	
	zkr - wyzkr 45	zkr - zkrw 7
	znh - wyznw 39	
	ḥwh - wyštḥww 19	
		ḥkh - ḥkw 13
	ḥnp - wtḥnp 38	
	ḥrb - wyḥrb 9	
	ḥrh - wyḥr 40	
	ḥšb - wtḥšb 31	
	ṭm' - wyṭm'w 39	
	yšʿ - wywšyʿm 8.10	
		ytr - nwtr 11
	knʿ - wyknʿw 42	
	ksh - wyksw 11	
	- wtks 17	
	kʿs - wykʿysw 29	
lhṭ - tlhṭ 18		
	lḥṣ - wylḥṣwm 42	
	lmd - wylmdw 35	
	m's - wym'sw 24	
		mhr - mhrw 13
	mwr - wymyrw 20	
	mkk - wymkw 43	
mrh - ymrw 43	mrh - wymrw 7	
	mšl - wymšlw 41	
	nḥm - wynḥm 45	
	nsh - wynsw 14	
nṣl - yṣylm 43		
	nś' - wyś' 26	
	ntn - wytn 15.46	
	- wytnm 41	
	ʿbd - wyʿbdw 36	
	ʿmd - wyʿmd 30	
	ʿṣr - wtʿṣr 30	
	ʿrb - wytʿrbw 35	
ʿśh - yʿśw 19		
	pll - wypll 30	
	prṣ - wyprṣ 29	
ptḥ - tptḥ 17		
	ṣmd - wyṣmdw 28	
	qn' - wyqn'w 16	
	qṣp - wyqṣypw 32	
	r'h - wyr' 44	
	rgn - wyrgnw 25	
	rʿʿ - wyrʿ 32	
		śkl - hśkylw 7
šyr - yšyrw 12		
		škḥ - škḥw 13.21
	šlḥ - wyšlḥ 15	
		šmd - hšmydw 34
		šmʿ - šmʿw 25
	špk - wyšpkw 38	
	tʿb - wytʿb 40	

As in the two previous poems the verbal system here is that of standard poetic Hebrew, though this poem differs from them in the virtually exclusive use of the w-pref conj. Of the ten instances of the suff conj, five are parallel with w-pref forms:

v. 7 hśkylw // zkrw // wymrw
11 wyksw // nwtr
24 wym'sw // h'mynw
25 wyrgnw // šm^{c}w

Of the 54 w-pref forms, 30 are initial and 24 medial:

Medial				*Initial*			
v. 7	wymrw	v. 30	wypll	v. 8	wywšy^{c}m	v. 29	wyk^{c}ysw
9	wywlykm	32	wyr^{c}	9	wyg'r	30	wy^{c}md
9	wyḥrb	33	wybṭ'	10	wywšy^{c}m	31	wtḥšb
10	wyg'lm	35	wylmdw	11	wyksw	32	wyqṣypw
14	wynsw	36	wyhyw	12	wy'mynw	35	wyt^{c}rbw
15	wyšlḥ	38	wtḥnp	14	wyt'ww	36	wy^{c}bdw
17	wtbl^{c}	39	wyznw	15	wytn	37	wyzbḥw
17	wtks	40	wyt^{c}b	16	wyqn'w	38	wyšpkw
19	wyštḥww	41	wymšlw	18	wtb^{c}r	39	wytm'w
28	wy'klw	42	wykn^{c}w	20	wymyrw	40	wyḥr
29	wyprṣ	43	wymkw	23	wy'mr	41	wytnm
30	wt^{c}ṣr	45	wynḥm	24	wym'sw	42	wylḥṣwm
				25	wyrgnw	44	wyr'
				26	wyś'	45	wyzkr
				28	wyṣmdw	46	wytn

All six of the pref forms are parallel with w-pref forms:

v. 12 wy'mynw // yšyrw
17 tptḥ & wtbl^{c} // wtks
18 wtb^{c}r // tlhṭ
19 y^{c}św // wyštḥww
43 yṣylm // ymrw // wymkw

In spite of this fact, however, it is probable that the two in v. 43 should be taken as frequentatives, since they are modified by the expression "many times." It should also be noted that in the case of *yšyrw* in v. 12 three Hebrew MSS, G, Hie, and S read the conjunction. Its loss is credible in that it would have occurred in the series *ywwy*, four very similar letters. The remaining three are best taken as having preterit force.

4. *Miscellaneous Shorter Passages*

a. *Genesis 49 and Deuteronomy 33*

Four of the short poems collected in Gen 49 and Dt 33 refer to the settlement of Israel as a whole or of one of its tribes. Gen 49:15 tells Issachar's story, 49:23-24 Joseph's, Dt 33:21 Gad's, and 33:27b-28 speaks in a summary way of all Israel. Since the verbal patterns in all of these poems match those found in standard poetic Hebrew, they are considered together. Only *yᶜrpw* in Dt 33:28 needs to be omitted, because it describes the nature of Palestine, not an event in the conquest.

Gen 49:15

w-pref (3)
hyh - wyhy 15
nṭh - wyṭ 15
r'h - wyr' 15

Gen 49:23-24

w-pref (4)	w-suff (1)
yšb - wtšb 24	
mrr - wymrrhw 23	
pzz - wypzw 24	
	rbb - wrbw 23[2]
śṭm - wyśṭmhw 23	

Dt 33:21

w-pref (2)	suff (1)
'th - wyt' 21	
	ᶜśh - ᶜśh 21
r'h - wyr' 21	

Dt 33:27b-28

w-pref (3)
'mr - wy'mr 27
grš - wygrš 27
škn - wyškn 28

Not only in the overwhelming predominance of the w-pref conj but in its positioning and its parallels, the pattern in these four poems is like that of standard poetic Hebrew. In Dt 33:21 a w-pref is parallel with a suff form: Dt 33:21 *wyt' // ᶜśh*. Of the twelve w-pref forms eight are initial and four medial:

Medial		*Initial*	
Gen 49:15	wyhy	Gen 49:15	wyṭ
:23	wyśṭmhw	:15	wyr'
:24	wypzw	:23	wymrrhw
Dt 33:27	wy'mr	:24	wtšb
		Dt 33:21	wyt'
		:21	wyr'
		:27	wygrš
		:28	wyškn

2. The reading of the Sam, *wyrybhw*, supported by the G, may well be correct.

b. *Psalm 40*

In verses 2-4a of this individual petition psalm the psalmist tells of a past deliverance wrought by Yahweh. No verbs are omitted.

w-pref (5)	suff (2)
	kwn - kwnn 3
nṭh - wyṭ 2	
ntn - wytn 4	
^{c}lh - wy^{c}lny 3	
	qwh - qwyty 2
qwm - wyqm 3	
šm^{c} - wyšm^{c} 2	

Twice w-pref are parallel with suff forms:

v. 2 qwyty // wyt & wyšm^{c}
3 wyqm // kwnn

Three of the w-pref forms are initial, two medial:

Medial	*Initial*
v. 2 wyṭ	v. 3 wy^{c}lny
2 wyšm^{c}	3 wyqm
	4 wytn

As far as the overall pattern is concerned, the above poems definitely resemble standard poetry. But Pss 78, 105 and 106 contain pref forms referring to single events in the past, a characteristic of early poetry. Since they are isolated anomalies embedded within a pattern essentially like that of standard poetic Hebrew, they can legitimately be labelled archaisms.

On the basis of the received text, the above conclusion seems sane enough. But there is another possibility. What if many or most of the conjunctions on pref forms in these five poems were added in the course of scribal re-editing, as is surely the case with 2 S 22 = Ps 18? Then the pattern found in them would be like that of early poetry. As it is, however, there is no manuscript or versional support for the wholesale deletion of conjunctions in these psalms. The G supports the MT in practically every case. In the absence of such evidence it is best to rest with the conclusion stated above.

C. *Poems Whose Relationship to Early or Standard Poetry is Equivocal*

For two reasons the relationship between the verbal patterns found in all the remaining undatable passages of past narrative and the patterns of early or standard poetry is equivocal. The first reason is that the suff conj is present in both. Any undatable passages containing exclusively or almost exclusively suff forms does not resemble the one more than the other. It is true, however, that in Ugaritic poetry having few conjunctions, both pref and suff forms are as a rule found; whereas in standard poetry containing few conjunctions, the suff conj is overwhelmingly predominant. A good example of this is Lam 2:2-8, considered above in the section on standard poetic Hebrew. It is probable, then, that passages where the suff conj is almost exclusively used resemble standard poetry. This argument applies to such passages as the following:

1. Ct 3:1-4 plus 5:3-7 where 25 suff forms and but one pref form occur.
2. Ps 124:3-5.7 which contains seven suff forms.
3. Ps 85:2-4 which has six suff forms.
4. Ps 22:5-6.10-11 which contains six suff forms along with one w-pref and one w-suff.
5. Ps 118:5.10-14.18.22.23 where fourteen suff forms and one w-pref occur.[3]
6. Ps 74:12-17 where eight suff forms and one pref occur.

Whether it would apply to passages like Ps 89:11.12b,13a which has four suff forms is debatable. Certainly it does not apply to passages having even less suff forms, like Ps 51:7 with two and Ps 102:26 with one.

The second reason is the stipulation that a pattern be discernible. We have already seen, on the one hand, how standard poetic Hebrew occasionally has verbal forms characteristic of early poetic Hebrew, and, on the other, how poems whose overall pattern resembles the latter manifest forms characteristic of the former. Therefore, even the presence of only one set of features in very short passages cannot be used as evidence in dating. Nor is verbal syntax of any value in dating quite lengthy poems which combine both sets of features in such a way that no pattern is discernible. There is no need to list all such passages here. Simply to identify them would be a monumental task.

But, because an appraisal of the cumulative weight of linguistic evidence in dating early Hebrew poetry will be made in chapter four, it is necessary to attempt to compile an exhaustive list of undatable poems containing forms characteristic of early poetic Hebrew. Since suff forms and w-pref forms in medial position are characteristic of standard as well as early poetic Hebrew, and since w-suff forms are characteristic of neither, though found sparingly in both, this task is limited to the detection of all pref forms with preterit rather than frequentative force. All of the following poems contain at least one pref form, but no definite pattern is observable:

1. 2 S 1:19-27
   pref (1) *tšwb* 22
   w-pref medial (1) *wy'bdw* 27
   suff (4) *nplw* 19.25.27, *nśwg* 22

3. The three pref forms from the root *mwl* in the *ky* clauses of vv. 10.11.12 occur in a cultic formula, and, hence, probably do not refer to past time.

pref // suff (1) *nśwg* // *tšwb* 22
w-pref // suff (1) *nplw* // *wy'bdw* 27

2. Ps 24
pref (1) *ykwnnh* 2 (*ky* clause)

3. Ps 30
pref (2) *'tḥnn* and *'qr'* 9
w-pref (2) *wt'zrny* 12 and *wtrp'ny* 3
suff (9) *'mrty* 7, *hyyty* 8, *hpkt* 12, *ḥyytny* 4, *hstrt* 8, *hᶜlyt* 4, *hᶜmdth* 8, *ptḥt* 12, and *šwᶜty* 3
w-pref // suff (2) *šwᶜty* // *wtrp'ny* 3, *hpkt* // *ptḥt* & *wt'zrny* 12

4. Ps 32
pref (1) *'wdyᶜk* 5
suff (5) *'mrty* 5, *blw* 3, *nhpk* 4, *ksyty* 5, *nś't* 5
pref // suff (1) *'wdyᶜk* // *ksyty* 5

5. Ps 44
pref (1) *trᶜ* 3
w-pref medial (2) *wtṭᶜm* and *wtšlḥm* 3
suff (3) *hwršt* 3, *sprw* 2, *šmᶜnw* 2
pref // w-pref // suff (1) *hwršt* & *wtṭᶜm* // *trᶜ* & *wtšlḥm* 3

6. Ps 66
pref (2) *yᶜbrw* and *nśmḥh* 6
suff (4) *hpk* 6, *qr'ty* 17, *hqšyb* 19, *šmᶜ* 19
w-suff (1) *wrwmn* 17
pref // suff (1) *hpk* // *yᶜbrw* // *nśmḥh* 6
suff // w-suff (1) *qr'ty* // *wrwmm* 17

7. Ps 74
pref (1) *ttnrw* 14
suff (8) *bqᶜt* 15, *hwbšt* 15, *yṣrtm* 17, *hkynwt* 16, *hṣbt* 17, *pwrrt* 13, *rṣṣt* 14 and *šbrt* 13
pref // suff (1) *rṣṣt* // *ttnrw* 14

8. Ps 77
pref (3) *ythlkw* 18, *yḥylw* 17, *yrgzw* 17
w-pref medial (1) *wtrᶜš* 19
suff (8) *h'yrw* 19, *zrmw* 18, *ndᶜw* 20, *nḥyt* 21, *ntnw* 18, *r'wk* 17.17, *rgzh* 19
pref // suff (2) *r'wk* // *r'wk* & *yḥylw* // *yrgzw* 17
zrmw // *ntnw* // *ythlkw* 18
w-pref // suff (1) *h'yrw* // *rgzw* & *wtrᶜš* 19

9. Ps 80
pref (3) *tgrš* 9, *tsyᶜ* 9, *tšlḥ* 12
w-pref medial (3) *wtml'* 10, *wtṭᶜh* 9, *wtšrš* 10
suff (2) *ksw* 11 and *pnyt* 10
pref // w-pref (1) *tsyᶜ* // *tgrš* & *wtṭᶜh* 9
w-pref // suff (1) *pnyt* // *wtšrš* // *wtml'* 10

10. Ps 95
pref (1) *'qwṭ* 10
w-pref initial (1) *w'mr* 10

11. Ps 99
pref (2) *ydbr* 7 and *yᶜnm* 6
suff (3) *hyyt* 8, *ᶜnytm* 8, *šmrw* 7

12. Ps 114
 pref (1) *ysb* 3
 w-pref medial (1) *wyns* 3
 suff (3) *hyth* 2, *r'h* 3, *rqdw* 4
 pref // w-pref // suff (1) *r'h* & *wyns* // *ysb* 3

13. Ps 116
 pref (2) *'mṣ'* 3 and *'qr'* 4
 suff (2) *'ppwny* 3 and *mṣ'wny* 3
 pref // suff (1) *'ppwny* // *mṣ'wny* // *'mṣ'* 3

14. Ps 138
 pref (1) *trhbny* 3
 w-pref medial (1) *wtᶜnny* 3
 pref // w-pref (1) *wtᶜnny* // *trhbny* 3

15. Ps 139
 pref (2) *yktbw* 16 and *tskny* 13 (*ky* clause)
 suff (3) *nkḥd* 15, *r'w* 16, *qnyt* 13 (*ky* clause)
 pref // suff (2) *r'w* // *yktbw* 16, *qnyt* // *tskny* 13 (*ky* clause)

16. Prv 8
 pref (1) *yᶜbrw* 29
 w-pref medial (1) *w'hyh* 30
 w-pref initial (1) *w'hyh* 30
 suff (4) *ḥwllty* 24.25, *nskty* 23, *qnny* 22

17. Ct 3:1-4 plus 5:3-7
 pref (1) *'rpnw* 3:4
 suff (25 in all)

Several comments on this list are in order. It is very likely that at least one of the pref forms listed above has frequentative force (*'qwṭ* in Ps 95:10) for it is accompanied by the adverbial expression of time "for forty years." Further, it is likely that at least two of them can be considered as archaisms (*ttnnw* in Ps 74:14 and *'rpnw* in Ct 3:4) for the large number of suff forms in these poems is suggestive of standard poetic Hebrew. On the other hand, in several the verbal pattern may be that of early poetry (e.g. Ps 66, 99, 116, and 139) but the passages are too short to be sure.

Summary

Verbal syntax in past narrative can be used with no little confidence as evidence of an early date for Ex 15, Jud 5, Hab 3, 2 S 22 = Ps 18, Dt 32 and Job. With less confidence because of their brevity it can be used in dating Pss 81 and 104 early. The similarities between these poems and standard poetry are either non-existent or negligible, and cannot easily be taken as evidence of archaizing. Possibly they are evidence that standard poetic Hebrew was just beginning to influence poetic diction when these poems were composed.

Verbal syntax can be used with great confidence as evidence in dating Pss 78, 105 and 106 shortly before or sometime after the eighth century. With less confidence because of their brevity it can be used in dating Ps 40 and several of the smaller units within Gen 49 and Dt 33 during this same period. With still less confidence because suff forms are exclusively or almost exclusively found in them, it can be used to date two poems within Canticles and Pss 22, 74, 85, 118, and 124 to this same period. Any similarities within these poems to early poetic Hebrew can confidently be labeled archaisms.

And, finally, though pref forms referring to simple events in past time occur sporadically in other poems of unknown date, it is impossible to tell whether they reflect a genuinely early dialect or are archaistic.

CHAPTER THREE
MORPHOLOGY

Problems of Procedure

In this chapter undatable poetry is compared with early and standard poetry with respect to a number of morphological variants which differentiate the latter two.[1] These morphemes are divisible into two groups. The first is composed of those whose existence in biblical Hebrew is recognized by the Massoretes and which, as a result, are indicated in the Massoretic pointing. Thus, an essentially accurate list of the total number of occurrences can be compiled with a minimum of textual emendation and with little or no involvement of the linguist's own judgment.

The morphemes in the second group are not recognized by the Massoretes and, hence, are not indicated by their pointing. Positing their existence in biblical Hebrew, then, involves alteration of the pointing, though generally not of the consonantal text. Text-critically speaking, such alteration does not constitute a drastic change of the received text. But it does mean that for every proposed emendation the merits of the received text must be weighed against the merits of the altered text. And a decision will depend, in the final analysis, upon the judgment of the linguist. Thus, the means by which a reasonably accurate list of the occurrences of a given morpheme is compiled differ radically for the two groups.

Group I

A. *The Preservation of the y/w of a Final y/w Root When it Opens a Syllable*

It is highly probable that in early poetic Hebrew the y/w of a final y/w root was preserved when it opened a syllable. This is precisely the

---

1. Morphemes which are characteristic of standard poetic Hebrew but are not present in Ugaritic or the Amarna glosses, such as the relative pronoun *'šr*, the particle *'t*, and the article *h-*, are not considered. Arguing for an early date from their absence is an argument from silence. Such arguments are always risky, but are doubly so in this case, because these morphemes are also absent from a rather large portion of standard poetic Hebrew. On the other hand, arguing for a late date from their presence is likewise problematical. Granted, they are not present in Ugaritic or the Amarna glosses. But Hebrew poems datable to the early period on non-linguistic evidence are needed to establish that they also were not present in early poetic Hebrew.

situation which obtains in Ugaritic, with some very few exceptions.[2] A syllable-closing y/w forms with the preceding vowel a diphthong, and so is lost. But the vowel following a syllable-opening y/w prevents the formation of a diphthong, and so the y/w is preserved. And the presence in biblical poetry as a whole of a rather considerable number of words from final y/w roots with a syllable-opening y/w retained constitutes the necessary confirmation that the Ugaritic practice once obtained in Hebrew as well.

Certain y/w's which are syllable-opening in Ugaritic, however, probably were not so in early poetic Hebrew. In Ugaritic final short vowels on singular nouns and indicative verbs are preserved, and so a y/w preceding them is syllable-opening. But in Hebrew it is likely that these final vowels were dropped before the period of early poetic Hebrew,[3] and, therefore, that a y/w preceding them had become syllable-closing. Once the y/w had been lost in the singular noun, it was concomitantly lost in the plural, for the plural endings were affixed to the y/w-less singular, even though the addition of the plural ending would allow the y/w to be syllable-opening.

In all likelihood, then, the situation in early poetic Hebrew was this: the y/w of a final y/w root was preserved when it opened a syllable. But, because of the loss of final short vowels, a y/w in a noun or in those verbs which once ended in a short vowel had become syllable-closing. A y/w remained syllable-opening only in verbal forms with afformatives beginning with a vowel, that is, in the 3fs and 3mpl suff conj, the 3mpl and 2mpl pref conj, and the fs and mpl imperatives, and so was preserved only in this position.

In standard poetic Hebrew, on the other hand, by elision in intervocalic position even a syllable-opening y/w of a final y/w root has been

---

2. Exceptions are fs and mpl imperatives and a few 3ms indicative pref forms. Why the y/w is not written in the case of the imperatives is very much of a puzzle, for the final long vowels of these forms would seemingly prevent the formation of diphthongs. It may be that the few 3ms pref forms have been mistakenly confused with apocopate forms.

3. The argument in support of this position runs as follows: theoretically, two reasons why a y/w of a final y/w root might be lost can be advanced, one, by the elision of the y/w in intervocalic position; and, two, by the loss of a final short vowel following it. We know that a y/w preceding a long vowel verbal ending was lost by elision. And we find a substantial number of y/w's in this position preserved in biblical poetry as a whole, suggesting that elision took place in the not too distant past. If a y/w preceding a short vowel ending, either verbal or nominal, was lost by elision, the number of y/w's preserved in this position should also be substantial. In fact, such is not the case. The number of y/w's retained on nouns are exceedingly rare, confined almost exclusively to the noun *śdh(y)*, and only three are preserved on verbal forms which once ended in a short vowel, *ḥby* (Isa 26:20), *hḥly* (Isa 53:10) and *tmḥy* (Jer 18:23). The logical conclusion is that a y/w preceding a short vowel was lost by a different process and at an earlier date.

lost. Accordingly, as a rule it is not present even in verbs with afformatives beginning with a vowel. Hence, with respect to these verbal forms, early and standard poetic Hebrew present contrasting pictures. In the latter, however, there are some exceptions to the rule. Before we can determine how many it is necessary to exclude certain examples of the retention of a y/w which cannot legitimately be used for dating early poetry. They are:

a. nine forms derived from the root *'th*. Verbal forms with afformatives beginning with a vowel from this root are without exception written with the y/w preserved. Thus, it seems that this root was excepted from the linguistic development which other final y/w roots underwent.

b. two forms which occur in prose, *hmsyw* in Jos 14:8 and *yrbyn* in Dt 8:13.

In addition to these eleven examples, one is textually too dubious to include: the *Qere* of Ps 73:2. Here the *Kethibh* reads a ms passive participle *nṭwy*, while the *Qere* reads a 3mpl suff form, *nṭyw*. Evidently the rationale behind the *Qere* is the desire to produce concord between the plural subject *rgly* "my feet" and its predicate. In the parallel stichos, the plural subject *'šry* "my steps" likewise has a singular predicate in the *Kethibh* but a plural one in the *Qere*. The question is, then, whether *rgly* and *'šry* demand plural predicates. The answer is that they do not. For is Pss 37:31 and 44:19 plural forms of *'šr* receive singular verbs. Evidently, the plural of this noun can be taken collectively, meaning something like "way of life" rather than "footsteps". Such is undoubtedly the case here, not only with *'šry* but also with *rgly*. Therefore, the change of both verbs in the *Qere* to plurals is weak and unnecessary.

On the other hand, *dlyw* of Prv 26:7, in spite of certain difficulties, must not be excluded. Although the Massoretic punctuation *dalyū* is puzzling, and many commentators suggest reading *dallū* from the root *dll* "hang low", it is best to give the *yodh* of the consonantal text weight over against the *pathah* of the vocalization, and take *dlyw* from the root *dlh*. To this it is objected that the meaning of the root *dlh* "draw water" is not appropriate in the context, which demands something like the "hang low" of the root *dll*. This objection, however, cannot be allowed to stand. For in certain stems of the Arabic verb one can see that the basic idea connoted by the root *dlw* is the same as that connoted by the root *dll*, "to hang down". According to Lane[4] *dlw* means in I "to pull (a bucket) up or out", in II "to let down a thing, make it hang down", in IV "to let down (a bucket)" and in V "to hang down; be let down". How *dll* and *dlw* can have identical basic meanings is easily understandable according to the theory of biconsonantal roots. Although

---

4. E. W. Lane, *Arabic-English Lexicon* (New York, 1955), vol. I, part 3, pp. 908f.

the root *dlw* becomes specialized in Aramaic, Hebrew, Akkadian, and for the most part in Arabic to mean "let a bucket hang down", that is, "draw water", the meaning demanded by the context in Prv 26:7 can be obtained from it. The exact significance of the pointing remains in doubt.[5]

Now we are in a position to state the number of syllable-opening y/w's which are retained in standard poetry. There are nine:

Isa 17:12	yhmywn
21:12	tbᶜywn
21:12	bᶜyw
26:11	yḥzywn
31:3	yklywn
33:7	ybkywn
40:18	tdmywn
40:25	tdmywny
46:5	tdmywny

Since as a rule a syllable-opening y/w is not retained in standard poetry, all of these can be labelled as archaisms.

Practically all of the examples of the preservation of y/w in poetry of unknown date occur in poems which also manifest examples of the loss of y/w, allowing us to conclude that in all probability they too are archaisms:[6]

Dt 32

With y/w	Without y/w
ḥsyw 37	hbw 3
	yštw 38
	r'w 39

Ps 36

With y/w	Without y/w
yḥsywn 8	dḥw 13
yrwyn 9	

Ps 57

With y/w	Without y/w
ḥsyh 2	krw 7

Ps 77

With y/w	Without y/w
w'hmyh 4	r'wk 17.17

5. C. H. Toy, *A Critical and Exegetical Commentary on the Book of Proverbs* (New York, 1899) *ad loc.*

6. In compiling a list of the examples of the loss of y/w in the poems which follow, forms from roots middle and final *yodh* are not considered.

Ps 78

With y/w	Without y/w
yštywn 44	hṭw 1
	zrw 30
	ymrwhw 40
	htww 41
	qnth 54

Ps 122

With y/w	Without y/w
yšlyw 6	ʿlw 4

Job

With y/w	Without y/w
yšlyw 12:6	r'w 3:16
twgywn 19:2	etc.
ybkywn 31:38	

Prv 25-29

With y/w	Without y/w
dlyw 26:7	r'w 25:7
	nsw 28:1
	yrbw 28:28
	yr'w 29:16

But a few occur in poems which do not manifest examples of the loss of y/w.

Ex 15

With y/w
yksymw 5

Balaam Oracles Num 23-24[7]

With y/w
nṭyw 24:6

Ps 39

With y/w
yhmywn 7

Ps 83

With y/w
yhmywn 3

---

7. In this study the four Balaam Oracles concerning Israel are considered as a unit, Num 23:7-10, 23:18-24, 24:3-9, and 24:15-19. The miscellaneous oracles which are appended to these in 24:20-24 are considered separately.

Theoretically, these poems resemble early poetry. But that they contain only one verb in which a y/w would open a syllable drastically reduces the evidential value of its preservation in this one verb. A poem must contain a cluster of verbs in which the y/w is retained before we can be confident that it resembles early poetry.

B. *The Use of z as a Relative Pronoun*

Ugaritic and rare forms within Hebrew poetry as a whole here again converge to show that derivatives of the proto-semitic element <u>d</u> probably functioned as the ordinary relative pronouns in early poetic Hebrew.[8] In Ugaritic the relative pronouns are <u>d</u> and <u>d</u>*t*, both derived from <u>d</u>; and forms of *z*-, also derived from <u>d</u>, used in this same capacity are occasionally met in biblical poetry. Whether either of the other two relative pronouns found in biblical poetry are present in early poetic Hebrew is difficult to determine. Since forms of *š*- are found not only in late biblical and post-biblical Hebrew but also in poems which are thought to have a northern Israel provenance, no good reason can be adduced why it may not have been characteristic of the dialect of northern Israel from very early times. It is also possible that *'šr* became a relative pronoun at a very early date. But the process of its development from a noun meaning "a place" to a relative pronoun probably has not begun in Ugaritic,[9] and its relative scarcity in biblical poetry as a whole bespeaks its late arrival on the scene. Therefore, the use of *'šr* beside forms of *z*- is possibly a sign of archaizing, though one cannot be sure.

---

8. Two other linguistic arguments of a more technical nature offer further corroboration. First, the use of derivatives of <u>d</u> as relative pronouns is a regular feature of all west semitic languages except Amorite, where Akkadian influence may have prevailed, Phoenician, except for the pre-5th century Bylos dialect (cf. Z.S. Harris, *A Grammar of the Phoenician Language* [New Haven, 1936], p. 55), and Hebrew. The Byblos dialect uses *z*, Aramaic *zī* which becomes *dī*, and, in Syriac, *dᵉ*, Arabic *ḏū/ḏātu*, etc., and *'allaḏī/'allatī*, etc., Old South Arabic <u>d</u>/<u>d</u>*t*, and Ethiopic *za*. Therefore, that <u>d</u> as a relative is proto-west semitic seems very likely, and the few remnants of it in biblical Hebrew and its use in the Byblos dialect show that it was not lost by the Canaanite dialects in hoary antiquity, but was preserved in them until the late 2nd millenium. (Cf. Z.S. Harris, *The Development of the Canaanite Dialects* [New Haven, 1939], p. 70 and J.M. Allegro, "Uses of Semitic Demonstrative Element z in Hebrew," VT 5 [1955] 310 and 311, n. 4.)

Second, in most west semitic languages the element <u>d</u> is also used in the formation of the singular near demonstrative pronoun. Aramaic attests *dᵉnā/dā*, Arabic *(hā)ḏā/ (hā)ḏihi*, etc., Sabaean *ḏn/ḏt* and Ethiopic *ze(ntū)/ zā(tī)*. This fact leads to the conclusion that, as a general rule, in west semitic the relative pronoun derives its form from the demonstrative pronoun. Since Hebrew, Phoenician, and Amorite attest derivatives of <u>d</u> as a demonstrative element, it is logical to conclude that they also once possessed a relative element <u>d</u>, and that such forms as *s*- and *'sr* are the result of external influences or peculiar internal development.

9. C.H. Gordon, *Ugaritic Manual* (Rome, 1955), p. 244, #296.

Three forms of *z*- are used as relative pronouns in biblical Hebrew, *zw* (pronounced *zū*), *zw* (pronounced *zō*) and *zh* (pronounced *ze*). The last two can be considered together. Since they are declinable, *ze* being the masculine and *zō* the feminine, it is natural to associate them with the singular near demonstratives and to derive them ultimately from *d̲i* and *d̲a*, respectively. Neither of them occurs in standard poetic Hebrew as a relative.[1] Therefore, barring signs of archaizing, the presence of either of them in a poem of unknown date can be used as evidence of an early date. But evidence is forthcoming that seven of the eight examples are archaistic, for each of these is used along side of *'šr*:

Ps 78

ze v. 54
'šr vv. 3.4.5.11.42.43.68

Ps 104

ze vv. 8.26
'šr vv. 16.17

Ps 132

zō v. 12
'šr v. 2

Job

ze 15:17 and 19:19
'šr 3:23, 4:19, etc.

Prv 22:17-24:34

ze 23:22
'šr 22:28, 23:1

Only in Ps 74 is evidence of archaizing absent, *ze* being the sole relative pronoun used. But because it occurs only once (in v. 2), its use as evidence for an early date is severely restricted.

In addition to being a relative *ze* is also twice used as a determinative pronoun, both times in the phrase *yhwh/'lhym zh syny* "Yahweh/God the one of Sinai" of Jud 5:5 and Ps 68:9. In neither can a cogent case be made for

---

1. The use of *zō* as a demonstrative pronoun in Hos 7:16 is a question not of an archaic syntactical use but of an archaic pronunciation and orthography, and so is not relevant here. *Ze* in Isa 25:9 *'lhynw zh qwynw lw* is often listed as a relative, but the parallel stichos *zh yhwh qwynw lw* "this is Yahweh for whom we wait" shows that it is a demonstrative, the stichos being translated "our God this is for whom we wait". *Ze* as a relative does occur once in prose (Ex 13:8) but in a cultic response whose age is impossible to gauge.

archaizing. To be sure, in Jud 5 both *'šr* and *š-* are also found as relative pronouns. But the one example of *'šr* (v. 27) is in a line which very prosaically repeats the thought of the preceding line, and which, consequently, probably should be deleted. And as was remarked above, the presence of *š-* and derivatives of *ḏ* within the same poem does not indicate the mixture of an earlier with a later dialect. Therefore, in all probability, evidence of archaizing is absent from this poem. Nor is it present in Ps 68, for there *ze* and another derivative of *ḏ* (*zū*) are the only pronouns used. But, again, that *ze* is found only once in each of these poems is a decided hindrance to its use as evidence of an early date. Furthermore, we are obviously dealing with a cultic formula, and such formulae are notorious for perpetuating archaic forms of speech.[2]

The other form of *z-* which is found as a relative in biblical Hebrew is *zū*. It, unlike *ze* and *zō*, is indeclinable, and is to be associated with the Arabic determinative pronoun *ḏū*, though it is declinable. But *ḏū* does occur as an indeclinable relative pronoun in the *Tayya'* dialect.[3] As a relative pronoun *zū* occurs fourteen times in biblical poetry,[4] of which three are in poetry datable to the eighth century or afterwards (Isa 42:24, 43:21 and Hab 1:11). All three can without hesitation be called archaistic, since *'šr* is the relative pronoun in ordinary use in poetry of this date (e.g. in Isa 41:8.9.22 etc. and Hab 2:5). In two poems of unknown date containing *zū*, *'šr* is also found:

Ps 9-10
zū 9:16, 10:2
'šr 10:6

Ps 31
zū 5
'šr 8.20

In all of the remaining *zū* is the only relative found:

Ex 15 zū 13.16	*Ps 68* zū 29
Ps 17 zū 9	*Ps 142* zū 4

---

2. Allegro, VT 5 (1955) 310-11, has proposed several other examples of derivatives of *ḏ* as determinative pronouns (e.g. Mic 5:4, Ps 34:7 and Ps 12:8) but none is convincing.

3. Cf. W. Wright, *A Grammar of the Arabic Language* (3rd ed. 2 vols. Cambridge, 1955) 1, 270.

4. Like *zō*, *zū* is found once as a demonstrative pronoun (Ps 12:8).

Ps 32
zū 8

Ps 143
zū 8

Ps 62
zū 12

But, once again, we have to face the problem that *zū* occurs but once in all of these poems save Ex 15, and there only twice. And its value as evidence for an early date is hardly enhanced by this dual occurrence.

C. *-anhū and -annū*

In Ugaritic affixing the 3ms pronominal suffix *-hū* to the pref conj by means of the infix *-an-* yields two forms: an older *-anhū* and a younger *-annū*, with the *he* of the suffix assimilated to the *nun* of the infix. In the consonantal orthography of Ugaritic the former is written *-nh* and the latter *-n* and *-nn*. The two occur in more or less equal distribution. The vestigial remains of the older form in biblical poetry as a whole justify the conclusion that in early poetic Hebrew, as in Ugaritic, it probably was as frequently used as the younger. In standard poetic Hebrew, however, the younger form has almost totally supplanted its ancestor, the lone survival of the latter appearing in Jer 5:22 (*y*^{c}*brnhw*). Thus, an early poem should manifest examples of the older form on a par with examples of the younger, whereas a poem of the eighth century or after should yield scarcely any examples of the older.

In no undatable poem is there an impressive accumulation of the older form. Dt 32 contains three (*ysbbnhw*, *ybwnnhw*, and *yṣrnhw* in v. 10), but their concentration in one verse makes poetic style (rhythm, euphony, or the like) as cogent an explanation as an early date. In addition, Ex 15 (*w'rmmnhw* in v. 2) and Ps 72 (*ybrknnw* in v. 15) contain one each.

D. *The 3mpl Pronominal Suffix -mw (-mō/-mū)*

That the 3mpl pronominal suffix *-mw* is a characteristic feature of early poetic Hebrew cannot be established by correlating its presence as a rare poetic form in biblical poetry as a whole with its presence in Ugaritic, for the 3mpl suffix in Ugaritic is always *-hm*. Nevertheless, *-mw* occurs often enough as a vestigial form in biblical poetry to suggest that it did not fall into disuse in the remote past but much more recently. Hence, the position that it was current in early poetic Hebrew is a tenable one.

It can be affixed to nouns, verbs and prepositions. On the first two it is not present in standard poetry, but is found there on certain prepositions. For this reason it is necessary to divide the discussion of its value for dating into two parts: one, affixed to nouns or verbs, and two, affixed to prepositions.

Since on nouns and verbs *-mw* does not occur in standard poetry, the contrast between early and standard poetic Hebrew is total: it is prevalent in the former but absent in the latter. Therefore, its presence in a poem of unknown date will count as evidence of an early date. But we must also attempt to control for archaizing, and in order to do so we must define the relationship between the two poetic dialects concerning the two 3mpl suffixes that are present in standard poetic Hebrew: *-hm* and *-m*. With regard to the former it is virtually certain that the two dialects do not differ. This suffix is the only one in Ugaritic, and it is reasonable to suppose that without hiatus it continued in use throughout the biblical period. Therefore, the presence of *-hm* along side of *-mw* is not a sign of archaizing.

With regard to *-m* the relationship of the two poetic dialects is much more obscure. If *-m* is derived from *-mw* by the dropping of the final vowel, then there would be good reason to suppose that the former was not present in early poetic Hebrew. In this case the convergence of both of them in one poem would constitute evidence of archaizing. But, since *-mw* is generally vocalized *-mō*,[5] it is a plausible hypothesis that it derives from the Proto-Semitic dual suffix **-humā*, whereas *-m* is a derivative of Proto-Semitic **-humu*, with syncope of the *he* in both. If so, both *-m* and *-mw* may have been present in early poetic Hebrew, with *-mw* dropping out of use by the time of standard poetic Hebrew. In this case the presence of both in one poem would not be evidence of archaizing.

If a mixture of *-mw* and *-m* is a sign of archaizing, then we have tangible evidence that *-mw* is archaistic the majority of the time.

Dt 32
-mw 27.32.37.38
-m 5.20.26.29.30.31.32.33.35.35. 38

Ps 2
-mw 3.3.5
-m 9.9

Ps 5
-mw 11
-m 10.10.10.11

Ps 11
-mw 7
-m 2.6

Ps 17
-mw 10.10
-m 14.14.14

5. For reasons of euphony it is vocalized *-mū* in Ex 15:5 (*y^e^kasyūmū*).

Ps 21
-mw 10.11.13
-m 10.10.11

Ps 35
-mw 16
-m 6.6.7.13.25

Ps 49
-mw 12
-m 7.7.9.11.12.12.12.14.15.15

Ps 59
-mw 12.12.13.13.14
-m 12.13

Ps 73
-mw 5.6.7
-m 4.9.17.18.20

Ps 80
-mw 6
-m 6

Ps 83
-mw 12.12.12
-m 5.9.16.16

Ps 89
-mw 18
-m 10.12.13.33

Ps 140
-mw 4.10.10
-m 4.11

Job
-mw 27:23
-m 4:19.19, 5:5, etc.

Evidence that *-mw* is anachronistic is lacking only in the following five poems:

Ex 15
-mw 5.7.9.9.10.12.15.17.17

Dt 33
-mw 29

Ps 22
-mw 5

Ps 45
-mw 17

Ps 58
-mw 7.7

In summary, assuming the presence of *-m* side by side with *-mw* is a mark of archaizing style, the value of *-mw* for dating can be assessed as follows: first, its presence in the poems in the first of the above lists is worthless because of the evidence of archaizing. Second, the paucity of examples in Dt 33 and Pss 22, 45, and 58 render its presence in them of negligible value. But third, the multitude of examples in Ex 15 coupled with the absence of evidence of archaizing makes its presence there a cogent argument for an early date.

If, however, *-m* is not a mark of archaizing, then the mere presence of *-mw* is evidence of an early date, as was stated above. But its value is in direct proportion to the number of times it occurs in a poem. The significance of one or two occurrences should not be pressed. But the nine examples of it in Ex 15 are very significant. Its appearance five times in Ps 58 and four times in Dt 32 may be significant, possibly also its threefold appearance in Pss 2, 21, 73, 83, and 140.

The suffix *-mw* is found on three prepositions, *l-*, *ᶜl*, and *'l*, each of which must be separately considered. On the first of these it occurs fifteen times in standard poetry:[6] Isa 16:4, 23:1, 26:14.16, 30:5, 35:8, 43:8, 44:7, 48:21, 53:8, Hab 2:7, Lam 1:19, 22, 4:10.15. Therefore, any difference between early and standard poetic Hebrew can only be slight, possibly a difference of relative frequency of occurrence. That is, one might expect more examples of *lmw* in the former than in the latter. But, since we are examining poetry of unknown date poem by poem, the presence in one of them of *-mw* on *l-*, unless in great numbers, cannot be significant for dating. The presence of *lhm* together with *lmw* cannot be used as evidence of archaizing, since there is every reason to believe that both have co-existed from earliest times.

Despite this stricture on the use of *lmw* for dating, certain instances of it possibly receive a modicum of significance in that they occur in poems already manifesting *-mw* on nouns or verbs. Under this category are the following: Dt 32:32.35, 33:2.2, Ps 2:4, 49:14, 58:5.8, 59:9, 73:6.10.18, 80:7, Job 3:14, 6:19, 14:21, 15:28, 22:17.19, 24:16.17, 30:13, 39:4. The

6. Regarding *lmw* in Isa 44:15 as in prose.

remainder of the examples of *lmw* are found in poems not exhibiting *-mw* on nouns or verbs: Gen 9:26.27, Ps 28:8, 44:4.11, 55:20, 56:8, 64:6.6, 66:7, 78:24.66, 88:9, 99:7, 119:165, Prv 23:20.

On *^{c}l* and *'l* *-mw* does not occur at all in standard poetry, so any example of *^{c}lymw* or *'lymw* is potentially significant for dating. This is especially true since both the one instances of the latter (Ps 2:5) and all of the examples of the former (Dt 32:23, Ps 5:12, 55:16, 64:9, Job 6:16, 20:23, 21:17, 22:2, 29:22, 30:2.5) occur in poems which manifest other examples of *-mw*.

When the incidence of *-mw* on nouns, verbs, and all three prepositions is totaled, the greatest concentration is found in Ex 15 (9 exx.), Dt 32 (7 exx.), Pss 59 and 73 (6 exx.), Ps 2 (5 exx.), and Job (19 exx.). Of course, in evaluating these totals adjustment must be made for the greater size of Job and the almost total restriction in it of *-mw* to prepositions.

E. *-y(-i)*

One occasionally encounters in Hebrew poetry[7] a *-y* (pronounced *-ī*) affixed to a noun or participle. Since final long vowels are not indicated in Ugaritic orthography, it is not possible to tell whether this morpheme is found there. But its position as a rare poetic form in biblical Hebrew is sufficient to demonstrate the probability that it was a regular feature of early poetic Hebrew, and the Amarna glosses possibly provide confirmation. Moran reports that he has isolated in these letters three participles with a final *-i* which may be identical with the Hebrew *-y*.[8]

There have been a proliferation of theories of the origin and function of this morpheme, but none of them commands assent. In light of this situation, it is best to proceed or the basis of a purely descriptive analysis of the form and function[9] of the phrases in which it occurs. The parts of speech to which it is affixed are as follows:

---

7. This morpheme is found twice in prose, both in Gen 31:39. Four others are most likely errors. The *yodh* on the bound inf *lhwšyby* in Ps 113:8 is the result of linear dittography, *yodh*'s occurring on participles in the lines immediately above and below it. The *yodh* on *qwly* in Ps 116:1 and on *r^{c}y* in Zc 11:17 is intended to signify the 1s suffix "me" rather than the morpheme under consideration here. In 2 K 4:23 the *yodh* on *hlkty* probably results from the influence of the *yodh* on the preceding *'ty*.

8. W. L. Moran, "The Hebrew Language in its Northwest Semitic Background," *The Bible and the Ancient Near East*, ed. G. E. Wright (Garden City, New York, 1961), p. 60.

9. These two words are used as technical terms in this study. "Form" refers to the internal structure of a syntactical construction, "function" to the relationship of the construction to the larger construction(s) of which it is a part.

1. Participles				
	Ex 15:6	N ms	of the root	*'dr* "to be mighty"[1]
	Hos 10:11	B fs act		*'hb* "to love"
	Gen 49:11a	B ms act		*'sr* "to bind"[1]
	Ps 113:5	H ms act		*gbh* "to be exalted"
	Gen 31:39.39	B fs pass		*gnb* "to steal"
	Ps 114:8	B ms act		*hpk* "to overturn"
	Isa 22:16a	B ms act		*ḥṣb* "to hew"
	Isa 22:16b	B ms act		*ḥqq* "to carve"
(K)	Jer 10:17	B fs act		*yšb* "to dwell"
(K)	Jer 22:23a	B fs act		"
(K)	Ezk 27:3	B fs act		"
	Ps 113:9	H ms act		"
	Ps 123:1	B ms act		"
(K)	Lam 4:21	B fs act		"
	Ps 101:5	L ms act		*lšn* "to slander"
	Isa 1:21	B fs act		*ml'* "to be full"
	Zc 11:17	B ms act		*ᶜzb* "to forsake"
	Ps 113:7	H ms act		*qwm* "to rise"
(K)	Jer 22:23b	D fs pass		*qnn* "to nest"
	Dt 33:16	B ms act		*škn* "to dwell"
	Jer 49:16a	B ms act		"
(K)	Jer 51:13	B fs act		"
	Ob 3	B ms act		"
	Mic 7:14	B ms act		"
	Ps 113:6	H ms act		*špl* "to be low"
	Jer 49:16b	B ms act		*tpś* "to grasp"
2. Nouns				
	Gen 49:11b	ms		*bn* "son"
	Ps 110:4	fs		*dbrh* "order"
	Ps 30:8	ms		*hr* "mountain"
	Lam 1:1a.1b	fs		*rbh* "great one" (f.)
	Lam 1:1c	fs		*śrh* "princess"

---

1. In Ex 15:6 *n'dry* and Gen 49:11a *'sry* are pointed as participles in the MT. But Cross and Freedman (JNES 14 [1955] 245) have suggested that both should be pointed as absolute infinitives *ne'dōrî* and *'āsōrî*. This suggestion is based on the work of Moran ("The Use of the Canaanite Infinitive Absolute as a Finite Verb in the Amarna Letters from Byblos," JCS 4 [1950] 169-72) who thinks he has discovered several absolute infinitives with an *-i* ending in the Amarna letters. Though Moran's work has been severely challenged by J. Obermann ("Does Amarna Bear on Karatepe?" JCS 5 [1951] 58-61), his rebuttal ("Does Amarna Bear on Karatepe? -- An Answer," JCS 6 [1952] 76-80) effectively counters most of Obermann's objections.

In Ex 15:6 the main argument in favor of reading the absolute infinitive is that, because *ymynk* in stichos b is the subject of a verb, one expects *ymynk* in stichos a to function likewise. And *n'dry* pointed as a participle cannot easily be the desiderated predicate, because it is masculine whereas *ymynk* is feminine. (To alleviate the discrepancy in gender some have suggested taking the *-y* as the feminine ending *-ay*, but this is most improbable. See F. E. König, *Lehrgebäude der Hebräischen Sprache* [2 vols., Leipzig, 1881-97] 2, 226). According to the MT *n'dry* must modify *yhwh*, leaving *ymynk* predicateless, "The right hand of Yahweh, who is exalted in power, // the right hand of Yahweh shatters the enemy." If, however, *n'dry* is repointed as an absolute infinitive, it can be the predicate of *ymynk*, as absolute infinitives can substitute for finite verbs. The translation would then read, "The right hand of Yahweh is exalted in power // the right hand of Yahweh shatters the enemy." If this interepretation is accepted, the Massoretic reading of *n'dry* in v. 6 but *n'dr* in v. 11, where Yahweh is indisputably the noun modified, can be

On the basis of this list the following generalizations can be made: usually *-y* occurs on a participle (27 times) but may also be found on nouns (six times). The participle in question can be from any stem of the verb (B, N, D, H, and L are attested), active or passive, masculine or feminine, but only singular, not plural. The noun in question can be of either gender, but again only singular in number.

The following is a description of the syntactical form of the phrase in which *-y* occurs:

I. Affixed to Participles
   A. Pattern: Ptc-*y*+Noun
      1. Participle is bound form
         Gen 31:39.39 *gnbty ywm wgnbty lylh* "stolen by day or stolen by night"
         Dt 33:16 *wrṣwn škny snh* "and the bounty of the bush dweller"
      2. Participle is bound form or governing as a verb takes an object
         Isa 1:21 *ml'ty mšpṭ* "filled with justice"
         Jer 49:16b *tpśy mrwm gbᶜh* "who grasps the height of the hill"
         Zc 11:17 *ᶜzby hṣ'n* "who forsakes the flock"

   B. Pattern: Ptc-*y*+Noun+Noun
      1. Participle governs as verb with both nouns its objects
         Ps 113:9 *mwšyby ᶜqrt hbyt* "he who gives the barren a home"
         Ps 114:8 *hhpky hṣwr 'gm mym* "he who turns rocks into gushing water"
      2. Participle governs as verb with the second noun its object and the first noun a noun modifier
         Isa 22:16a *ḥṣby mrwm qbrw* "who hews out his tomb on high"

---

adequately accounted for. The latter is a participle, the former an absolute infinitive. In Gen 49:11a the principal argument in favor of repointing the text is that *'sry*, if a participle, is separated from its antecedent *yhwdh* by two lines of poetry. Cross and Freedman maintain that a smoother translation is achieved by reading *'sry* as an absolute infinitive substituting for a finite verb and parallel with the suff form *kbs* in v. 11b. This reading may be intended by the Sam *'swry*, though the vowel letter *waw* could also represent the *-ū-* of the passive participle.

These arguments are indeed forceful, but not entirely persuasive. There are several difficulties. One, all of the sure examples Moran has culled from the Amarna letters occur in what are logically subordinate clauses, best translated by "if" and "when." (In EA 287.45-48 Moran thinks he has found an example in what cannot possibly be a subordinate clause, but the reading of the signs is uncertain.) And Ex 15:6a and Gen 49:11a are unquestionably independent clauses. Moran in replying to Obermann says that, even though the clauses containing examples of absolute infinitives with *-ī* are best translated by English subordinate clauses, in light of the semitic preference for paratactic constructions it is possible to consider them as independent clauses. This is true, but it may be that the infinitive itself is the sign of subordination. At present, insufficient evidence exists to decide the issue. Two, the Sam reading in Ex 15:11 *n'dry* may well be correct. If so, since *n'dry* here must be a participle, the chances are that *n'dry* in v. 6 is also a participle. Three, and by far the most important, the overwhelming majority of *-y*'s in Hebrew occur on participles used as adjectives in appositional position. Both *n'dry* and *'sry* can without serious obstacles be read as participles in this position. Therefore, the odds favor such a reading.

C. Pattern: Ptc-*y*+Prepositional Phrase

Ex 15:6 — *n'dry bkḥ* "who art exalted in strength"
(K) Jer 10:17 — *yšbty bmṣwr* "you who live under seige"
(K) Jer 22:23a — *yšbty blbnwn* "who live on Lebanon"
(K) Jer 22:23b — *mqnnty b'rzym* "who are nested among the cedars"
Jer 49:16a — *škny bḥgwy hslᶜ* "who dwells in the clefts in the rock"
(K) Jer 51:13 — *škntỵ ᶜl mym rbym* "who dwells at the many waters"
(K) Ezk 27:3 — *hyšbty ᶜl mbw't ym* "who dwells at the seaports"
Hos 10:11 — *'hbty ldwš* "who loves to thresh"
Mic 7:14 — *škny lbdd yᶜr* "who dwells alone in the forest"
Ob 3 — *škny bḥgwy slᶜ* "who dwells in the clefts of the rock"
(K) Lam 4:21 — *ywšbty b'rṣ ᶜws* "who dwells in the land of Uz"
Ps 113:5 — *hmgbyhy lšbt* "who sittest down on high"
Ps 113:6 — *hmšpyly lr'wt* "who stoopest to see"
Ps 123:1 — *hyšby bšmym* "who dwellest in the heavens"

D. Pattern: Ptc-*y*+Prepositional Phrase+Noun, the Noun being the object of the ptc

Gen 49:11a — *'sry lgpn ᶜyrh* "who binds to the vine his ass"
Isa 22:16b — *ḥqqy bslᶜ mškn lw* "who carves in the rock his home"
Ps 101:5 — *mlwšny bstr rᶜhw* "who slanders in secret his neighbor
Ps 113:7 — *mqymy mᶜpr dl* "who raisest from the dust the poor"

II. Affixed to Nouns

A. Pattern: Noun-*y*+Noun, with Noun-*y* a bound form

Gen 49:11b — *bny 'tnw* "the colt of his ass"
Ps 30:8 — *hᶜmdth lhrry ᶜz* "thou hast set me up as a mountain of strength"
Ps 110:4 — *ᶜl dbrty mlky ṣdq* "according to the order of Melchizedek"
Lam 1:1a — *rbty ᶜm* "mighty one of peoples"

B. Pattern Noun-*y*+Prepositional Phrase

Lam 1:1b — *rbty bgwym* "mighty one among the nations"
Lam 1:1c — *śrty bmdynwt* "princely one among the cities"

On the basis of this list one can say that a participle to which -*y* is affixed may be the bound member of a bound phrase, may goven one or two objects, may be followed by a preposition (*b*- is attested eight times, *l*- four and *'l* twice), or a combination of these may obtain. In other words, regarding the relationship between a participle and its modifiers, a participle with -*y* functions as does any other participle. A noun to which -*y* is attached may be, like any other noun, bound or free.

A description of the syntactical function of the phrase containing -*y* is given in the list below:

I. Apposition

A. With a noun

Gen 49:11a — *'sry* with *yhwdh* (v. 10)
Ex 15:6 — *n'dry* with *yhwh*
Isa 1:21 — *ml'ty* with *qryh*
(K) Ezk 27:3 — *hyšbty* with *ṣwr*
Hos 10:11 — *'hbty* with *'prym*
Mic 7:14 — *škny* with *ᶜm*
Zc 11:17 — *ᶜzby* with *rᶜy*
Ps 113:5.6.7.9 — *hmgbyhy*, *hmšpyly*, *mqymy*, *mwšyby* with *yhwh*

Ps 114:8 *hhpky* with *'lwh y^c qb*
Lam 1:1a.1b.1c *rbty, rbty, śrty* with *h^c yr*
(K) Lam 4:21 *ywšbty* with *bt 'dwm*

B. With a pronominal suffix
Gen 31:39.39 *gnbty, gnbty* with 3fs *-h*
Isa 22:16a.16b *ḥṣby, ḥqqy* with 2ms *-k*
(K) Jer 10:17 *yšbty* with 2fs *-k*
(K) Jer 22:23a.23b *yšbty, mqnnty* with 2fs *-k*
Jer 49:16a.16b *škny, tpśy* with 2ms *-k*
(K) Jer 51:13 *šknty* with 2fs *-k*[2]
Ob 3 *škny* with 2ms *-k*
Ps 123:1 *hyšby* with 2ms *-k*

C. With an independent pronoun
Ps 101:5 *mlwšny* with *'wtw*[2]

II. Object of a preposition
Ps 30:8 *lhrry ^c z* "as a strong mountain"
Ps 110:4 *^c l dbrty mlky ṣdq* "according to the order of Melchisedek"

III. Object of a participle
Gen 49:11b *'sry .... bny 'tnw* "who binds .... the colt of his ass"

IV. Free noun in a bound phrase
Dt 33:16 *wrṣwn škny snh* "and the bounty of the bush dweller"

Twenty-nine times the noun/participle to which *-y* is affixed is in apposition with a noun or pronoun and, hence, functions as an adjectival modifier of it. In addition, *-y* may be attached to a word which is the object of a preposition, the object of a participle, or the free noun in a bound phrase.

From the first and third of the above lists it is clear that, functionally speaking, *-y* is generally associated with participles in apposition functioning as adjectives. This generalization applies to 26 of the 33 attested examples. And three of the remainder, Lam 1:1a.1b.1c can be subsumed under it, for in this verse *-y* is affixed to nouns rather than participles, but they are in apposition functioning as adjectives. It is also clear that the *-y* in these 29 cases cannot be a remnant of the genitive case ending, as a large number of scholars have maintained.[3] For in at least ten of the 29 the word to which *-y* is affixed would not be in the genitive case (Gen 31:39.39, Isa 1:21, Hos 10:11, Ob 3, Mic 7:14, Lam 1:1.1.1 and Lam 4:21). From the second list it is equally apparent that the *-y* in these examples does not somehow exphasize the bound relationship,[4] since the word to which it is attached is incontro-

---

2. In these cases the word to which *-y* is affixed precedes the pronoun with which it is in apposition.

3. Cf. W. Gesenius, *Hebrew Grammar*, ed. by E. Kautzsch, trans. by A. E. Cowley (Oxford, 1910), 90k.

4. Cf. J. Barth, "Die Casusreste im Hebräischen," ZDMG 53 (1899) 593-99.

vertibly in the bound state only three times (Gen 31:39.39 and Lam 1:1a) though it may possibly be in the bound state three more times (Isa 1:21, Jer 49:16b and Zc 11:17). One might conjecture that the *-y* in these 29 examples is related to the morpheme *-y* which converts nouns into adjectives (e.g. *nkry* "strange" from *nkr* "strangeness") or into actor nouns (e.g. *rgly* "footman" from *rgl* "foot"), cardinals into ordinals (e.g. *ššy* "sixth" from *šš* "six"), and proper names into a gentilic (e.g. *mw'by* "moabite" from *mw'b* "Moab"). Although the two morphemes can be descriptively distinguished, they are tangent at the point of being associated with the adjectival state.

In none of the remaining four examples of *-y* (Gen 49:11b, Dt 33:16, Ps 30:8 and Ps 110:4) is the word to which it is affixed in apposition, and in only one case (Dt 33:16) is it attached to a participle. Functionally, three times it is affixed to a word which would be in the genitive case (Ps 30:8 and Ps 110:4 after a preposition and Dt 33:16 as a free noun in a bound phrase) and one time to a word which would be in the accusative case (Gen 49:11b after the participle *'sry*). Therefore, it is doubtful that the *-y* in these four examples can be understood as a vestige of the old genitive case ending.

In spite of the evidence to the contrary which Gen 49:11b provides, Cross and Freedman take the *-y* both there and in Dt 33:16 as the genitive ending.[5] They can explain the *i* vowel instead of an *a* vowel, which would appear in Hebrew as *ō*, in the former by appealing to the indiscriminate use often made of the case endings in numerous semitic languages when they are in the process of being lost.[6] And they further buttress their argument by suggesting that there are several more examples of the survival of the genitive case endings in biblical Hebrew. Two of their suggestions, *šmšy* for *šmš* in Dt 33:14 *metri causa*[7] and *hry* for *hr* in Dt 33:19 with the Sam,[8] cannot be given much credence. Our knowledge of the scansion of Hebrew poetry is far too scanty to support a textual emendation involving the restoration of an archaic case ending, and the *yodh* on *hry* in the Sam can more easily be explained as the result of dittography, since the following word begins with a *yodh*.

Three of their proposals, however, deserve serious consideration. In Dt 33:17 the MT reads *wqrny r'm qrnyw* "and the horns of a bull are his horns" but the Sam reads *wqrny r'my qrnyw*, with the same translation. Cross

---

5. Cross, SAYP, p. 160 n. 40 and p. 229 n. 53 (Cf. F.M. Cross, Jr. and D. N. Freedman, "The Blessing of Moses," JBL 67 [1948] 206 n. 53).

6. Cf. Akkadian and Bedouin Arabic. Also see G-K-C 90k.

7. Cross and Freedman, JBL 67 (1948) 206 n. 53 (Cf. SAYP, p. 229 n. 53).

8. Ibid.

and Freedman suggest that the Sam is the original reading, that the *-y* is the genitive ending, and that it has been edited out of the MT.[9] They see the same process at work in the dual recension of the poem in 2 S 22 and Ps 18. In v. 44 2 S 22 reads *wtplṭny mryby* ᶜ*my* "and thou deliverest me in disputes with my people," but Ps 18 omits the *yodh* on ᶜ*m*. Their suggestion is that the text of 2 S 22 is correct, and that, since the 1s suffix makes no sense, the *-y* is the genitive ending.[1] Finally, they take the *yodh* on *m*ᶜ*wny* in 2 S 22:24 = Ps 18:24 *w'š̌tmr(h) m*ᶜ*wny* "and I kept myself from my iniquity" as the genitive case ending since also here the 1s suffix yields poor sense.[2]

In no one of these cases are their arguments strong enough to command assent, but they are plausible. If their readings are accepted, it would seem reasonable to conclude that the case for regarding the *-y* in Gen 49:11b, Dt 33:16, Ps 30:8 and Ps 110:4 as a survival of the genitive case ending is appreciably reinforced. Such a deduction is premature, however. For there is an important formal difference between these four and the three cited by Cross and Freedman. The word to which *-y* is affixed is a bound noun in all four of the former, but is a free noun in all three of the latter. In regard to syntactic form, then, the two groups are not comparable. Furthermore, one should remember that, even in regard to syntactic function, they are only partially comparable, in that *bny* in Gen 49:11b would be in the accusative not the genitive case.

This partial similarity functionally and the total dissimilarity formally causes one to search around for a more adequate explanation of the *-y* in the four passages of the first group. Because all four of the words to which *-y* is affixed are bound forms, it is best to have recourse to the explanation proposed by Barth for all examples of *-y*, namely, that it is a morpheme which strengthens the bound relationship. It seems that Barth had a good insight, but overgeneralized it. He was right in seeing that *-y* sometimes emphasizes the bound state, but was wrong in stating that it always has this force. That this explanation is correct receives impressive corroboration from the fact that it applies also to the morpheme *-w*, to be discussed in the next section.

The upshot of the foregoing discussion is that we are dealing with two morphemes, not one. One is associated with the appositional state and the other with the bound state. Clearly their value for dating must be assessed independently. For the sake of convenience, the morpheme associated with nouns or participles in apposition will be labeled *-y* I and the one reinforcing the bound state will be called *-y* II.

---

9. Cross and Freedman, JBL 67 (1948) 206 n. 53 (Cf. SAYP, p. 229 n. 53).

1. Cross and Freedman, JBL 72 (1953) 33 n. 99 (Cf. SAYP, p. 316 n. 99).

2. Ibid., p. 28 n. 58 (Cf. SAYP, p. 299 n. 58).

The former is found often in standard poetry: Isa 1:21, Jer 10:17(K), 22:23a(K).23b(K), 49:16a.16b, 51:13, Ezk 27:3(K), Hos 10:11, Ob:3, Mic 7:14, Zc 11:17, Lam 1:1a,1b.1c, 4:21(K). Therefore, the only difference between early and standard poetic Hebrew is that *-y* I would supposedly occur more frequently in the former. This means that its appearance in Gen 49:11a, Ex 15:6, Pss 101:5, 114:8 and 123:1 is insignificant for dating, since it occurs only once in each of them. Only its manifold appearance in Ps 113 (vv. 5.6.7.9) is likely to be valuable for dating.

The morpheme *-y* II is never found in standard poetry. Thus, its occurrence in Gen 49:11b, Dt 33:16, Pss 30:8 and 110:4 is evidence for an early date, though use of this evidence must be tempered by the recognition that only one example is found in each poem.

F. *-w(-ō)*

Biblical Hebrew also manifests the nominal affix *-w*. As with *-y* Ugaritic orthography precludes our knowing whether it is found there. Heretofore, it has not been found in the Amarna letters. So the only evidence for its antiquity is the fact that, with one exception (Gen 1:24), it is exclusively a rare poetic form.

A descriptive analysis of the form and function of the words to which it is affixed yields the following information. It is attached only to nouns, which may be masculine or feminine, but only singular.

Num 23:18	ms	of the word *bn* "son"
Num 24:3.15	ms	"
Gen 1:24	fs	*ḥyh* "beast"
Isa 56:9a.9b	fs	"
Zp 2:14	fs	"
Ps 50:10	fs	"
Ps 79:2	fs	"
Ps 104:11.20	fs	"
Ps 114:8	ms	*mʿyn* "fountain"

In eleven of the twelve cases the noun is the bound member of a bound phrase, in the other is followed by a prepositional phrase.

A. Pattern: Noun-*w*+Noun, with Noun-*w* a bound form

Gen 1:24	*ḥytw 'rṣ* "beasts of the earth"
Num 23:18	*bnw ṣpr* "son of Zippor"
Num 24:3.15	*bnw bʿr* "son of Beor"
Isa 56:9a	*ḥytw śdy* "beasts of the field"
Zp 2:14	*ḥytw gwy* "beasts of the nation"
Ps 50:10	*ḥytw yʿr* "beasts of the forest"
Ps 79:2	*ḥytw 'rṣ* "beasts of the earth"
Ps 104:11	*ḥytw śdy* "beasts of the field"
Ps 104:20	*ḥytw yʿr* "beasts of the forest"
Ps 114:8	*m ynw mym* "fountain of water"

B. Pattern: Noun-*w*+Prepositional Phrase

Isa 56:9b	*ḥytw byʿr* "beasts in the forest"

Functionally, six times the noun to which *-w* is affixed is the free member of a bound phrase; two times it is the object of a preposition; once it is in apposition; and three times it is found in the standard name formula "N son of N."

A. Free noun in a bound phrase

Isa 56:9a	*kl ḥytw śdy*	"all the beasts of the field"
Isa 56:9b	*kl ḥytw byᶜr*	"all the beasts in the forest"
Zp 2:14	*kl ḥytw gwy*	"all the beasts of the nation"
Ps 50:10	*kl ḥytw yᶜr*	"all the beasts of the forest"
Ps 104:11	*kl ḥytw śdy*	"all the beasts of the field"
Ps 104:20	*kl ḥytw yᶜr*	"all the beasts of the forest"

B. Object of a preposition

Ps 79:2	*lḥytw 'rṣ*	"to the beasts of the earth"
Ps 114:8	*lmᶜynw mym*	"into a fountain of water"

C. Apposition

Gen 1:24	*twṣ' h'rṣ npš ḥyh lmynh bhmh wrmś wḥytw 'rṣ* "let the earth produce living creatures according to their kinds, cattle and creeping things and beasts of the earth"

D. Name formula

Num 23:18	*blq // bnw ṣpr*	"Balak // son of Sippor"
Num 24:3.15	*blᶜm bnw bᶜr*	"Balaam son of Beor"

From the above lists it is clear that *-w* relates not to the function of the word to which it is affixed but to its form. Like *-y* II it seems to emphasize the bound state. The one place where it is not on a bound form (Isa 56:9b) is in a passage dated by most to the post-exilic period, and, hence *ḥytw byᶜr* is probably to be explained as a corruption of a stereotyped phrase.

It is found three times in standard poetry: Isa 56:9a.9b, Zp 2:14. Thus, the difference between early and standard poetic Hebrew is once more a matter of relative frequency of occurrence. As a result, the lone examples of *-w* in Pss 50:10, 79:2, 114:8 are not significant for dating. Its double and triple appearance in Ps 104:11.20 and the Balaam Oracles (Num 23:18 and Num 24:3.15), respectively, may be somewhat significant. But another factor is involved here. Out of a total of twelve examples, eight times *-w* occurs in the set phrase "beasts of/in the ...," including all three of the examples in standard poetry. It may be that by the time of standard poetic Hebrew *-w* had survived only in this one phrase. If so, its significance in Ps 104 is cancelled. This leaves the Balaam oracles, and even there its value is depreciated by the fact that it occurs only in proper names, which frequently perpetuate archaic forms.

Group II

None of the morphemes in this group is indicated by the Massoretic pointing of the text. Simply to locate them is, therefore, a laborious and complicated task. In essence, it consists of comparing the MT with the text emended so as to exhibit the morpheme in question, in order to determine which is the better reading. In this comparison certain guidelines can be laid out.

Because the Massoretes failed to recognize the existence of these morphemes and subsequently mispointed the text, it is in the nature of the case that most of them will be found in passages having some kind of problem, whether textual, syntactical, semantic or lexical. It is, of course, theoretically possible that one of them might be concealed in a flawless text, but the chances of this happening must always be slim. For in the assimilation of the unrecognized morpheme into the Massoretic version of the text, it is almost inevitable that a lexical, syntactical, or semantic problem will result, which may in turn lead to textual corruption. Therefore, one principle to be used in determining where these unrecognized morphemes occur is that where the MT presents no major difficulties the probability is against reading one of them.

If the MT is difficult, then this difficulty must be weighed against the difficulty involved in postulating the presence of morphemes so rare that the Massoretes do not attest to their existence. After all, they otherwise preserved scores of archaic morphemes. Thus, too easy adoption of one of the unrecognized morphemes cannot be justified. On the other hand, their presence in Ugaritic and/or the Amarna correspondence makes it likely that they were once in general use in Hebrew, too. If so, there is no logical reason why they should not have continued in use as archaistic survivals in literary poetry. Hence, to refuse to recognize their presence because they do not appear in the MT also cannot be justified.

In nearly every case the difficulty in the MT consists of the use of some unusual form or construction. A word may be a *hapax legomenon* or seem to have a peculiar meaning, out of harmony with its use in other passages. The syntactical construction of the MT may deviate in some way from normal usage. Or the passage is irreproachable in these respects but seems not to make acceptable sense. And the principal argument for reading one of the unrecognized morphemes in any one of these cases is that doing so eliminates the difficulty in the MT and restores normal Hebrew usage.

Therefore, the crucial question is this: which is more likely, that a poet employed an unusual word, phrase, or construction, or that he followed more normal Hebrew usage but employed a rare particle whose existence in biblical Hebrew is not acknowledged by the Massoretes. Put in this way, it is possible to see the dilemma before us. We are put in the position of arguing for one unusual form on the basis that the text contains another. This is not a happy position, but an unavoidable one. Thus, a second principle is that one should not read an unrecognized morpheme unless doing so is less difficult than reading the MT. This means that it is not legitimate to read one just because the

MT presents some sort of difficulty. The magnitude of the difficulty must be assessed.

And at this point a third principle comes into play. Even if the MT is adjudged the more difficult, before reading an unrecognized morpheme the possibility of accounting for the difficulty by internal corruption of the MT must be explored.

A final principle needs stating because it is so often flouted. Reading an unrecognized morpheme must not in solving one problem spawn a host of others. For example, more than once scholars have suggested reading an enclitic *-m* even though doing so entails substantial modification of the consonantal text.

In locating these unrecognized morphemes, evaluation of versional and MS readings is extremely tricky. If MS traditions agree with the MT and the readings of the versions presuppose it, this cannot be used as evidence against reading one of them. For, presumably, since the Massoretes did not recognize their existence, neither did copyists or translators. On the other hand, omission of a consonant suspected of being an unrecognized morpheme in a MS tradition or in the *Vorlage* of one of the versions can, with proper caution, be used as supporting evidence for reading it. For in the transmission of the text, a letter whose function is no longer understood is more likely to be dropped than a letter integral to the text. But alternative explanations of the omission may be possible. Perhaps a scribe felt uneasy about an unusual word, phrase or construction which was nevertheless the original reading and brought the text in line with more normal Hebrew usage. Perhaps a translator read the MT but glossed over the difficulty in his translation, giving the illusion that he had a text different from the MT before him. It is necessary, therefore, to exercise extreme caution in evaluating MS and versional variants.

In what immediately follows and in the *Excursus* at the end of this chapter, an analysis is made of texts heretofore alleged to contain certain morphemes present in Ugaritic and/or the Amarna letters but not recognized by the Massoretes as present in biblical Hebrew. In discussing each morpheme the texts are grouped according to the type of difficulty exhibited by the MT. Since we must speak in terms of probability, the examples falling under each type of difficulty are collected in the following groups: Group A, texts where the probability favors reading an unrecognized morpheme; Group B, texts where the probability favors reading the MT or explaining the difficulty within it by textual corruption; Group C, texts where the probability favoring the above two alternatives is about even; and Group D, texts where the difficulty in the MT is so acute that confidence in any emendation is undermined.

A. *Enclitic -m̱*

At this point in the study we are concerned only with unrecognized morphemes whose existence we can postulate as a regular feature of early poetic Hebrew, or, in other words, which have not already become archaic even in the early period. According to the methodology we are employing, this means that we must demonstrate not only that one of these morphemes exists in Ugaritic or the Amarna letters, but also that it occurs frequently enough as a rare form of biblical poetry as a whole that we are justified in assuming that it became a rare form not in the remote but in the recent past. There is only one morpheme which meets both of these requirements, enclitic *-m*. All of the others are found in Ugaritic or the Amarna glosses but occur, if at all, in biblical poetry so infrequently that we must conclude that they became archaic long before the Israelites appeared as a cohesive cultural and political unit on the historical scene. These will be discussed in the *Excursus* at the end of this chapter.

The existence of enclitic *-m* in the Amarna letters and in Ugaritic has been proven beyond doubt. Following the lead of H.L. Ginsberg[3] many have pointed to possible examples in biblical Hebrew. In 1957 H. D. Hummel[4] published a list of all the alleged cases prior to that time, and included a long list of his own suggestions. Since then such scholars as Pope, Dahood, Sarna and Calderone have tossed others into the pot.[5] The first order of business is to decide where the reading of an enclitic *-m* is likely, and where unlikely. As has already been said, the texts are grouped according to the type of difficulty in the MT.

1. *Apposition: Noun-Noun*

In certain texts where the enclitic *-m* allegedly exists two nouns are juxtaposed with one modifying the other, but the relationship between them cannot be explained as that of a clause (that is, one is subject and the other predicate) or a bound phrase. If the MT is to be preserved, the relationship must be explained as one of apposition. The question is whether such an explanation is legitimate in light of the use of apposition in Hebrew. If it is not legitimate, and scribal error is unlikely, then reading an enclitic *-m* can be considered probable.

A. There are four cases where reading an enclitic *-m* is probable. Two of these cases concern the use of apposition to designate a locality. Generally

---

3. H. L. Ginsberg, *Kitvê Ugarit* (Jerusalem, 1936) pp. 20, 29, 63, 74 *et al.*

4. H. D. Hummel, "Enclitic *Mem* in Early Northwest Semitic," JBL 76 (1957) 85-107.

5. See below for references.

localities are designated in Hebrew by a bound phrase, e.g. *'rṣ knᶜn* "the land of Canaan." But occasionally apposition is employed for the same purpose, e.g. *h'rṣ knᶜn* "the land Canaan."[6] The question is whether *bhrrm śᶜyr* in Gen 14:6 "in their mountains, Seir" and *w't hnḥlym 'rnwn* in Num 21:14 "and the wadis Arnon" are examples of this use of apposition. In both cases the evidence is strongly against such an explanation.

The syntactical problem involved is the same in both. When apposition is used to designate a locality there is always numerical concord between the noun and the proper name. Such concord is lacking in both of these examples. Furthermore, there is corroborative evidence against the readings of the MT. For Gen 14:6 this evidence is lexical, contextual, and textual. Lexically, the plural of *har* "mountain" can be used to designate "hill country, mountain district, mountain range," etc., but in such cases it is always in a bound phrase. Contextually, the 3mpl suffix is not employed elsewhere in this list of peoples conquered by Chedorlaomer and his allies. Textually, the Sam G (followed by V), and S all read the bound plural. Since reading the suffix would not produce syntactical problems in either Greek or Syriac, there is good reason to assume that the Hebrew texts they translated did not contain it. Therefore, the evidence favors reading with Moran *bhrr-m śᶜyr* "in the hill country of Seir."[7]

For Num 21:14 the corroborative evidence is only lexical. Not only is the plural of *nḥl* never used to designate one particular wadi, but also the plural is never used to designate the tributaries of a wadi. In light of this and the fact that the article is attached to *nḥlym* the reading *hnḥl-m 'rnwn* "the wadi Arnon" is to be preferred to Hummel's *nḥly-m 'rnwn* "the wadis of the Arnon."[8]

The third case where reading an enclitic *-m* is probable is Dt 33:11 *mḥṣ mynym qmyw* "strike the loins--those who rise up against him." Albright is certainly right in reading *mtny-m qmyw* "the loins of those who rise up against him."[9] In specifying the person to whom a part of the body belongs the bound phrase is always used in Hebrew, never an appositional phrase. It is also possible to take *mtnym* as a verbal modifier, and translate the clause, "Strike those who rise up against him on the loins." It is, however, very rare

---

6. See G-K-C 131f and S. R. Driver, *A Treatise on the Use of the Tenses in Hebrew*, 3rd ed. (Oxford, 1892), section 190.

7. W. L. Moran, "The Putative Root ᶜtm in Isiah 9:18," CBQ 12 (1950) 154.

8. Hummel, p. 97.

9. W. F. Albright, "The Oracles of Balaam," JBL 63 (1944) 319 and "The Old Testament and Canaanite Language," CBQ 7 (1945) 22.

indeed for a noun used as a verbal modifier to intervene between a verb and its object. These considerations plus the fact that Sam reads *mtny qmyw* "the loins of ..." make reading an enclitic *-m* the most likely of the several alternatives.

And, lastly, reading an enclitic *-m* is probable in Job 31:11 *ᶜwn plylym* "iniquity, judges." Changing *ᶜwn* from the free to the bound state does not produce acceptable sense, for the meaning demanded by the context is "iniquity to be brought before the judges" not "iniquity of the judges." In light of *ᶜwn plyly* "libelous iniquity" in v. 28 doubtless we should read with Pope *ᶜwn plyly-m.*[1]

B. Reading an enclitic *-m* is improbable in the following cases. In three of these an abstract noun is placed in apposition with another noun:[2] *'lhym 'mt* in Jer 10:10 "the true God;"[3] *'mrym 'mt* in Prv 22:21 "true words;"[4] and *mym lḥṣ* in Isa 30:20 and 1 K 22:27 = 2 Chr 18:26 "oppressive waters."[5] In each case the suggestion is to take the final *mem* on the first word of the phrase as an enclitic and read bound phrases. For several reasons this suggestion should not be adopted. Most important is the fact that one of the best attested characteristics of Hebrew grammar is the use of abstract nouns where adjectives would normally occur. Thus, one finds abstract nouns in predicate position (e.g. *mšpṭy yhwh 'mt* "the judgments of Yahweh are true" in Ps 19:10) and in attributive position (e.g. *ᶜd 'mt wn'mn* "a true and reliable witness" in Jer 42:5).[6] Therefore, in none of the above expressions is the syntax abnormal.

This basic consideration can be reinforced by observations on the individual phrases involved. One never finds in biblical Hebrew *my lḥṣ* "waters of oppression;" in all three instances of the phrase *mym lḥṣ* is found. And, furthermore, all three are in prose, where one would least expect to find rare morphemes. And it is not surprising to find in Prv 22:21 *'mry 'mt* "words of

---

1. M. H. Pope, *Job* (New York, 1965), p. 203.

2. Hummel, p. 99, also takes *ḥyym* in the expression *'lhym ḥyym* as an abstract noun and reads *'lhy-m ḥyym* "God of life." But *ḥyym* is here an adjective, as is proved by the expressions *'l ḥy* and *'lhym ḥy* "the living God."

3. Hummel, p. 99.

4. M. Dahood, *Proverbs and Northwest Semitic Philology* (Rome, 1963), p. 47.

5. P. J. Calderone, "The Rivers of *Masor*," *Biblica* 42 (1961) 428 n. 1.

6. See G-K-C 131c and Driver, *Treatise*, section 189 for numerous other examples.

truth" along side of *'mrym 'mt* "true words" since in Ezk 47:4 *mym`brkym* "knee high water" occurs along side *my mtnym* "waist high water."

In addition to these four expressions, Hummel suggests that *'lhym ṣb'wt* "God Sabaoth" in Ps 59:6, 80:5.8.15, and 84:9 be read *'lhy-m ṣb wt* "God of Hosts."[7] It is almost certain, however, that this phrase results from the substitution of *'lhym* for *yhwh* in the second and part of the third book of the Psalter.

C. A very difficult problem is posed by *hrym gbnnym* "many-peaked hills" in Ps 68:17. Albright has proposed reading *hry-m gbnnym* "hills of many peaks."[8] The phrase as it occurs in the MT cannot be fitted conveniently into any of the well-attested uses of apposition. It does not designate a locality, it does not specify a measure or number, nor specify the material of which the hills are composed, nor state the species of a certain genus, nor, finally, is it an abstract noun used attributively. Certainly, it comes closest to fitting into the last of these categories. But the use of non-abstract nouns in attributive position is rare indeed. Possibly *hᶜrym hmbdlwt* "separate cities" of Josh 16:9 is a parallel. The fact that *gbnnym* occurs in v. 16 in a bound phrase with *hr* tends to support the case for reading enclitic *-m*. But already two examples of apposition side by side with a bound phrase in the same verse have been cited (Prv 22:21 and Ezk 47:4). In the final analysis a decision is difficult because the evidence is ambiguous.

2. *Apposition: Pronoun-Noun*

B. Grammatically speaking, the construction in which a pronoun is directly followed by a modifying noun is also apposition. It is identical with the construction in which noun modifies noun except that the head word of the phrase is a pronoun. It is a common construction in Hebrew, G-K-C 131 l-n listing one example where the head word is an independent pronoun, twelve where it is a verbal suffix, and twelve where it is a nominal suffix. And this list is nowhere near exhaustive. Hence, it is better to read this construction in Ps 83:12 *šytmw ndybmw kᶜrb* "make their nobles like Oreb"[9] and Isa 19:12 *'ym 'pw' ḥkmyk* "where, then, are your wise men"[1] than to read an enclitic *-m*. That the G did not reproduce the suffix in Ps 83 probably only means that the translator

---

7. Hummel, p. 97.

8. W. F. Albright, "A Catalogue of Early Hebrew Lyric Poems (Psalm 68)," HUCA 23 (1951) 24.

9. J. H. Patton, *Canaanite Parallels in the Book of Psalms* (Baltimore, 1944) p. 13.

1. Hummel, p. 102.

followed his own native idiom. For the same reason the RSV does not translate it.

3. *Abstract Noun as Predicate*

C. Just as abstract nouns can be used in attributive position in place of the corresponding adjective, so it can also be used in predicate position. In this position it can precede or follow the subject. The question is, then, whether *ᶜz mlk* in Ps 99:4 can be better accounted for by taking it as an example of this construction, or by adopting Hummel's suggestion that *ᶜz-m lk* "thou hast strength" be read.[2] What makes opting for the former alternative difficult is the lack of an article on *mlk*. Normally when the predicate is an abstract noun the subject is definite, not indefinite. And a definite subject is certainly to be expected in this verse. A statement of limited not universal application is being made. All kings are not strong, only *the* King is. Just how serious this omission of the article should be considered is very difficult to estimate. It is not legitimate, especially when dealing with Hebrew poets, to lay down hard and fast rules which admit no exceptions. Much is a matter of feeling and nuance in cases like this one. Since we are not native speakers of biblical Hebrew, we can make no final judgment. All we can say is that, on the basis of analogy with other examples of abstract nouns used as predicates, *ᶜz mlk* appears awkward.

Supporting the rendering of *ᶜz* as a predicate noun is the pointing of *'hb* as 3ms pref conj *'āhēb* "he loves." Thus, *mšpṭ 'hb* "he loves justice" is a statement about Yahweh in the 3rd person, and does not blend with Hummel's reconstruction *ᶜz-m lk*, a statement about Yahweh in the 2nd person. One can, however, skirt this difficulty by pointing *'hb* as *'ōhēb*, the ms participle, and by taking *'th* "thou" as its subject, translating, "Thou hast strength, thou who lovest justice." The pointing of *'hb* cannot settle the matter.

4. *Concord: Noun-Adjective*

B. Both the examples in this category concern the concord of adjectives with so-called "intensive" plurals, and in neither case is reading an enclitic *-m* probable. Normally in Hebrew "intensive" plurals take singular attributives.[3] Thus for *'lhym špṭym* in Ps 58:12 Hummel wishes to read *'lhym špṭ-m* "God who judges."[4] If *'lhym* in this phrase refers to Yahweh, then, omitting cases where foreigners are the speakers (e.g. 1 Sam 4:8) this is one of only six passages in which *'lhym* with singular reference receives a plural adjective, the

---

2. Hummel, p. 102.

3. G-K-C 132h.

4. Hummel, p. 103.

others being *'lhym ḥyym* in Dt 5:23, I Sam 17:26.36, Jer 10:10 and 23:36 and *'lhym qdšym* in Jos 24:19. But *'lhym* quite often takes a plural verb (e.g. 2 Sam 7:23, 1 K 19:2, 20:10 and often in the E strange of the Pentateuch). Hence, its modification by a plural adjective cannot be considered ungrammatical, though rare.

But *'lhym* in this verse probably does not refer to Yahweh at all. Because *'lym* "gods" are addressed in v. 2 (emended text) and because v. 12 is put in the mouth of *'dm* "mankind" and not in the mouth of a Hebrew, most likely *'lhym* refers to gods. If so, the plural *šp̣tym* is perfectly normal.

In Isa 19:4 *'dnym qšh* "a hard overlord" the normal Hebrew practice prevails and the "intensive" plural receives a singular adjective. Hummel, however, is suspicious of the noun *'dnym* because it is an "intensive" plural referring not to God but to a human being.[5] But *'dnym* in the absolute state occurs as a designation of a human lord also in Gen 42:30, where the prose narrative makes the presence of an enclitic *-m* unlikely. And with certain pronominal suffixes the plural often refers to human overlords, as does the plural of *bᶜl* with suffixes. And in these cases both words take singular verbs (e.g. Ex 21:4 and 29). Therefore, the plural of *'dn* with singular reference cannot be considered abnormal, and surely is a more likely reading than *'dn-m*.

5. *Concord: Subject-Predicate*

B. In none of the four examples in this section should an enclitic *-m* be read. One of them can be dismissed straightaway. In Ps 125:1 *hbṭḥym byhwh khr ṣywn l' ymwṭ lᶜwlm yšt* O'Callaghan suggests reading *hbṭḥ-m* "he who trusts' for *hbṭḥym* "those who trust" to go with the singular verbs *ymwṭ* and *yšb*.[6] But the subject of the verbs is "Mount Zion," not "those who trust." It is Mount Zion which is thought of as literally "never being moved--remaining forever." "Those who trust" remain forever only figuratively. Thus, the two verbs are part of the figure, not main verbs. That a plural "those who trust" is here compared with a singular "Mount Zion" should cause no uneasiness, for in Hebrew, as in English, what is compared with a singular object can be in the singular or plural (e.g. Ps 1:4 where wicked men are compared with chaff).

In Jer 22:6 *ᶜrym l' nwšbh* (Q: *nwšbw*) Hummel proposes to read *ᶜr-m* to go with the singular verb *nwšbh*.[7] But his proposal should not be adopted. For this clause is an example of the use of a feminine singular predicate to agree with a feminine or masculine plural subject which states the name of an

---

5. Hummel, p. 101.

6. R. T. O'Callaghan, "Echoes of Canaanite Literature in the Psalms," VT 4 (1954) 170-71.

7. Hummel, p. 103.

animal or a thing. This usage is quite common in Hebrew, G-K-C 145k naming over 25 examples. For our purposes the following three are instructive:

ydynw l' špkh (Q:*špkw*) "our hands did not shed..." Dt 21:7
whmṣdwt ntpśh (Oriental Q:*ntpśw*) "and the strongholds will be seized
Jer 48:41
ᶜryw nṣth (Q:*nṣtw*) "his cities are in ruins" Jer 2:15

In all three of these examples the predicate follows the subject, as in Jer 22:6, and one or another of the *Qere*'s read the plural, as in Jer 22:6. In the last of the three in another passage from Jeremiah *ᶜrym* "cities" is construed as a singular as in Jer 22:6. But in none of these three cases can the syntactical difficulty be avoided by postulating an enclitic *-m*. Thus, the odds are heavily against reading enclitic *-m* in Jer 22:6. Undoubtedly the Massoretes, like Hummel, were concerned about the discrepancy in number, but with as little reason.

The last two examples concerning concord of subject and predicate present a problem similar to the one presented by several cases where there is lack of concord between a pronoun and its antecedent, and so will be considered in the next section.

6. *Concord: Pronoun-Antecedent*

B. In all the examples in this section there is lack of numerical concord between a pronoun and its antecedent. In none is reading an enclitic *-m* a likely way to avoid the discrepancy. Three of them may be conveniently grouped together: Ps 102:18 *hᶜrᶜr....wl' bzh 't tpltm* "the destitute....and he will not despise their prayers;" Ps 109:13 *šmm* "their name" and v. 15 *zkrm* "their memory" where the antecedent *ršᶜ* "the wicked" is to be found in v. 2. In all three Hummel suggests reading the 3ms suffix and the enclitic *-m*.[8] Supposedly the 3ms suffix *-w* would not have been indicated in the orthography, though positive proof that such would be the case is lacking.

Since the antecedents of these pronouns are collectives, the suggestion of Hummel loses all force. For the number of times collectives are supplied with plural verbs or suffixes is legion.[9] For example, *ršᶜ* takes a plural verb in Ps 10:2 and Prv 28:1 and plural suffixes in Ps 9:6 (where, it is interesting to observe in the light of Ps 109:13, the text reads *šmm* "their name") and Prv 28:4. To be sure, one might suggest reading enclitic *-m* in these last two cases as Hummel has suggested doing for Pss 109:13 and 15. But the question we are confronted with is this: which is more probable, that a rare particle was used on four different occasions after a 3ms suffix referring to

8. Hummel, pp. 99-100.

9. G-K-C 145b-g.

the common collective *rš*ᶜ, or that the 3mpl suffix was used? The latter is more probable.

In two more examples of lack of concord between pronoun and antecedent and in two examples of lack of concord between subject and predicate[1] precisely the opposite of the above situation obtains. In these four cases a noun designating a class of people, and, hence, when in the singular often supplied with a plural pronoun or verb, is in the plural but supplied with a singular pronoun or verb. In all four it is suggested that we read enclitic *-m*'s instead of plurals. The examples are, where the lack of concord is between pronoun and antecedent: Ec 10:15 ᶜ*ml hksylym tyg*ᶜ*nw* "the toil of fools wearies him"[2] and Isa 5:23 *wṣdqt ṣdyqym ysyrw mmnw* "and the right due the righteous they turn aside from him;"[3] and where the lack of concord is between subject and predicate: Prv 28:1 *wṣdyqym kkpyr ybṭḥ* "the righteous are as bold as a lion"[4] and Prv 21:27 *zbḥ rš*ᶜ*ym tw*ᶜ*bh // 'p ky bzmh yby'nw* "the sacrifice of wicked men is taboo // especially when he offers it in sin."[5]

While plurals of collectives taken as singular are not as common as singulars of collectives taken as plural, nevertheless they are quite numerous, certainly numerous enough to make reading enclitic *-m*'s in the cases under discussion improbable.[6] The fact that the G reads singular nouns in Ec 10:15, Isa 5:23 and Prv 28:1 probably means nothing. The translator had to make the noun singular or the verb plural in order to produce concord in his own language, and in these cases he chose to change the noun.

In Jer 10:4 too there is a lack of concord between pronoun and antecedent. The antecedent of "them" is *yḥzqwm* "they fasten them" is either *m*ᶜ*śh* "work" or ᶜ*ṣ* "tree" in v. 3 or more likely simply "idol" understood. Whatever the antecedent, it is resumed in v. 4a by a 3ms suffix and in v. 4b receives a singular verb. Hence Hummel suggests reading an enclitic *-m* with either no suffix or with the 3ms suffix *-w* obscured by the *-m*.[7] But it must be noted that in v. 5 the pronouns and verbs are plural again. These several

---

1. See above, p. 85.

2. M. Dahood, "Canaanite-Phoenician Influences in Qoheleth," *Biblica* 33 (1952) 154.

3. H. L. Ginsberg, "Some Emendations in Isaiah," JBL 69 (1950) 54.

4. Hummel, p. 102.

5. For some reason, other commentators have failed to notice the similarity between this example and the others.

6. For lists of instances see G-K-C 145 l-m and S. R. Driver, *The Book of the Prophet Jeremiah* (London, 1906), p. 362 n.a.

7. Hummel, p. 104.

verses are a perfect example of the vacillation in number so characteristic of Hebrew.[8]

7. *3mpl Suffix // 1pl Suffix*

B. In Isa 33:2 *zrᶜm // yšwᶜtnw* "their arm // our deliverance" and Mic 7:19 *ḥṭ'wtm // ᶜwntynw* "their sins // our iniquities" a 3mpl suffix is parallel with a 1pl one. In both of these cases Dahood has suggested reading enclitic *-m*'s instead of the 3mpl suffixes.[9] This leaves the nouns in question without suffixes, but to extricate himself from this difficulty he appeals to G. R. Driver's demonstration that a suffix in one half of a poetic line may be understood but not expressed in the other.[1]

There is another more likely explanation of the discrepancy in the suffixes of these two verses, however. R. Weiss has shown convincingly that often an original *nw* at the end of a word is represented by a closed *m*, and vice versa.[2] Many of his examples come from prose, and in most of those from poetry there is no possibility of reading an enclitic *-m*. Hence his hypothesis is not endangered by those who wish to see a proliferation of enclitic *-m*'s throughout the MT. Instead of 3mpl suffixes in the above verses Weiss wishes to read 1pl ones. And he finds support from the versions. In Isa 33:2 T, S, and V read "our arm" and in Mic 7:19 G, S, and V read "our sins." Weiss' explanation is far more convincing than Dahood's.

Probably Ps 12:8 should also be understood in terms of Weiss' hypothesis. As the text stands a 3mpl suffix is followed by a 3ms one: *tšmrm tṣrnw* "do thou protect them, do thou guard him." Hummel deduces that because the second verb has a singular suffix the first one originally had no suffix, only an enclitic *-m*.[3] Actually, however, the antecedent of these two pronouns is the plural *ᶜnyym // 'bywnym* "afflicted // needy" in v. 6. Hence, even if the MT is correct, the 3mpl suffix is entirely in order, and the 3ms suffix can be subsumed under the rule that the plural of a noun designating a class of people may take a singular suffix.[4] But the MT is probably wrong.

---

8. Cf. Driver, *Jeremiah*, p. 362 and notes. It is interesting to note that M. Held in an unpublished dissertation from Johns Hopkins has shown that in Ugaritic suffixes in the two halves of the same line often disagree in number.

9. M. Dahood, "Some Ambiguous Texts in Isaias," CBQ 20 (1958) 45-46.

1. G. R. Driver, "Hebrew Studies," JRAS (1948) 194-65.

2. R. Weiss, "On Ligatures in the Hebrew Bible (*m=nw*)," JBL 82 (1963) 188-94.

3. Hummel, p. 103.

4. See above, pp. 84ff.

In light of Weiss' investigations, both suffixes should be either *-nw* "us" or *-m* "them." It is hard to decide which of these alternatives is correct. On the basis of the context either is acceptable. A few Hebrew MSS, G and Jerome read 1pl suffixes. On the other hand T and two *midrashim* read both suffixes as 3mpl.[5] It is not necessary to make a decision here, for either alternative excludes an enclitic *-m*.

8. *3mpl Suffixes without Antecedents*

A. In all the passages discussed in this section 3mpl suffixes occasion difficulty because they are apparently without antecedents. In two cases it is probable that an enclitic *-m* should be read instead of the suffix. The first of these is Ps 29:6, which reads *wyrqydm kmw ᶜgl lbnwn // wśryn kmw bn r'mym* "he makes Lebanon to skip like a calf, and Sirion like a young ox." The only possible objects of the action of the verb are Lebanon and Sirion. Hence, if the 3mpl suffix on *wyrqydm* is correct, it must be an anticipatory suffix. But that a plural suffix would anticipate two singular objects, one in the first half of the line and one in the second, is highly unlikely. Ginsberg has suggested taking the *-m* as an enclitic, and he is probably right.[6]

The second of these is Jer 18:15, which reads:

v. 15 *ky škḥny ᶜmy // lšw' yqṭrw*
wykšlwm bdrkyhm // šbyly ᶜwlm
llkt ntybwt // drk l' slwlh
v. 16 *lśwm 'rṣm lšmh // šrwqt ᶜwlm*

"But, my people have forgotten me // they burn incense to powerless (gods). And they make them stumble in their ways // in the old roads by going into byways // not highways, by making their land a blight // a thing forever hissed at."

If the MT is correct, then the subject of *wykšlwm* is *šw'* understood as "idols" and the 3mpl suffix refers to "my people," that is, Israel. But it is abundantly clear from 15c and 16a that Israel is the understood subject of the infinitives *llkt* and *lśwm*. Thus, Israel should also be the subject of *wykšlwm*. This reading is supported by G, S and V, all of which take the verb intransitively with "my people" as the subject. Hummel suggests that the best way to explain the *mem* and thus the resulting corruption of the text is to take it as an enclitic.[7] It seems likely that he is right.

---

5. See Weiss, p. 192.

6. Ginsberg, *Kitvê Ugarit*, pp. 129-31.

7. Hummel, p. 104.

B. In two more cases reading an enclitic *-m* is not probable. One is Ex 15:9. While there is no expressed antecedent for the suffixes on *tml'mw* and *twryšmw* "my throat will be sated with them" and "my hand will dispossess them," it is easily supplied from the context. Since the Egyptians are the speakers, the Israelites are the obvious objects of their attack. Thus, Cross and Freedman are probably wrong in proposing that the suffixes be read as enclitic *-m*'s.[8]

The other passage is Isa 10:5 *hwy 'šwr šbṭ 'py // wmṭh hw' bydm zᶜmy* "Woe to Assyria, rod of my anger // and the club (it is in their hands) of my wrath." In order to repair the defective second stich Ginsberg has suggested reading the *mem* on *bydm* as enclitic.[9] The verse would then read, "Woe to Assyria, rod of my anger, and it [i.e. Assyria] is a club in the hand of my wrath." To be sure, Ginsberg's suggestion does produce a clause capable of translation according to the rules of Hebrew syntax, for, as the text stands, it is difficult to relate syntactically *bydm* and *zᶜmy*. But the resulting phrase is most odd. For one thing, the expression "in the hand of my wrath" is bizarre, and not attested elsewhere. For another, what we expect is another bound phrase modifying Assyria and parallel to "rod of my anger." The desired bound phrase can be read by omitting the words *hw' bydm*. This leaves "and the club of my wrath," a perfect parallel to "the rod of my anger." Since *hw' bydm* is a clause and, therefore, can stand on its own, and since it can easily be understood as a marginal gloss prosaically explaining what Isaiah states more imaginatively, this is a most natural expedient. The resulting line can be understood as 2-2-2, so that the deletion does not upset the poetic symmetry.

In the above two examples, at least something of an argument can be mounted for reading an enclitic *-m*, even though the arguments in rebuttal are more persuasive. The same cannot be said for the following examples. Here the MT presents such flawless Hebrew that it seems pointless to defend it at length. Thus, the instances are simply listed without comment, giving first the proposed emendation and then the MT:

Num 21:18 *bmḥqq bmšᶜnt-m* "with a rod, with staves" for MT *bmšᶜntm* "with their staves."[1]

Isa 47:14 *'yn gḥlt lḥm-m* "no coal for warmth" for MT *lḥmm* "for warming themselves."[2]

---

8. F. M. Cross and D. N. Freedman, "The Song of Miriam," JNES 14 (1955) 246 n. 25 (Cf. SAYP, p. 115 n. 25).

9. Ginsberg, JBL 69 (1950) 54.

1. Hummel, p. 101.

2. Ibid., p. 103.

Hos 9:2 *grn wyqb l' yd^c-m* "threshing floor and vat shall not flow (*yd^c=yz^c*) for MT *yr^{c}m* "shall not feed them."[3]

Ps 78:3 *'šr šm^{c}nw wnd^c-m* "which we have heard and known" for MT *wnd^{c}m* "and known (them)."[4]

Ps 89:10 *bšw' glyw 'th tšbḥ-m* "when its waves rage thou stillest" for MT *tšbḥm* "thou stillest them."[5]

Ps 147:20 *wmšpṭym bl yd^{c}w-m* "just actions they do not know" for MT *yd^{c}wm* "they do not know (them)."[6]

Job 8:8 *wkwnn lḥqr 'bwt-m* "consider the lore of the fathers" for MT *'bwtm* "their fathers."[7]

Lam 4:20 *nlkd bšḥytwt-m* "we are seized by (our) boils" for MT *nlkd bšḥytwtm* "he was captured in their pits."[8]

C. In Ps 65:10 it is very difficult to decide whether an enclitic *-m* should be read. The suffix in the clause *tkyn dgnm* "thou preparest their grain" has no expressed antecedent. Hummel has suggested taking the *mem* as enclitic.[9] The context describes how Yahweh blesses the earth with rain, so the 3mpl suffix, if original, must refer to the inhabitants of the earth. The mental act involved in switching from the earth to its inhabitants is understandable, but nevertheless the change is abrupt, and reading an enclitic *-m* must not be ruled out.

D. In the following passages the text is so difficult that intelligent judgment is rendered impossible:

Isa 33:23 *bl yḥzqw kn trn-m* "it does not hold the mast straight" for MT *trnm* "their mast."[1]

Ps 42:5 *'dd-m* "I move" for MT *'ddm* "I lead them."[2]

Ps 49:9 *wyqr pdywn npš-m/npšw-m* "and precious is the soul's ransom/ransom of his soul" for MT *npšm* "of their soul."[3]

---

3. Dahood, PNWSP, p. 21 n. 2.
4. Hummel, p. 103.
5. Ibid.
6. Ibid., p. 104.
7. Pope, *Job*, p. 65.
8. Dahood, PNWSP, p. 28 n. 2.
9. Hummel, p. 102.
1. Ibid.
2. T. Gaster, "Psalm 29," JQR 37 (1946) 65 n. 32.
3. Hummel, p. 102.

9. *Semantic Problems Created by the 3mpl Suffix*

B. In Job 17:7 *wtkh mkᶜś ᶜyny // wyṣry kṣl klm* "my eyes fail from vexation // and my limbs, all of them, are like a shadow" Sarna wishes to read *kullām* as *kālū-m*, 3mpl suff B stem from the root *klh* here meaning "to fail."[4] His justification is that the second stichos needs a verb to parallel *wtkh*. But in light of the very common practice of following a noun, either immediately or at some interval, by *kl* plus a suffix referring back to the noun, the MT is the superior reading.

10. *Participles Governing as Verbs*

B. In Isa 19:9 *w'rgym ḥwry* "those who weave *ḥoray*" and Jon 2:9 *mšmrym hbly šw'* "those who heed vain idols" Hummel suggests reading bound plural participles followed by enclitics.[5] Since participles in Hebrew govern as verbs as well as nouns, and, hence, can take an object, this proposal can be dismissed straightaway.

11. *The Vocative*

B. A. D. Singer has tried to show that the enclitic *-m* is one of the proven syntactic means of expressing the vocative in Ugaritic.[6] Following this lead Dahood has suggested reading the enclitic in Prv 5:7 where the plural *bnym* "sons" appears in the MT instead of the more usual *bny* "my son".[7] Since the plural occurs three other places in Prv 1-9 (4:1, 7:24, and 8:32) he would undoubtedly read the enclitic there too. It appears, however, that Singer overstates the facts. Out of more than ten examples of proper names used in the vocative the enclitic is found in no more than four. It is also used on proper names which are not vocative. Thus, a more accurate statement is that enclitic *-m* may be attached to proper names whether or not they are in the vocative. Therefore, it probably has nothing to do with signaling the vocative.[8]

If enclitic *-m* is not a sign of the vocative, then Dahood's argument loses its force. For it is not likely that a rare particle would fall at random four times on the same word within the space of nine chapters. Such a happening is believable only if the enclitic once had a specific vocative force.

---

4. Sarna, N.M., "Some Instances of the Enclitic *-m* in Job," JJS 6 (1955) 110.

5. Hummel, pp. 98-99.

6. A. D. Singer, "The Vocative in Ugaritic," JCS 2 (1948) 1-10.

7. Dahood, PNWSP, p. 12.

8. See M. H. Pope, "Ugaritic Enclitic *-m*," JCS 5 (1951) 123 n. 8.

12. *The Preposition min in Bound Phrases*

B. In two passages where the preposition *min* occurs in a bound phrase between the bound and free noun Hummel has suggested taking the *mem*'s as enclitics.[9] These passages are Isa 28:9 *gmwly mḥlb ᶜtyqy mšdym* "weaned from milk and taken from breasts" and Hos 7:5 *hḥlw šrym ḥmt myyn* "the princes become sick with the heat of wine." In neither of these cases is the reading of an enclitic likely. Prepositions in bound phrases are not at all uncommon in the MT.[1] The preposition *min* occurs three other places where there can be no question of reading the enclitic: Gen 3:22 *'ḥd mmnw* "one of us;" Jer 23:23 *h'lhy mqrb // 'lhy mrḥq* "a god nearby // a god far away;" and Ezk 13:2 *lnby'y mlbm* "to the prophets (who prophesy) from their own hearts." It is important to note that in all the above examples one of the common meanings of *min* is expressed, and that the sense of the *min* is appropriate to the phrase in which it is found. The same can be said about Isa 28:9 and Hos 7:5. "Weaned from" and "taken from" are most natural. Likewise, the use of *min* to indicate the origin from which the heat comes is in accord with normal Hebrew usage, though elsewhere only the bound phrase is used to express where *ḥmh* comes from.

13. *The Preposition min on Verbal Objects*

B. In four passages where the preposition *min* follows a verb which ordinarily takes an object Hummel proposes that the enclitic be read instead.[2] In Ps 85:4 *hšybwt mḥrwn 'pk* "thou didst turn back from thy burning wrath" the verb in question is the H stem of *šwb*. Admittedly, the H stem of *šwb* usually does take an object, but twice elsewhere it is followed by *min*, Ezk 14:6 (*mᶜl*) and Ezk 18:30. Furthermore, the sense of separation expressed by the *min* compliments the meaning of *šwb* "to turn away or back."

In Isa 25:2 *ky śmt mᶜyr lgl* "for thou hast made the city a heap" there can be no doubt that the text is in error. But a solution easier than postulating an enclitic *-m* is readily at hand. Since *mᶜyr* occurs in v. 2, *mᶜyr* for *ᶜyr* in v. 1 is perhaps a result of vertical dittography.

The verb in question in Lam 3:17 *wtznḥ mšlwm npšy* "my appetite shuns plenty" is *znḥ* "spurn, repell, reject, shun" etc. If the MT is correct, the preposition can be defended on the grounds that it goes well with a verb expressing a drawing back in disgust. But the MT does not yield suitable sense. For the psalmist is describing not how he himself was repulsed by prosperity, but how Yahweh took prosperity from him (Cf. vv. 15, 16). Hence the G

---

9. Hummel, pp. 98-99.

1. Cf. G-K-C 130a.

2. Hummel, pp. 103, 104, 105.

kai apōsato eX eirēnēs psuXēn mou "he has removed my soul from peace" probably reflects the correct reading, *wyznḥ* instead of *wtznḥ*. In this case *npšy* is the object of the verb and the prepositional phrase a verbal modifier.

And, finally, the preposition *min* in the phrase *sqlw m'bn* "clear of stones" can easily be defended on the grounds that it compliments the verb "clear (of) stones."

D. Both Gaster[3] and Cross and Freedman[4] suggest reading *yś'-m dbrtyk* "that they may receive Thine utterances" (Gaster) or "they carry out Thy decisions" (Cross and Freedman) for the MT *yś' mdbrtyk* in Dt 33:3. But the context is too obscure to permit sound judgment.

14. *Lexical and Semantic Problems Created by the Preposition Min*

A. In all the passages in this section lexical or semantic considerations are adduced as reasons why the preposition *min* should be read as the enclitic *-m*. In two cases the argument for the enclitic is very persuasive. In Num 24:19 *wyrd myᶜqb* Albright suggests attaching the *mem* to the verb and taking Jacob as the subject.[5] There can be little doubt that he is right. *'ybyw* "his enemies" of v. 18a almost certainly should be transposed from its present position and placed after *myᶜqb*. Not only does it not make sense in v. 18a but it also makes the stich there too long. Verse 19a, on the other hand, is too short. Such a transposition produces the following clause: *wyrd myᶜqb 'ybyw*. Whether the verb is from *yrd* "go down" or from *rdh* "rule," there is no doubt that Jacob, not "his enemies," must be its subject. For the context speaks of Israelite victory in war, v. 18b reading "and Israel does valiantly" and v. 19b reading "and he destroys survivors from the city." Verse 18a must be read either "and Jacob rules his enemies" or "and Jacob goes down to his enemies." Either reading fits well in the context. If *yᶜqb* is the subject of the clause, the *mem* attached to it cannot be the preposition *min*. It is most likely an enclitic *-m* and should be affixed to the verb *wyrd*.

Likewise, the MT in Job 15:18 *'šr ḥkmym ygydw // wl' kḥdw m'bwtm* "which the wise men declared // and they did not hide from their fathers" is obviously corrupt, for the idea of the wise men hiding their wisdom from their fathers is clearly non-sensical. Wisdom passes from father to son, not vice versa. Pope suggests taking the *mem*'s before and after *'bwt* as enclitics.[6]

---

3. Gaster, JQR 37 (1946) 65 n. 32.

4. Cross and Freedman, JBL 67 (1948) 201 n. 17 (Cf. SAYP, p. 212 n. 17).

5. Albright, JBL 63 (1944) 221 n. 93.

6. Pope, *Job*, p. 110.

The latter, however, can easily be understood as a 3mpl suffix referring to the wise men. But the former cannot be understood as the preposition *min*, and so must be affixed to *kḥdw*. In this position it could possibly be taken as a 3mpl suffix complimenting the relative particle *'šr*, yielding the translation "what the wise men declared // and their fathers did not hide (them)." Not only is this reading forced, but the first stichos contains no resumptive pronoun. It is better to take the *mem* as enclitic.

Also the MT is seemingly corrupt in Jer 18:14 *hyᶜzb mṣwr śdy // šlg lbnwn* "does the snow of Lebanon forsake the cliffs of the steppe."[7] The answer to this question is yes, but the context demands a negative answer. If we make *ṣwr* and *šlg* parallel subjects, the desired sense is obtained: the steppe always has its rocky crags and Lebanon its snow. This reading can be effected merely by attaching the *mem* on *ṣwr* to *hyᶜzb*.[8]

B. In three other instances the case against reading an enclitic *-m* is persuasive. In Job 5:15 *wyšᶜ mḥrb mpyhm // wmyd ḥzq 'bywn* "he delivers from their mouths from the sword // and from the power of the strong the needy" the MT is clearly corrupt. The first stichos must originally have contained a parallel to *'bywn*. In light of the present consonantal text the most likely candidate is *ptyym* "the simple." This leaves the initial *mem* of *mpyhm* unaccounted for, and Pope attaches it to *mḥrb* as the enclitic.[9] But an easier explanation is available. The *mem* can be attached to *mḥrb* as Pope suggests but understood as the 3mpl suffix referring to the "crafty, cunning, devious ones" of vv. 12-14.

Hummel wishes to take the *mem* from *'ps* in Isa 40:17, attach it to the last word in the preceding stichos, and regard it as enclitic.[10] It is indeed difficult to discern precisely what the force of the *min* is here, but the legitimacy of the combination of *min* and a substantive expressing negation to mean "nothing" is confirmed by Isa 41:24, where *m'yn* and *m'pᶜ* (either an error or a dialectical variant of *m'ps*) occur with exactly the same force as *m'ps* has here.

Practically all commentators transpose the *mem* on *'šr* "Asshur" at the beginning of Gen 49:20 to *ᶜqb* at the end of verse 19, citing the G, S and V for support. Cross and Freedman suggest that, while the transposed *mem*

---

7. Cf. M. H. Pope, *El in the Ugaritic Texts* (Leiden, 1955) p. 67 and A. Heidel, "A Special Usage of the Term *ŠADÛ*," JNES 8 (1949) 233-35.

8. S. M. Dahood, "Philological Notes on Jer 18:14-15," ZAW 74 (1962) 207-09.

9. Pope, *Job*, p. 44

10. Hummel, p. 100.

might be taken as the adverb *-ām*, it might also be the enclitic.[1] But a third alternative exists which is more likely than either of these: to take the *mem* as the 3mpl pronominal suffix referring back to the collective *gdwd* "raiders."[2] In any case, it is readily apparent that both the first and the last of these alternatives are easier than the middle one.

In the following there are no good grounds for suspecting that the MT conceals an enclitic *mem* under the guise of the preposition *min*:

Num 24:17 *kwkb(y)-m yᶜqb // šbṭ(y)-m yśr'l* "stars of Jacob // scepters of Israel" for MT *kwkb myᶜqb // šbṭ myśr'l* "star from Jacob // scepter from Israel."[3]

Isa 10:2 *lhṭwt-m dyn dlym* "to pervert the cause of the poor" for MT *lhṭwt mdyn dlym* "to turn aside the poor from justice."[4]

Isa 17:13 *wns-m mrḥq* "it will flee far away" for MT *wns mmrḥq* "Ibid."[5]

Isa 24:18 *ky 'rbwt-m mrwm npthw* "for the windows of heaven opened" for MT *ky 'rbwt mmrwm npthw* "for the windows above opened" or "the windows opened from above."[6]

Isa 24:22 *wsgrw ᶜl msgr-m // rb ymym ypqdw* "they will be shut up in a prison // they will be punished for many days" for MT ...*msgr // wmrb ymym ypqdw* "in a prison // and after many days will be punished."[7]

Isa 29:4 *whyh k'wb-m 'rṣ qwlk* "and your voice will be like a ghost of the underworld" for MT *k'wb m'rṣ* "like a ghost from the underworld."[8]

Isa 65:20 *l'yhy(h)-m šm ᶜwd ᶜwl ymym* "never again will an infant die there" for MT *mšm* "ibid."[9]

Ps 74:12 *w'lhym mlk-m qdm* "God is the Ancient King" for MT *w'lhym mlky mqdm* "God, my King, is of old."[1]

Ps 77:6 *ymy-m qdm* "days of old" for MT *ymym mqdm* "ibid."[2]

---

1. SAYP, p. 171 n. 68.

2. Cf. E. A. Speiser, *Genesis* (Garden City, New York, 1964) *ad loc.*

3. Albright, JBL 63 (1944) 219 n. 83.

4. Ginsberg, JBL 69 (1950) 54.

5. Hummel, p. 104.

6. Ibid., p. 98.

7. Ibid., p. 102.

8. Ibid., p. 99.

9. Ibid., p. 104.

1. Ibid., p. 97

2. Ibid., p. 98.

Ps 107:39 *wyšḥw-m ᶜṣr rᶜh wygwn* "they are brought low by oppression, evil, and sorrow" for MT *wyšḥw mᶜṣr* "they are brought low by oppression..."[3]

Job 11:8 *gbhy šmym // ᶜmqh-m š'wl* "heights of Heaven // depth of Sheol" for MT .... // *ᶜmqh mš'wl* "deeper than Sheol."[4]

Job 28:9 *hpk-m šrš hrym* "he overturned the root of the mountains" or "he overturned the mountains rootwise" for MT *hpk meršš hrym* "he overturned the mountains from the root up."[5]

Prv 20:4 *ḥrp ᶜṣl l' yḥrš* "in winter the sluggard does not plow" (the *mem* on *ḥrp* being attached to the preceding line) for MT *mḥrp* "ibid."[6]

C. In Jer 3:23 *'kn lšqr mgbᶜwt // hmwn hrym* "truly from the hills is a delusion // the mountains are a hubbub" Hummel suggests taking the *mem* on *gbᶜwt* as the enclitic particle.[7] If the MT is read, there is good reason to accept his suggestion. According to it both stichoi are independent clauses. The two predicates *lšqr* and *hmwn* are parallels. If the *mem* on *gbᶜwt* is removed, the subject of the second stichos *hrym* finds a perfect parallel in the first *gbᶜwt*. Taking the *mem* as enclitic eliminates the necessity of changing the consonantal text at all.

But nowhere else is *hmwn* used as a parallel to any of the numerous Hebrew words for "in vain." Furthermore, the G, S, and V take *hmwn* as a bound form with *hrym* "the hubbub of the mountains," and they find support from 36 Hebrew MSS. If this reading is adopted, then it is not the "hills // mountains" which are a delusion, but what is practiced upon them, a statement much more in line with ordinary speech habits. *lšqr* is left as the sole predicate, and *hmwn hrym* as a parallel subject. But parallel to what? The first stichos has no subject. Since there is no manuscript or versional evidence that a word has dropped out, the only way to supply a subject is to take the expression "from the hills" as elliptical for "what is from the hills," that is, idolatrous practices or perhaps even the idols themselves.

A third alternative is to follow the versions in the first stichos as well as the second, taking "hills" as the subject and *hmwn hrym* as an explanatory parallel to it. This would supply the first stichos with a subject and eliminate the parallism of *hmwn* with *lšqr*. The superfluous *mem* could then

---

3. Hummel, p. 104.

4. M. Dahood, "Northwest Semitic Philology and Job," *The Bible in Current Catholic Thought* (New York, 1962), pp. 57-58.

5. Hummel, p. 103.

6. Dahood, PNWSP, p. 43.

7. Hummel, p. 103.

be taken as the enclitic particle. All in all, it seems that the weight of the evidence favors the first or third of the above alternatives, but some doubts linger.

The MT in Job 7:15 is to say the least somewhat peculiar. It reads *wtbḥr mḥnq npšy // mwt mᶜṣmwty* "my soul chooses strangulation // death rather than my bones." The traditional remedy is to emend the *mem* in *ᶜṣmwty* "my bones" to a *beth*, reading *ᶜṣbwty* "my pains."[8] Since the alteration of *mem* to *beth* is an easy textual change, this solution is a fairly happy one. But also quite cogent is the proposal of Sarna to regard the initial *mem* of *mᶜṣmwty* as enclitic to *mwt*, and translate "my soul chooses strangulation // my bones death."[9] The plural of *ᶜṣm* is often used to designate the self, so there is no problem there. The parallelism which results from Sarna's solution makes it very attractive. In the final analysis, it is difficult to decide between it and the traditional solution.

Also, the MT in Job 8:18 is not exactly smooth-flowing. It reads *'m yblᶜnw mmqwmw // wkḥš bw l' r'ytyk*. The problem resides in the *yblᶜnw*. It can be understood in one of two ways. One is to take God as the implied subject, yielding the translation, "If he [God] swallows him up from his place // then it [his place] will deny him, 'I have never seen you'." The other is to take the subject as the indefinite "one," a common device for expressing the passive, and translate, "If he is swallowed up from his place // then it will deny him, 'I have never seen you'." Either of these translations is grammatically passable, but it must be conceded that they are somewhat awkward. Thus, most welcome is Sarna's suggestion to take the initial *mem* of *mmqwmw* as enclitic to *yblᶜnw*, *mqwmw* then becoming its subject, with the translation "If his place swallow him up..."[1] Since, however, either of the first two alternatives is possible, we cannot unconditionally accept Sarna's proposal.

D. The following two passages are too difficult to permit confident appraisal:

Dt 33:2 *w't-m rbbt qdš* "with him were the myriads of holy ones" for MT *w'th mrbbt qdš* "and he came from the holy myriads." (?)[2]

Ps 49:15 *š'wl-m zbl lw* "Sheol will be his dwelling" for MT *š'wl mzbl lw* "Sheol from his dwelling."[3]

---

8. Cf. BH^3 *ad loc.*

9. Sarna, JJS 6 (1955) 109.

1. Ibid.

2. Cross and Freedman, JBL 67 (1948) 198 n. 8 (Cf. SAYP, p. 203 n. 8).

3. Hummel, p. 102.

15. *"Intensive" Plurals*

B. In several passages it has been suggested that "intensive" plurals should be read as singulars plus enclitic *-m*'s. But in no case are the arguments adduced convincing. Pope thinks that in Job 17:1 *qbrym* "grave" may have originally been singular.[4] But the mpl of *qeber* referring to one grave is attested in 2 K 22:30 = 2 Chr 34:28, 2 Chr 16:14 (both of a royal tomb), and Job 21:32. In light of this evidence the plural rather than the enclitic is more likely the original reading in Job 17:1.

In Job 21:22 Dahood,[5] followed by Pope,[6] argues that *rmym* refers to God, not the angels, and that the correct reading is *rām/rōm-m*. Probably *rmym* does refer to God. But in light of the use of the plural adjective *qdwšym* to refer to God, e.g. Hos 12:1, Prv 9:10, etc., it is not at all surprising to find the plural adjective *rmym* used in the same way. This is more likely than reading an enclitic.

Finally, Hummel suspects *myšrym* in Ps 58:2, *ᶜwlmym* in Ps 61:5, *šlwmym* in Jer 13:19, and *tmrwrym* in Hos 12:15 of being originally singulars plus enclitics.[7] But these words are so frequently attested that his suspicion is unwarranted.

16. *Lexical and Semantic Problems Created by the Masculine Plural Ending -im*

A. In the passages in this section lexical or semantic considerations are adduced as reasons why the plural ending *-(y)m* should be read as the enclitic particle *-m*. In two instances the arguments in favor of reading the enclitic are very cogent. In Ps 89:51 the text reads as follows: *zkr 'dny ḥrpt ᶜbdyk/ś'ty bḥyqy kl rbym ᶜmym* "Remember, O Lord, the ignominy of thy servant // how I bore in my bosom all the many peoples." There is, of course, no grammatical problem here, for if the text is correct, this is one of numerous examples of *rbym* or *rbwt* preceding its noun in the manner common to numerals. But it must be admitted that the phraseology is passing strange. To be sure, it is possible to make sense of the MT. "Many peoples" is a common expression for the enemy in the Psalter, and here, if correct, is a circumlocution for the injury, shame, etc., inflicted by these enemies. But the proposal of Hummel is a much more attractive alternative. He reads *kl rby-m ᶜmym* "all the strife of the nations."[8]

---

4. Pope, *Job*, p. 120.

5. M. Dahood, "Some Northwest Semitic Words in Job," *Biblica* 38 (1957) 316-17.

6. Pope, *Job*, p. 146.

7. Hummel, pp. 100-01.

8. Ibid., p. 98.

The sense given to *ryb* here finds an exact parallel in Ps 18:44 *tplṭny mryby ᶜm* "thou didst deliver me from strife with the people." Other commentators have suggested reading *klmt ᶜmym* "the reproach of the nations," and they see in *kl* the remnant of the beginning of this word. But Hummel's reading necessitates no change in the consonantal text, and so is preferable.

Similarly, one can make sense of the MT in Isa 10:1. The text *hwy hḥqqym ḥqqy 'wn // wmktbym ᶜml ktbw* can be translated, "Woe to those who inscribe iniquitous decrees // and to the writers who write trouble." But the parallelism between *'wn* and *ᶜml* almost certainly indicates that *ḥqqy* and *mktbym* should be parallel too. This can be accomplished by taking, with Ginsberg, *mktby* as the bound plural of *mktb* "decree" and the *mem* as the enclitic.[9]

B. In most of the examples where it is suggested that *-im* be read as enclitic *-m*, the case against the latter is persuasive. In Hab 3:8 Albright has suggested that instead of *nhrym* "rivers" *nhr-m* "river" be read as a better parallel with *ym* "sea."[1] But *nhrm* as well as *nhr* occurs in Ugaritic meaning the primordial deep.[2]

Pope suggests that in Job 24:5 the subject of *yṣ'w* "they go out" is "the destitute of the earth" of v. 4 and that *pr'ym* "wild asses" is used adverbially. Accordingly he reads the singular *pr'* and takes the *mem* as enclitic.[3] He is probably right that *pr'ym* is used adverbially, but there is no need to change it to a singular. A noun or adjective used to modify adverbially a plural verb may often be singular (e.g. Job 24:10, Isa 20:4)[4] but also may be plural (e.g. 1 S 2:33 and 2 K 5:2).

Hummel questions *'yšym* in Isa 53:3. He wishes to read *'yš-m* and translate "despised and rejected was the man."[5] But there are no objective grounds for questioning *'yšym*. It is attested in Phoenician, and twice elsewhere in Hebrew, Ps 141:4 and Prv 8:4, where it is paralleled by plurals.

In Ps 29:1 and 89:7 Hummel thinks that *'lym* in the phrase *bny 'lym* may be singular plus enclitic because in Ugaritic mythology El is the father

---

9. Ginsberg, JBL 69 (1950) 54.

1. W. F. Albright, "The Psalm of Habakkuk," *Studies in Old Testament Prophecy* (Edinburgh, 1950), p. 15.

2. Cf. Gordon, UM, p. 295 #1219.

3. Pope, *Job*, p. 160

4. Cf. G-K-C 118o.

5. Hummel, p. 101.

of the gods.[6] But the parallel expression *bny 'lhym* shows that the Hebrews were accustomed to refer to the host of divine beings as sons of the gods. And there is no reason to question the form *'lym*, for *'lm* is the common plural of *'l* in Ugaritic.

The text of Ps 38:20 *w'yby ḥyym ᶜṣmw // wrbw śn'y šqr* "my enemies - living - are numerous // and those who hate me wrongfully are great" is without doubt corrupt. Hummel suggests reading the final *mem* of *ḥyym* as the enclitic particle, repointing *'yby* as *'ōyᵉbē*, and translating, "The enemies of my life are numerous."[7] His suggestion does have the advantage of not changing the consonantal text. But in light of the frequent parallelism between *šqr* and *ḥnm* (e.g. Pss 35:19 and 69:5, cf. also 109:2-3) almost certainly the latter should be read here for *ḥyym*. Thereby, a perfect parallelism is achieved.

Jirku regards the *mem* on *ṣwpym* in the MT of 1 S 1:1 *wyhy 'yš 'ḥd mn hrmtym ṣwpym mhr 'prym* as an enclitic *-m* and translates the word "a Suphite."[8] While he is almost certainly right that the correct reading is *ṣwpy*, the additional *mem* can be more easily explained by dittography of the initial *mem* of *mhr*.

In Hos 14:3 *wnšlmh prym śptynw* "and we will repay with bulls our lips," O'Callaghan wishes to regard the final *mem* of *prym* as enclitic and to repoint *śptynw* as *šᵉpattēnū*, equating this word with *šptym* of Ps 68:14, understanding both to mean "cattle enclosure," and translating, "the bullocks of our pens."[9] But it is far easier to transpose the *mem* of *prym* on to *śptnw* and vocalize *pᵉrī miśᵉpātēnū* "the fruit from our lips," with both the G and S.

The one case where the dual ending *-(y)m* has been alleged to be an enclitic *-m* can be conveniently considered under this section. In Ec 10:18 *bᶜṣltym ymk hmqrh // wbšplwt ydym ydlp hbyt* "through two lazy things the roof sinks in // through indolent hands the house leaks" Dahood reads the abstract noun *ᶜṣl(w)t* plus enclitic *-m* to parallel the abstract noun in the second stichos *šplwt*.[1] For some reason scholars have a difficult time accepting the dual here as genuine. But for all their reticence it is, in parallelism with the dual *ydym* "hands," an outstanding example of the use of inflectional morphology for poetic effect.

---

6. Ibid.

7. Ibid., p. 99.

8. A. Jirku, "Eine Renaissance des Hebräischen," FF 32 (1958) 212.

9. R. T. O'Callaghan, "Echoes of Canaanite Literature in the Psalms," VT 4 (1954) 171.

1. Dahood, *Biblica* 33 (1952) 194-95.

In the following cases the MT needs no explicit defence:

Isa 3:13 *wᶜmd ldym ᶜm(w)-m* "he stands to judge his people" for MT *ᶜmym* "the peoples."[2]

Jer 8:19 = Isa 33:17 *m'rṣ mrḥq-m* "from a distant land" for MT *m'rṣ mrḥqym* "ibid."[3]

Ps 10:17 *t'wt ᶜnw-m* "the desire of the humble man" for MT *t'wt ᶜnwym* "the desire of the humble."[4]

Ps 18:28 *wᶜyny-m rmym* "and the eyes of the haughty" for MT *wᶜynym rmwt* "and haughty eyes."[5]

Ps 77:18 *zrmw my-m ᶜbwt* "the water of the clouds pours forth" for MT *zrmw mym ᶜbwt* "the clouds pour forth water."[6]

Ps 88:7 *bmḥšk-m mṣlwt* "in the darkness of the depths" for MT *bmḥškym bmṣlwt* "in the darkness, in the depths."[7]

D. The following texts are too difficult for confident analysis:

Dt 33:3 *'p ḥbb ᶜm(w)-m* "yea, he loves his people" for MT *ᶜmym* "the peoples."[8]

Isa 28:1 *'šr ᶜl r'š gy' šmny-m hlwmy yyn* "which is on top of the rich valley of those overcome by wine" for MT *gy' šmnym hlwmy yyn* "of the rich valley-those overcome by wine."[9]

Job 33:22 *lmy mwt-m* "to the waters of death" for MT *lmmtym* "to the killers."[1]

17. *The Interrogative Particle m(h)*

B. There are two passages where Hummel suggests reading enclitic *-m* for the interrogative particle *mh*. His suggestion is surely wrong in Prv 30:13 *dwr mh rmw ᶜynyw* "a generation - how lofty are their eyes."[2] The use of *mh* to turn a statement into an exclamation is a favorite device of the wise men, occurring

---

2. Hummel, p. 100.

3. Ibid., p. 101.

4. Dahood, PNWSP, p. 28 n. 2.

5. Cross and Freedman, JBL 72 (1953) 28 n. 63 (Cf. SAYP, p. 301 n. 63).

6. O'Callaghan, VT 4 (1954) 170-71.

7. Hummel, p. 98.

8. Ibid., p. 99.

9. Ibid., p. 98.

1. Pope, *Job*, p. 219.

2. Hummel, p. 102.

elsewhere in Prv 15:23, 16:16, 20:24 and 25:8.

His suggestion has a little more plausibility in Ps 21:2 *wbyšw ᶜtk mh ygyl m'd* "in thy victory how he [the king] does greatly rejoice."[3] The G (followed by Jerome) and the S do not contain an equivalent of *mh*. The Q reads the short form of the pref conj in place of the long form of the K. The reading of the Q might be due to rhythmical reasons.[4] But in light of the versions it seems more likely that the Q-K represents a double reading. Q, G, Jerome, and S reflect a text without the *mh*, the K a text with the *mh*. Taking the *mh* as an expansion of an original enclitic *-m* would provide a convenient way of accounting for the double tradition, for it is more likely that a no longer understood *-m* would drop out of the text than that the well understood *mh* would. In the tradition which stands behind the K the *-m* was retained but pointed as the interrogative particle. In the final analysis, however, this reasoning is not substantial enough to warrant reading a rare particle. The Q-K may not represent a double tradition and the *mh* fits very well in a context where the psalmist is demonstrating the king's loyalty to Yahweh in order to motivate Him to intervene on the king's behalf in battle.

18. *Preformative m- on Nouns*

B. Certain nouns formed by prefixing the preformative morpheme *m-* have been suspected of concealing enclitic *-m*'s. In Ps 60:11 Hummel reads *ᶜyr-m ṣwr* "city of rock" (i.e. Petra) for the MT *ᶜyr mṣwr* "entrenched city."[5] But the reading *ᶜyr mbṣr* in the parallel recension of this verse in Ps 108:11 conclusively confirms the correctness of the MT.

Likewise, Hummel's suggestion that *ᶜry mᶜzw* "the cities of his stronghold" in Isa 17:9 be read *ᶜry-m ᶜzw* "cities of his strength" is wide of the mark.[6] For the noun *ᶜyr* often occurs in a bound phrase with a noun formed by the addition of the morpheme *-m* in which the free noun acts as an adjectival modifier of the bound noun (e.g. *ᶜyr mṣwr* and *ᶜyr mbṣr* cited just above). Hence, *ᶜyr mᶜwz* and *ᶜyr ᶜz* are identical in meaning. In this particular case the entire phrase is modified by the 3ms pronominal suffix. According to the rules of Hebrew syntax, pronominal suffixes must be affixed to the free noun. Thus *ᶜyr mᶜzw* is not syntactically strange as Hummel suggests, but perfectly normal.

In Joel 1:17 Gaster reads the initial *mem* on *mgrwt* "storehouses" as

---

3. Ibid., p. 99.

4. Cf. G-K-C 109k.

5. Hummel, p. 97.

6. Ibid., p. 98.

the enclitic.[7] To be sure, *mmgrwt* is almost certainly wrong. *mgwhr* is attested in Hg 2:19. Whether the root of this word is *gwr* or *'gr* (cf. Arabic *māgūr* "trough") the initial *mem* is certainly not radical but the preformative morpheme *m*-. One can account for *mmgrwt* in Joel 1:17, then, only by assuming that another *m*- has been prefixed to *mgwhr*. But the prefixing of two *mem*'s is not attested elsewhere in Semitic as a means of forming nouns. Hence, it is best to regard *mmgrwt* as corrupt. Dittography, however, is an easier way to account for the two *mem*'s than by postulating the rare enclitic -*m*.

In Jer 50:26 *m'bsyh* "her granaries" is difficult to evaluate because of the uncertainty of our knowledge of the root *'bs*. Hummel[8] and Albright[9] read *ptḥw-m 'bsyh*. Their rationale for doing so is twofold. First, Albright thinks that *'bws* means "granary," like the Akkadian *abussu* "storehouse," and not "crib," that is, that it designates a place for storing grain, not a receptacle out of which domestic animals eat it. And, since *'bws* means granary, another word formed by prefixing the morpheme *m*- to *'bws* also meaning granary is superfluous. But, despite Albright, *'bws* probably means "crib" not "granary." It occurs only two times in the OT:[1] Isa 1:3, "The ox knows its owner, the ass the *'bws* of its master," and Job 39:9, "Is the wild ox willing to serve you / will he spend the night at your *'bws*?" In both of these places granary is possible, but it is more natural to take it as designating the place where or the place out of which the animal eats. These last two meanings are the only alternatives in post-biblical Hebrew, for there *'bws* means either a crib or a stall.[2] And its meaning in post-biblical Hebrew is given added significance because, being a technical agricultural term, it is less likely to undergo change of meaning over a long period of time. Also it is interesting to note that *'bws* in both Isa 1:3 and Job 39:9 is translated in the G by *phatnē* "crib" and that *m'bs* in Jer 50:26 is translated by *apothēkē* "storehouse." In determining the meaning of *'bws* in Hebrew the post-biblical Hebrew usage and the G constitute much more valuable evidence than does Akkadian usage. The logical conclusion is that *'bws* means "crib" in biblical Hebrew, and that *m'bs* as a designation of the place where feed is stored is a natural companion to it.

---

7. Gaster, JQR 37 (1946) 65 n. 32.

8. Hummel, p. 104.

9. W. F. Albright, "Canaanite-Phoenician Sources of Hebrew Wisdom," *Supplements to Vetus Testamentum* 3 (1955) 11 n. 3.

1. In Prv 14:4 *'bws* is an error for *'ps*.

2. M. Jastrow, *A Dictionary of the Targumim, the Talmud Babli and Yerushalmi, and the Midrashic Literature* (2 vols. New York, 1950) 1, 4.

Second, Albright, against Goetze,[3] thinks that *'bws* is a Hurrian loan word. As such its three consonants *'bs* probably would not be treated by the Hebrews as a tri-consonantal root, and hence, would not be subject to the inflectional changes which produce nouns, verbs, etc. One such inflectional modification is the prefixing of the morpheme *m-*. Therefore, *m'bs* must be viewed as an unlikely nominal formation from the loan word *'bws*. But this argument is also inconclusive. That *'bws* is a Hurrian loan word is in dispute. But even assuming that it is, there is evidence that it has been assimilated into the Hebrew inflectional system, for a verb meaning "fatten," probably denominative from *'bws*, is attested. If a verb can be formed from *'bws*, why not also a noun of place? In conclusion then, it is Albright and Hummel who cannot substantiate their claim that *m'bsyh* conceals an enclitic *-m*.

The word *mṣwr (māṣōr)* occurs four times as an indication of a geographical district, taken by most modern commentators as Egypt: Isa 19:6, Mic 7:12,12 and counting Isa 37:25 = 2 K 19:24 as one. In all of these verses Calderone wishes to attach the initial *mem* on to the preceding word and read *ṣwr*, vocalized as *ṣur* "rock" in Isa 37:25 = 2 K 19:24, Isa 19:6 and Mic 7:12a and as *ṣor* "Tyre" in Mic 7:12b.[4] In the last case grammatical considerations make the proposed emendation unlikely. There *mṣwr* is preceded by the preposition *min*, and neither in Ugaritic nor in Hebrew is another example of enclitic *-m* on *min* attested.

In Isa 19:6 and Isa 37:25 = 2 K 19:24 lexiographical problems make Calderone's emendations difficult to accept. In both of these passages the phrase *y'ry mṣwr* occurs. In the former he reads "channels of rock," that is cataracts. But *ṣwr* generally designates a cliff or a mountain, not smaller rocks of the type that would be found in cataracts. In the latter he reads "mountains streams." But the only place *y'rym* refers to a channel other than a river bed is Job 28:10. And whatever "channels in the rock" refers to in that verse, drainage canals, mine shafts, or the like,[5] it is certain that mountain streams, that is, wadis, are not referred to, since the *y'rym* in Job 28:10 are man made.

Finally, in all four of these examples it is natural to connect *mṣwr* with Egypt, in Isa 37:25 = 2 K 19:24 and Isa 19:6 because of *y'rym* and in Mic 7:12 because of the frequent parallelism of Mesopotamia and Egypt in restoration oracles. It can be shown that these are the only places where an original *ṣwr* could have been taken as a geographical designation of Egypt. That in all

---

3. A. Goetze, "Hittite Courtiers and their Titles," *Revue Hittite et Asianique* 12 (1952) 5f, 12 n. 46.

4. Calderone, *Biblica* 42 (1961) 423-32.

5. Cf. Pope, *Job*, *ad loc*.

of them *ṣwr* would have been preceded by an enclitic *-m* is improbable. Thus the hypothesis of Calderone is not tenable.

The case for reading an enclitic *-m* is strong for both *mtbn* in Isa 25:10 "straw"[6] and *mšḥr* in Ps 110:3.[7] In both a very common word has a preformative *m-* with no concomitant alteration in meaning. In neither, however, can the reading of an enclitic *-m* be easily embraced. For in Ps 110:3 dittography of the final *mem* of *mrḥm* "from the womb" may account for the anomalous form. And one hesitates to read a rare particle in Isa 25:10 because the passage is almost certainly prose.

In the following passages the MT needs no explicit defense:

Jer 46:5 *wgbwryhm yktw-m // nws* (inf abs) *nsw* "their heroes are shattered // they have surely fled" for MT *wgbwryhm yktw / wmnws nsw* "their heroes are shattered / they have fled a flight."[8]

Ps 7:7 *ᶜwrh 'ly-m špṭ ṣwh* "awake, O God, O Judge, command" for MT *ᶜwrh 'ly mšpṭ ṣwyt* "Awake, O my God, do thou command judgment."[9]

Ps 46:9 *ḥzw-m pᶜlwt yhwh* "see the works of Yahweh" for MT *ḥzw mpᶜlwt yhwh* "ibid."[1]

D. The following passage is too difficult to evaluate:

Isa 30:27 *wkbdw-m ś'h* "his liver raging" for MT *wkbd mś'h*"?."[2]

19. *Preformative m- on Participles*

A. A preformative particle *m-* is used in the formation of the active and passive participles of all verbal stems except B and N. In the case of Job 4:20 Dahood,[3] followed by Pope,[4] is probably right in suggesting that *mbly mśym* "without taking (it to heart)" should be read *mbly-m šm* "without name." The participle *mśym* can be understood only by taking it as elliptical for *mśym lb* "one who takes to heart." But this stratagem is a dubious one. Dahood's suggestion does not change the consonantal text (except for the vowel letter y) and the resulting line makes perfect sense in the context.

---

6. Hummel, p. 104.

7. Ibid., p. 98.

8. Ibid., p. 104.

9. Ibid., p. 101.

1. Ibid., p. 103.

2. Ibid., p. 100.

3. Dahood, NWSPJ, p. 55.

4. Pope, *Job*, p. 38.

B. On the other hand, there is little chance that Hummel is right in reading *ᶜmy ngšyw mᶜwll* "my people's rulers act like children" in Isa 3:12 as *ᶜmy ngšyw-m ᶜwll* "my people's rulers are children."[5] The use of the denominative participle "those who act like children" instead of the noun meaning "children" is an effective satirical device.

The following text needs no explicit defense:

Num 23:22 and 24:8 *'l-m hṣ'h* "God brought out" for MT *'l mwṣy'm* (23:22) / *mwṣy'w* (24:8) "it is God who brought them/him out."[6]

C. The passive participle *mdbq* in *wlšwny mdbq mlqwḥy* "and my tongue is made to cling to my palate" of Ps 22:16 is extremely difficult to evaluate. Hummel's suggestion that *wlšwny-m dbq mlqwḥy* "my tongue clings to my palate" be read is certainly less tortuous than the H passive participle of the MT, and may well be right.[7]

20. *Passages Where Words Containing a* mem *Occasion Difficulty*

A. There are a few cases where an enclitic *-m* has allegedly been assimilated into a word. In Ps 18:16 the case for the presence of an enclitic is strong. The text there reads *'pyqy mym* "channels of water." But the parallel in 2 S 22 reads *'pyqy ym* "channels of the sea." There can be little doubt that the latter reading is correct, for the subterranean oceans are being referred to. Patton,[8] followed by Cross and Freedman,[9] suggests that the original text was *'pyqy-m ym*, the enclitic *-m* having been attached to *ym* in Ps 18 but having been deleted in 2 S 22. This hypothesis very well accounts for the facts.

B. The following texts need no explicit defense:

Gen 1:9 *mqw(h)-m 'ḥd* "one pool" for MT *mqwm 'ḥd* "one place."[1]

Isa 33:21 *mqw-m nhrym* "a reservoir of rivers" for MT *mqwm nhrym* "a place of rivers."[2]

---

5. Hummel, p. 100.

6. Albright, JBL 63 (1944) 215 n. 45.

7. Hummel, p. 99.

8. Patton, *Canaanite Parallels in the Book of Psalms*, pp. 12-13.

9. Cross and Freedman, JBL 72 (1953) 26 n. 41 (Cf. SAYP, p. 294 n. 41).

1. D. N. Freedman, "Notes on Genesis," ZAW 64 (1952) 193.

2. Hummel, p. 102.

C. In one passage the case for reading an enclitic is provocative, but not completely convincing. In Ps 31:12 Hummel reads *wlškny-m 'd // wpḥd lmydᶜy* "calamity to my neighbors // and the object of fear to my acquaintances" for the MT *wlškny m'd // wpḥd lmydᶜy* "very much to my neighbors // and the object of fear to my acquaintances."[3] The MT is obviously wrong. But there is one flaw in Hummel's proposal: *'yd* always designates the calacity itself and never the object from which calacity comes. On the other hand, the parallel *pḥd* often designates the object of fear. As a synonym of *pḥd*, *mr'* "fear" also often indicates the object of fear, and, in fact, in Dt 11:25 is used as a parallel to *pḥd*. And *mr'* can be read here with little violence to the text. The letters *d* and *r* are often confused in both the old Hebrew and in the square script. And metathesis of letters is not at all uncommon. Possibly the metathesis preceded the change from *r* to *d*, and was the cause of the latter. Because of the semantic difficulty with *'yd* this explanation must be considered just as likely as reading an enclitic *-m*.

D. The following are too difficult for confident evaluation:

Isa 9:18 *nᶜt-m 'rṣ* "the earth reeled" for MT *nᶜtm 'rṣ* "the earth ...."[4]

Isa 11:15 *bᶜ(h)-m rwḥw* "in the boiling up of his anger" for MT *bᶜym rwḥw* "....of his anger."[5]

Job 15:29 *mnl(w)-m* "his property" for MT *mnlm* "?."[6]

Job 29:25 *b'šr 'blm ynḥ(w)-m* "wherever I guided they were led" for MT *k'šr 'blym ynḥm* "according to the mourners he comforts."[7]

Summarizing the results of the previous investigation, we can say that an enclitic *-m* is likely contained in the following verses:

Group A.

1. Datable poetry
   - Isa 10:1
   - Jer 18:14.15
2. Undatable poetry
   - Num 24:19
   - Dt 33:11
   - 2 S 22:16 = Ps 18:16
   - Ps 29:6

---

3. Hummel, p. 99.

4. Moran, CBQ 12 (1950) 153-54.

5. M. Dahood, "Additional Examples of Enclitic *mem* in the Bible," Unpublished Manuscript, quoted by Hummel, p. 95.

6. Dahood, NWSPJ, pp. 60f.

7. Pope, *Job*, p. 187.

Ps 89:51
Job 4:20
Job 15:18
Job 31:11
3. Prose
Gen 14:6
Num 21:14[8]

Since three examples are found in standard poetic Hebrew, the contrast is only partial between it and early poetic Hebrew, where we have good reason to assume the enclitic *-m* was prominent. And there is not a sufficient concentration in any poem of unknown date for the examples which do not occur to be used reliably as evidence of an early date. Adding to the above list the examples in Group C does not alter this conclusion:

Group C.
1. Datable poetry
Jer 3:23
2. Undatable poetry
Ps 22:16
Ps 31:12
Ps 65:10
Ps 68:17
Ps 99:4
Job 7:15
Job 8:18

Enclitic *-m* also is affixed to certain prepositions in Hebrew, and in this position it is designated by the Massoretic pointing. Hence, strictly speaking, it should have been considered under Group I, but it seems preferable to discuss it here, in context with enclitic *-m*'s on other parts of speech. It occurs most often on the preposition *k-*. Of the total of 52 examples in poetry[9] sixteen are in standard poetry: Isa 26:17.18, 41:25.25, 51:6, Jer 13:21, 15:18, 50:26, Hos 7:4, 8:12, 13:7, Zc 9:15, 10:2.7.8, Lam 4:6. So once again the difference between early and standard poetic Hebrew is a matter of relative frequency of occurrence, and the clustering in none of the poems of unknown date is more pronounced than in standard poetry, with the exception of Ps 58 and Job. There are six in the former (Ps 58:5.8.8.9.10.10) and eleven in the latter (Job 6:15, 10:22.22, 12:3, 14:9, 19:22, 28:5, 31:37, 38:14, 40:17, 41:16).

The remaining instances in undatable poems are as follows: Ex 15:5.8, Hab 3:14, Ps 29:6.6, 61:7, 63:6, 78:13 (from Ex 15:8).69, 73:15, 79:5, 88:6, 89:47, 90:9, 92:8, 140:4, 141:7, Prv 23:7, Ct 6:10, 7:2.

---

8. See p. 8 n. 3 for a statement of why Num 21:14-15 should be considered prose rather than poetry.

9. Four examples are found in prose: Gen 19:15, Isa 30:22, Ezk 16:57 and Neh 9:11 (from Ex 15:5).

On the preposition *b*- enclitic *-m* occurs once in standard poetry (Isa 43:2) and six times in undatable poems, five in Job (9:30 [Q], 16:4.5, 19:16, and 37:8) and one in Ps 11:2.[1] Certainly the example of *bmw* in Ps 11 is not significant for dating, and possibly neither are the five examples in Job.

On *l*- enclitic *-m* occurs four times, all in Job (27:14, 29:21, 38:40 and 40:4) and hence may be tangible evidence of an early date for that book.

In Ugaritic *-m* also is affixed to the preposition *ᶜd*, and Hummel may be right in suggesting that *ᶜdy-m* be read in Jer 48:32 for the MT *ᶜd ym yᶜzr ngᶜw* "they reach the sea of Jazer," since Jazer appears not to have been on a lake or sea.[2] Since this passage is not in undatable poetry, no decision on the matter need be made here. His other suggestions for reading enclitic *-m* on prepositions are most problematical.

---

1. There are three examples in prose (Isa 25:10 [Q], 44:16.19).

2. Hummel, p. 105.

Excursus

The Old Testament contains remnants of numerous morphemes which had already become archaic even in early poetic Hebrew. The rationale for the utilization of these for dating is slightly different from that for the morphemes which have just been examined. This rationale will be expounded in chapter five, so there is no need to belabor the point by discussing it here. It is more convenient to list the most important of these morphemes here, however, rather than in chapter five. They are divided into Group I and Group II, corresponding to the two groups in the main body of the chapter.

Group I.

A. *The 3fs Suffix Conjugation Enging -t*[1]

The ending for the 3fs suff conj verbs in Ugaritic is *-t*, but it is virtually certain that this ending had become *-a* in Hebrew by the early period. The older ending is found only once in biblical Hebrew: Dt 32:36 *'zlt.*[2]

B. *The Retention of the he of the H Stem in the Prefix Conjugation*

Likewise, it is virtually certain that the infixed *-h-* of the H stem in the pref conj had elided before early poetic Hebrew. The archaic form is found twice in prose (1 S 17:47 and Neh 11:17) and three times in poems of unknown date (Ps 28:7, 45:18 and 116:6). The fact that *yhwšyᶜ* is found in two and *yhwdh* in three of these passages suggests that the *-h-* survived only in certain words.

C. *The 3ms Pronominal Suffix -ahū on Plural Nouns*

In Ugaritic *-h* (probably pronounced *-hū*) is the 3ms pronominal suffix on singular and plural nouns. Already in pre-early poetic Hebrew the *he* had elided, producing *-w* (vocalized *-ō*) in the singular and *-yw* (vocalized *-āw*) in the plural. On singular nouns, however, the older and younger suffixes continued in use throughout the biblical period, in prose as well as in poetry. Hence, the older form on singular nouns cannot be labelled an archaism. But on

1. The understanding of the feminine ending *-t* in nouns, whether vocalized *-at* or *-āt*, is so fraught with difficulties that it is the better part of wisdom to omit any consideration of it here. Cf. O'Callaghan, VT 4 (1954) 175 and G-K-C 80g.

2. The forms *wmškḥt* in Isa 23:15 and *wšbt* in Ezk 46:17 are best explained as Aramaisms.

plurals the older form almost completely fell into disuse, and so, when it does occur, can be labelled an archaism.

According to the Massoretic pointing the older form occurs on plural nouns seven times. Some doubts exist about the legitimacy of three of them, however. In two cases (1 S 30:26 and Job 42:10) it is attached to the plural of the noun *r*ᶜ "friend," yielding the form *rēᶜẹhū*, and one must seriously question whether there has been confusion with the singular noun, which with the 3ms suffix also yields the form *rēᶜẹhū*. In addition, the genuine archaic nature of *ma'ᵃlōṯẹhū* in Ezk 43:17 is doubtful, since it is the only example in biblical Hebrew of a 3ms suffix with an unelided *he* following the feminine -*t*, either -*at* of the singular or -*ōt* of the plural.

Twice in Nah 1 Albright, the MT to the contrary, reads the 3ms suffix *ẹhū* on plural nouns.[3] For *mᵉqōmāh* "its place" in v. 8 and *ṣārā* "disaster" in v. 9 he reads *miqqāmẹhū* "his enemies" and *ṣārẹhū* "his adversaries," respectively. This reconstruction does vastly improve the text. But the general disarray of the text of vv. 8 and 9 hinders unhesitating adoption of it.

In the following list Albright's suggestions are marked with an asterisk and the doubtful enclosed in parentheses:

1. Datable poetry
   Nah 2:4 *gbrhw*
2. Undatable poetry
   Hab 3:10 *ydyhw*
   Nah 1:8 **mqmhw*
   Nah 1:9 **ṣrhw*
   Job 24:23 *ᶜynyhw*
   Prv 29:18 *'šrhw*
3. Prose
   (1 S 30:26 *rᶜhw*)
   (Ezk 43:17 *wmᶜlthw*)
   (Job 42:10 *rᶜhw*)

Group II.

A. *The Energetic Ending -an(na)*

There have often been suggestions that certain 3/2fpl pref conj verbs be read as 3/2fs verbs plus the affix -*an*(*na*), the termination marking the energetic mood in Arabic. Few of these suggestions have received general scholarly approbation. With the discovery that this termination is quite common in Ugaritic,[4] however, a renewed effort was made to find examples of it in the MT. One characteristic of this renewed search is the suspicion that, in addition to 3/2fpl verbs, certain 3s, 1s/pl and 2ms verbs plus the suffixes -*nw* or

3. Albright, CBQ 7 (1945) 23 and notes 62, 63.

4. Gordon, UM 9.8.

-nh should be read as energetic forms. Since the *waw* and *he* of these suffixes are vowel letters, it could be argued without undue conjecture that they were added by later scribes who misunderstood the forms. Or in the case of *he*, one could maintain that it represents the final *a* in *anna*, which had undergone lengthening in order to be preserved, since all short final vowels in Hebrew were dropped or lengthened. To all appearances, this renewed search will fare somewhat better than did the older ones.

1. *Concord between Subject and Predicate*

A. All the examples under this category concern the agreement of a 3fpl verb with a 3fs subject. In four cases the argument for reading the energetic form of the verb is good. Isa 28:3 reads *brglym trmsnh ᶜṭrt g'wt škwry 'prym* "the proud crown of the drunkards of Ephraim will be trodden under foot." There is only one possibility for producing concord here, and that is to point *ᶜṭrt* as plural *ᶜaṭrōṯ* instead of the singular *ᶜaṭereṯ*. Since this alteration of the MT entails no change of the consonantal script, it is not a difficult one. But the singular is supported by the singular in the identical phrase in v. 1 and by the fact that all the versions read the singular in both places. Since no evidence that *ᶜṭrt* was ever taken collectively in Hebrew exists, taking the verb as 3fs plus the energetic ending *-an(na)* is the least cumbersome way to account for the consonantal text.

The other three examples can be grouped together because the same verb form *trnh* is present in each. It occurs in Prv 1:20 *ḥkmwt bḥwṣ trnh* "Wisdom cries in the streets;" in Prv 8:3 *mbw' ptḥym trnh* "at the entrances of the gates she (i.e. *ḥkmh* "Wisdom" of v. 1) cries;" and in Job 39:23 *ᶜlyw trnh 'šph // lhb ḥnyt wkydwn* "around him rattle the quiver // flashing spear and javelin." In the first two the context demands that the verb be singular, for the subject in both cases is personified Wisdom, in 1:20 called *ḥokmōṯ* and in 8:1 *ḥokmāh*. In the example from Job a feminine plural form is possible as predicates preceding compound subjects may be plural, but analogy strongly suggests a singular, since verbs preceding compound subjects are usually singular.[5] But, although we are led to expect singulars the Massoretes have vocalized the first two as 3fpl *tārōnnā* and only the last as singular *tirneh*. And this last vocalization compounds problems rather than solving any, for *tirneh* can only be from the root *rnh*, a by-form of *rnn* otherwise unattested in Hebrew.

Scholars who wish to deny the existence of the energetic form of the verb in Hebrew point the two in Proverbs to agree with the pointing in Job.[6] Their antagonists, relying on the fact that the root *rnh* is otherwise unattested,

---

5. Cf. G-K-C 146f,g.

6. E.g. G-K-C 47k.

argue that the Job occurrence should be pointed according to the two instances in Proverbs.[7] The latter have the most convincing case. Derivation of *trnh* from *rnn* (which is manifested as a verb over fifty times and in the two very common nouns, *rinnāh* and *r^e nānāh*) is patently more feasible than deriving it from the root *rnh*, unattested apart from *tirneh* in Job 39:23.

Thus, the only way to avoid adopting the energetic form is to account for the final *he* of *trnh* in some other way. Some have suggested emending Prv 1:20 to read *ḥkmwt bḥwṣt rnh* "as for Wisdom, her cry is in the streets."[8] But this expedient cannot be resorted to in Prv 8:3. Another possibility is to take the final *he* as the cohortative *-h* attached to the third person. Undisputed examples of this phenomenon occur only in Isa 5:19.19 *yḥyšh* and *wtbw'h*, both with jussive force, and in Ezk 23:20 *wtᶜgbh* in past narrative.[9] Another possible example is *tᶜph* in Job 11:17 in future narrative. One can understand how the cohortative ending might be transferred from the first person to the third when the verb has a jussive force, as in Isa 5:19.19. The *-h* of Job 11:17 and Ezk 23:20 is without analogy. And since none of the examples of *trnh* are jussives, great dubiety inheres in explaining the final *he* as the cohortative ending. Taking *trnh* in all three cases as energetic forms of the verb remains the most likely explanation.

B. In five more cases the arguments against reading *-an(na)* are decisive. Ex 1:10 reads *whyh ky tqr'nh mlḥmh wnwsp gm hw' ᶜl śn'ynw wnlḥm bnw* "and if war occurs, they [the Israelites] will join with our enemies and fight against us." The fs subject *mlḥmh* takes the 3fpl verb *tqr'nh*. The Sam, however, reads *tqr'nw* "if war befall us" and is supported by all the versions. Since there is no syntactical difficulty obstructing adoption of this reading, the verb *qrh* often taking an object in the B stem, and since the 1pl suffix is used twice in the same verse, the Sam has doubtless preserved the correct reading.

In Gen 49:26 *thyyn lr'š ywsp* "may they [*brkt* "blessings"] be upon the head of Joseph," Cross and Freedman suggest reading *tihyan(na)*, a 3fs form plus *-an(na)*, instead of the 3fpl *tihyēnā* of the MT.[1] Since the subject of the verb is the fpl *birkōt*, no justification for reading a singular resides in the context. They find justification from their brilliant interpretation of *tbw'th* in the parallel passage Dt 33:16. They suggest that this monstrosity is a double reading composed of *tābō'* and *t^e hī*, the latter being written

---

7. E.g. Dahood, PNWSP, p. 4 and Pope, *Job*, p. 263.

8. For the references see Toy, *Proverbs*, *ad loc.*

9. Cf. G-K-C 48d.

1. SAYP, p. 182 n. 84.

defectively according to the orthographic practices prior to the tenth century. Since in this parallel recension 3fs verbs are used, they propose that *thyyn* should also be considered as singular. Since 3fs verbs are often used with 3fpl subjects, especially when the verb precedes, such a reading presents no grammatical difficulty.[2]

This suggestion overlooks, however, a crucial difference between the two recensions. In Dt 33 the subject is *mgd* "excellence"(?) whereas in Gen 49 the subject is *birkōt* "blessings." Even granting that our knowledge of *mgd* is narrowly circumscribed (it occurs only in this passage and three times in Canticles as a masculine plural) one cannot help suspect that the difference in the number of the verbs is related to this difference in their subjects. Furthermore, of course, it is necessary to say that, as brilliant as Cross and Freedman's dissection of *tbw'th* is, it is based on a theory of orthographic practices in early Israel which is very difficult to substantiate. They can find only one document which actually embodies these early practices: the very difficult to date and to interpret Gezer Calendar. An emendation based on poorly documented conclusions about early Israelite orthographic practices is hardly firm grounds for reading an extremely rare verbal form.

In Job 17:16 *bdy š'l trdnh* "into the hands(?) of Sheol will they go down?" the Massoretes have pointed *trdnh* as 3fpl *tēradnā*. Dahood[3] and Pope[4] wish to read a 3fs verb plus *-an(na)*. The rationale for this is the fact that the subject of the verb *tqwty* "my hope" in v. 15 is singular. But *tqwty* occurs twice in v. 15, once in each half of the line. Such repetition is highly irregular in the poetry of Job, occurring elsewhere only in 8:3, where, as here, the G reads two different words. In both cases the G should be followed. Here it reads *ta agatha mou* "my good" for the second *tqwty*, probably reflecting *tōbātī* in the Hebrew. Hence, "my hope" and "my good" become the dual subjects of the plural verb in v. 16.

In Isa 27:11 *bybš qṣyrh tšbrnh* it is logically possible for the subject of *tšbrnh* to be either *ʿyr bṣwrh* "fortified city" of v. 10 or *qṣyrh* "boughs" of v. 11. Driver opts for the former.[5] In the first place, the gender of *ʿyr* is feminine, that of *qṣyr* evidently masculine, since in Job 14:9 and 18:16 it is used with 3ms verbs and in Ps 80:12 it has the masculine plural morpheme for bound nouns. In the second place, the subject of *tšbrnh* apparently is the antecedent of the 3fs pronoun *'wth* in the next line. If Driver

2. Cf. G-K-C 145k.

3. Dahood, PNWSP, p. 4.

4. Pope, *Job*, p. 122.

5. G. R. Driver, "Hebrew Notes on Prophets and Proverbs," JTS 41 (1940) 163-64.

is correct, the *-nh* of *tšbrnh* is best taken as the energetic ending. But, notwithstanding the apparent masculinity of *qṣyr*, it is a natural collective and as such could legitimately be construed with a plural verb. And *qṣyr* can be the subject of *tšbrnh* without at the same time being the antecedent of *'wth* in the following line, as the following translation shows, "When its [the city's] boughs are dry, they [the boughs] are broken up; woman come and set fire to it [the city]." Granting that the problems in this passage are tricky, nevertheless, this solution is easier than reading the rare energetic form.

In Isa 49:15 the MT reads as follows:

htškḥ 'šh ᶜwlh // mrḥm bn bṭnh
gm 'lh tškḥnh // w'nky l' 'škḥk

G. R. Driver, noting that the subject of *tškḥnh* must be the singular *'šh* in 15a, takes it as singular plus the energetic ending, and takes *'lh*, with the antecedents *ᶜwlh* and *bn bṭnh*, as its object.[6] This yields the translation "does a woman forget her child // not having mercy on the son of her womb? Though she forget these, // I will not forget you." This rendering finds support from the G *ei de kai tauta epilathoito gunē* "even if a woman should forget these..." But if the text is to be emended, a far easier option is available, namely, to repoint *mrḥm* as *m^e raḥēm*, a D participle, understood as a term for a woman. The D stem ms participle *muraḥim* is often used in this way in Arabic. Since the gender is implicit in the sense, the fact that the participle is ms presents no problem.[7] This emendation produces very good parallelism, *'šh* finding its counterpart in *mrḥm* and *ᶜwlh* in the ballast variant *bn bṭnh*, the extra word being used because the second stich lacks a verbal counterpart of *tškḥ*. If it is adopted, *tskḥnh* is supplied with a compound subject, and the antecedents of *'lh* can be either *ᶜwlh* and *bn bṭnh*, in which case it is the object of the verb, or *'šh* and *mrḥm*, in which case it is the subject.

C. In one case the arguments for and against reading the energetic form are about equally persuasive. It has often been suggested that *tšlḥnh* of Jud 5:26 *ydh lytd tšlḥnh* "her hand to the tent peg she stretched" should be read as 3fs plus the energetic ending. Recently, Cross and Freedman,[8] Freedman alone,[9] and Dahood[1] have defended this position with great vigor. It is, of

6. Ibid., p. 164.

7. Cf. G-K-C 122c.

8. SAYP, p. 37 n.r.

9. D. N. Freedman, "Archaic Forms in Early Hebrew Poetry," ZAW 72 (1960) 102.

1. Dahood, PNWSP, p. 4.

course, obvious that the MT is in error. But the alternative to reading the energetic form is not at all unattractive, namely, to take the final *-nh* as the 3fs suffix referring to *ydh* "her hand." The resulting syntactical construction, object - verb - suffix resuming object, is not uncommon in Hebrew, as the examples listed in G-K-C 143c attest. The objections to this expedient are threefold. One, the verb without the suffix is better stylistically. Two, no witnesses to the suffix can be found in the versions. Three, reading *tišlaḥanna* improves the meter, making both stichoi contain nine syllables. This last argument is the one espoused by Freedman in his article on archaic forms in early Hebrew poetry. He believes that early Hebrew poetry is characterized by a remarkable symmetry between the parallel stichoi, and that this symmetry is manifested in the equivalence or near equivalence of the number of syllables in the two, although he thinks it unlikely that the poets actually counted syllables. According to the examples he adduces, there is never a discrepancy of more than one between the number of syllables in the parallel stichoi. In Jud 5:26 he claims that there are seven syllables in the first and nine in the second. The former number is arrived at by reading *tišlaḥ*. Freedman achieves symmetry by adding *-anna* to it. If one reads *tišlaḥēnnā*, the 3fs form plus the 3fs suffix, however, symmetry is also attained, and the metrical argument for reading *tišlaḥanna* over *tišlaḥēnnā* is nullified.

The argument based on the versional reading is indecisive. The Greek translator may have read the *-nh* as the 3fs suffix, but chose not to translate it because of considerations of Greek style. That the Syriac translator omitted it is a little more striking, since the syntactical construction involved is quite common in Syriac. The V is dependent on the G and, hence, is of no value. The paraphrasing tendencies of the T make recourse to it useless in a case like this one. It must be admitted, however, that the total absense of witnesses to the reading of *-nh* as the 3fs suffix is an argument in favor of taking it as the energetic ending.

As for the argument based on Hebrew style, it is true that the construction object - verb - suffix resuming object is awkward--to English speakers! It is not so clear that it was felt as awkward by the Hebrews. The simpler construction, object - verb, is more common. But such stylistic considerations are a flimsy basis for reading a rare morpheme. The combination of objections one and two tip the scales ever so slightly in favor of reading the energetic ending, but doubts persist.

2. *2fpl // 2ms*

A. In v. 13 of Obadiah the MT reads as follows:

'l tbw' bšʿr ʿmy // bywm 'ydm
'l tr' gm 'th brʿtw // bywm 'ydw
w'l tšlḥnh bḥylw // bywm 'ydw

> "Do not enter into my people's gate // on the day of their disaster.
> Do not look - even you - on his misfortune // on the day of his disaster.
> And do not loot his goods // on the day of his disaster.

This command is addressed to Edom. The first two verbs are 2ms but the third, anomalously, is 2fpl, pointed *tišlaḥnāh*. Clearly the MT is wrong. The verb must be 2ms. But how, then, is the *-nh* to be explicated. Apart from taking it as the energetic ending, there have been two suggestions. One is to read it as the particle of entreaty *nā'*. This particle does occur with the negative *'l* in Jud 19:23, but in the context of a request. It is a sign of polite speech, and surely there can be no question of such here. Obadiah is not beseeching, "please do not ...," but categorically commanding "do not ..." The other one is to take the *-nh* as a corruption of an original *yd* "hand," which would be expected after the verb *šlḥ* "to stretch out."[2] But the ellipsis of the object *yd* after *šlḥ* poses no insuperable problem, for such is the case in 2 S 6:6 and 22:17 = Ps 18:17. Furthermore, the mutation of *yd* into *nh* is not an easy textual change. Since neither of these stratagems is particularly successful, it is best to regard *-nh* as the energetic ending.

3. *Verbal Suffixes without Antecedents*

B. In Num 23:9 *ky mr'š ṣrym 'r'nw // wmgbᶜwt 'šwrnw* "Yea, from the top of mountains I see him // and from hills I spy him" and in Num 24:17 *'r'nw wl' ᶜth // 'šwrnw wl' qrwb* "I see him, but not now // I spy him but not yet" the verbs *r'h* and *šwr* occur in the 1s pref conj with suffixes *-nw* "him." Albright has suggested that in every case the suffix is a mispointing of an original energetic ending.[3] He bases his case solely on the fact that the pronouns are without antecedents. And he is right, if one means by an antecedent a referent which literally comes before. But Hebrew and English and most other languages permit themselves certain license to mention a pronoun before its antecedent when the latter follows immediately or is obvious from the context. Both of these conditions are met here, as the obvious antecedents of these pronouns immediately follow in vv. 10 and 18, respectively, *ᶜm* "people" and *kwkb // šbṭ* "star // rod."

In Num 23:19 *hhw' 'mr wl' yᶜśh // wdbr wl' yqymnh* "does he [Yahweh] say and not do // or promise and not carry it out?" and in v. 20 *wbrk* (Sam: *'brk*) *wl' 'šybnh* "and he has blessed (Sam: I have blessed) and I will not annul it" H stem 3ms pref conj forms are found with 3fs suffixes *-nh* "it." Albright suggests reading energetic forms of the verb in both cases instead

---

2. Cf. G-K-C 47k.

3. Albright, JBL 63 (1944) 212 n. 23.

of the suffixes.[4] He bases his argument on the fact that none of the other verbs in the context has suffixes. Two considerations can be offered in rebuttal. One, it is quite common in Hebrew for the 3fs suffix to refer to the action or idea stated by a verb in a preceding clause.[5] This use of it is exactly parallel to the use made of the pronoun "it" in English. Two, and more decisive, the H stem forms to which the suffixes are attached by their very nature demand objects. The suffixes supply them.

4. *Semantic Problems Created by 3ms or 3fs Suffixes*

A. The passages included in this section present no grammatical or lexical problems. Rather the problem is that the MT does not seem to make good sense. In each it has been suggested that a 3ms suffix *-nw* or a 3fs suffix *-nh* be read as the energetic ending of the verb. In one case the arguments for doing so seem persuasive. That passage is Dt 33:7:

> šmᶜ yhwh qwl ydwdh // w'l ᶜmw tby'nw
> ydyw rb lw // wᶜzr mṣryw thyh
> "Hear the voice of Judah, O Yahweh // and to his people bring him."
> May his power be great // and be thou a help against his enemies."

Cross and Freedman propose reading *tāḇō'an(na)* "do thou come" instead of the MT *tᵉḇī'ēnnū* "bring him."[6] Their main argument is that it is difficult to understand precisely what "bring Judah to his people" could mean. Judah is here surely not thought of as a separate person apart from the tribe of Judah. Rather, it is the tribe on whose behalf supplication is made. This argument is buttressed nicely by two other ones. One, if *tāḇō'an(na)* is read, it becomes a perfect parallel to *thyh* in the following line "do thou come // do thou be." Two, the G understood the verb in precisely this way, translating *elthois an* "mayest thou come."

B. Lam 1:13 reads *mmrwm šlḥ 'š // bᶜṣmty wyrdnh* "from on high he [Yahweh] sent fire // into my bones he rules (?) it." Since the root *rdh* "rules" seems to make no sense here, Dahood suggests reading the B stem of *yrd* "go down" plus the energetic ending *-an(na)* (*wayyirdenna* [sic]) with *'š* as its subject.[7] The second stichos would then read "into my bones it descends." Since *'š* occasionally is masculine,[8] Dahood's reading is theoretically possible. But,

---

4. Ibid.

5. Cf. G-K-C 135p.

6. Cross and Freedman, JBL 67 (1948) 203 n. 25 (Cf. SAYP, p. 218 n. 25).

7. Dahood, PNWSP, p. 4.

8. E.g. Jer 48:45, Ps 104:4, Jer 20:9, and Job 20:26.

if the verb is to be repointed from the root *yrd*, another possibility is eminently more probable, namely, to repoint it as an H stem plus the 3fs suffix with Yahweh as its subject, *wayyōrīdennā* "he made it descend." This reading is supported by the fact that *'š* is habitually feminine, that Yahweh is the subject of all the other verbs in the stanza, and that this is the reading presupposed by the G and S.

C. Gen 49:19 reads *gd gdwd ygwdnw // whw' ygd ᶜqb* "As for Gad, raiders raid him, but he raids from the rear." Cross and Freedman point out that on the basis of analogy with the other tribal sayings where the tribe is characterized by a figure,[9] the play on words here (*gd* with *gdwd*) must turn on a characterization of Gad, not his enemies.[1] Thus, they translate "Gad is a band which raids // and he raids at the rear." This entails omission of the suffix on *ygwdnw*. They handle the superfluous *-nw* by saying the *nun* was originally the sign of the energetic ending but subsequently mispointed as the 3ms suffix. This argument is, indeed, ingenious, but, since the MT does make good sense, is not completely persuasive.

5. *Textual Corruption*

B. On the basis of their theory that final vowels were not indicated in Israelite orthography prior to the tenth century, Cross and Freedman have proposed the following restoration of Jud 5:21c: instead of the MT *tdrky npšy ᶜz* "march on, my soul, in strength" they read *tdrkn p(r)š ᶜz*, which they vocalize as *tidrᵉkan(na) paršē ᶜuzzō* and translate as "his mighty chargers pounded."[2] This reading makes only one change in the non-vowel letter consonantal text, the insertion of *resh*, and it produces a line which can be joined to v. 22, which speaks of the pounding of horses. Doubtless, this suggestion must be taken very seriously in any further work on the text of Jud 5, but at present the theory of the development of Israelite orthography on which it is based is too conjectural and the insertion of the *resh* too radical a change to permit its adoption.

6. *Assimilation of t and k in the HtL Stem*

B. Freedman has suggested repointing *tkwnn* (*tikkōnēn*) of Num 21:27 as *tikkōnanna*, that is, 3fs N stem plus the energetic ending, on the basis that the assimilation of the *taw* of the prefix with the *kaph* of the root is questionable.[3] But, since the HtL stem of *kwn* occurs twice elsewhere with assimilation

---

9. Cf. vv. 9, 14, 17, 21 and 27.
1. SAYP, p. 171, n. 66-67.
2. SAYP, p. 35 n.j.
3. Freedman, ZAW 72 (1960) 106.

of *taw* and *kaph* (Isa 54:14 and Ps 59:5) as opposed to only one instance of the unassimilated form (Prv 24:3) Freedman's proposal is most unlikely.

In summary, there is a total of six examples in Group A:

Dt 33:7	bw'
Isa 28:3	rms
Ob:13	šlḥ
Job 39:23	rnn
Prv 1:20	rnn
Prv 8:3	rnn

and two examples in Group C:

Gen 49:19	gwd
Jud 5:26	šlḥ

But the three examples on the root *rnn* are valueless for dating, for the preservation of the archaic energetic ending on these forms is probably a function of some special peculiarity of this root.

B. *3mpl Prefix Conjugation* *taqtulu*

In Ugaritic and the Amarna letters certain masculine plural nouns receive pref conj verbs with a *t-* prefix. Whether these verbs should be interpreted as 3fs forms, with the nouns understood as collectives, or as 3mpl has been the subject of great debate. Until the publication of Moran's article in JCS 1961, practically all of the supporters of the former position were pupils of Albright. Albright himself has spoken out in favor of this position repeatedly, beginning in 1945 with an article on the Old Testament and Canaanite language and literature,[4] followed by an article published jointly with Moran,[5] and by his article on Ps 68.[6] Cross and Freedman concurred with this position in their article on the Blessing of Moses.[7] Later G. R. Driver also wrote in favor of this position in the grammatical notes accompanying his text and translation of the Ugaritic texts.[8] All of these scholars base their judgment primarily on the fact that in West Semitic 3fs verbs occur quite regularly with certain types of masculine plural nouns, namely, those designating animals, things and abstract qualities. It seems best to them to interpret the usage in Ugaritic and Amarna Canaanite according to this known linguistic practice rather than postulate a verb form not otherwise attested in West Semitic.

---

4. Albright, CBQ 7 (1945) 22-23.

5. W. F. Albright and W. L. Moran, "A Re-interpretation of an Amarna Letter from Byblos (EA 82)," JCS 2 (1948) 243ff.

6. Albright, HUCA 23 (1950-51) 17.

7. Cross and Freedman, JBL 67 (1948) 200 n. 16 (Cf. SAYP, p. 208 n. 16).

8. G. R. Driver, *Canaanite Myths and Legends*, Old Testament Studies 3 (Edinburgh, 1956) 130.

Previous to Moran's article, C. H. Gordon was the principal supporter of the position that the verbs in question are 3mpl.[9] But it was Moran himself who, in an about face, offered the most convincing evidence in favor of this position.[1] Basing his conclusions primarily on a study of purpose clauses, he argued that most all of the *t*- prefix verbs with mpl subjects in the Amarna letters must be construed as mpl. He allowed, however, that there did remain some (actually he cites only one example)[2] which are 3fs. Moran's position has since been adopted by Dahood.[3] In addition, Gordon has reaffirmed his former stand.[4]

All, then, are agreed that in Northwest Semitic of the period c. 1500-c. 1300 there are mpl nouns which receive pref conj verbs with a *t*- prefix. If the nouns refer to things, animals or abstract qualities, it is best to take the verbs as fs in line with known West Semitic practice. If the nouns refer to persons (human beings, angels, gods, etc.) it is best to withhold judgment regarding the form of the verb. It appears that Moran has definitely proved that some of them are mpl. But according to him the alternative is also possible.

3fs verbs with mpl nouns referring to things, animals and abstracts are common throughout Hebrew, and, hence, of no relevance for dating. The important question is whether any *t*- prefix verbs with mpl subjects designating persons can be found in biblical Hebrew. As the following analysis will show, possibly one or two can be discovered, far too few to justify the supposition that they were a regular feature of early poetic Hebrew. If in the MT one of these verbs is pointed as plural, we can postulate that it is a 3mpl *taqtulū* form. If it is pointed as singular, two alternatives for understanding it are available, one, as 3fs, or two, as a 3mpl form whose final -*w* has been deleted in the course of transmission because the form was misunderstood or was never written because of early orthographic practices.

1. <u>*taqtulū*</u> *Forms with mpl Subjects*

B. Of the several alleged examples of *taqtulū* as a 3mpl form none are convincing.[5] In Dt 5:23-24 *wtqrbwn 'ly kl r'šy šbṭykm wzqnykm wt'mrw* Gordon wishes

---

9. C. H. Gordon, *Ugaritic Handbook* (Rome, 1948) 9, 10.

1. W. L. Moran, "New Evidence on Canaanite *taqtulu(na)*," JCS 5 (1951) 33-35.

2. Ibid., p. 35

3. Dahood, PNWSP, pp.5f.

4. UM 9.10.

5. In Job 19:15 (cf. UM 9.10) the problem is not the use of the <u>*taqtulū*</u> pattern as a 3mpl but its use as a 3fpl instead of the more usual *taqtōlnā*.

to translate "and all the heads of your tribes and your elders came to me and said" instead of the traditional "and you came to me, all the heads of your tribes and your elders, and you said to me."[6] Although the latter does not produce as smooth flowing an English translation, it is perfectly acceptable according to the rules of Hebrew syntax. In light of the highly convoluted style of Deuteronomy, it is questionable whether this clause should even be considered a stylistic irregularity. But even if it is, such irregularities are not a sufficient basis for reading an extremely rare form of the verb.

Gaster takes *tkw* (*tukkū*) in Dt 33:3 as a 3mpl pref conj form from the root *wk'*, attested in Arabic as *wk'* "recline."[7] This derivation is, however, questionable. A metaplastic *wky* must be postulated in order to make the connection between *tkw* and the root *wk'*,[8] and neither *wk'* or *wky* is attested in Northwest Semitic. Thus, reading the rare verbal form *taqtulū* from the unattested root *wky/wk'* is doubly jeopardous. And compounding the difficulties is the general obscurity of the context.

The only suggestion for reading a 3mpl form which sounds even credible is Dahood's proposal for Prv 1:22.[9] The MT reads as follows:

ᶜd mty ptym t'hbw pty
wlṣym lṣwn ḥmdw lhm
wksylym yśn'w dᶜt

Dahood suggests taking *t'hbw* as 3mpl, hence, eliminating the mutation in persons between the first stichos and the next two. This would, indeed, produce a more smooth flowing translation. But here again, as in Dt 5:23-24 above, what is stylistically difficult in English is not necessarily so in Hebrew. Vacillation between second and third person is common in Hebrew poetry, whether Yahweh, personal or national enemies, or some other person/s are addressed. Thus, disagreement in person between *t'hbw* on the one hand and *ḥmdw* and *yśn'w* on the other is not a sufficient reason to read such a rare verbal form.

2. *taqtul Forms with mpl Subjects*

A. Albright has suggested three *taqtul* forms as candidates for fs verbs with mpl subjects referring to persons. In Ps 68:3 his proposal is the only

---

The subject of *tḥšbny* is *w'mhty* "my maidservants." Likewise, the *taqtulū* pattern is used as a 3fpl in Jer 49:11, 2:19, Ezk 37:7 and Ct 1:6.

6. UM 9.10.

7. T. H. Gaster, "An Ancient Eulogy on Israel: Deuteronomy 33:3-5, 26-29," JBL 66 (1947) 57.

8. Cf. Cross and Freedman, JBL 67 (1948) 200 n. 16 (Cf. SAYP, p. 208 n. 16).

9. Dahood, PNWSP, pp 5f.

plausible alternative unless radical emendation is resorted to.[1] The text of vv. 2-3a reads:

> yqwm 'lhym ypwṣw 'wybyw // wynwsw mśn'yw mpnyw
> khndp ᶜšn tndp // khms dwng mpny 'š

> "God arises, his enemies scatter // and those who hate him flee from him.
> As smoke is driven.... // as wax melts before a fire."

The crucial form is *tndp*, vocalized by the Massoretes as *tindōp*, that is, a B stem pref conj 2ms or 3fs. If it is 2ms, it can only be taken as a jussive "do thou drive." But this is difficult in the extreme. First, a suffix would be expected designating who is driven. Compare Job 32:13 and Ps 1:4, the only other occurrences of the B stem of *ndp*, where suffixes are present. Second, if *tndp* is a jussive one would expect *yqwm* to be jussive also. Third, inspection of the context leads one to expect the descriptive statement about the enemies begun in v. 2 to continue in v. 3. If *tndp* is 3fs, it is without a subject. Hence, many[2] supply *rwḥ* "wind" as the subject on the analogy of Ps 1:4 and translate "like smoke is driven when the wind drives it." This recourse involves not only the insertion of *rwḥ* but also supplying *tndp* with a suffix. That both would have been lost in transmission is improbable.

Put in such desperate straits by the MT, Albright's suggestion to take *tndp*, repointed as N rather than as B stem, as a 3fs with a masculine plural subject is most welcome. This proposal involves no change in the consonantal text and makes perfect sense. Verse 3 can be translated "like smoke is driven they are driven // as wax melts before a fire."

B. In one case Albright's argument is clearly specious.[3] The MT of Nah 1:5b reads *wtś' h'rṣ mpnyw // wtbl wkl yšby bh*. Albright, following practically all modern commentators, reads *wattiššā* "became waste" for *wattiśśā'* "lifted up." This emendation is reasonable. But also for *wᵉtēbel* he reads *wattēbal*, a 3fs pref conj B stem verb from the root *'bl* "languish," and takes *kl yšby bh* as its subject, a procedure which entails omission of the *waw* on *kl*. He appeals to Amos 8:8 and 9:5 where the phrase *kl yšb(y) bh* is the subject of B stem derivatives of *'bl*. Moran has very cleverly countered the objection that Albright's reading necessitates the deletion of the *waw* before *kl*. He suggests attaching the *waw* to *wtbl* and reading the verb as a *taqtulū* 3mpl form.[4] But

---

1. Albright, HUCA 23 (1950-51) 17 n.e.

2. Cf. BH³.

3. Albright, CBQ 7 (1945) 22-23.

4. W. L. Moran, "The Hebrew Language," p. 71 n. 108.

this stratagem does not skirt the weightiest objection to Albright's theory, that his emendation is entirely superfluous. The MT is perfectly acceptable. *Tbl* and *'rṣ* are often found in parallelism, and, what is more, the phrase *tbl wyšby bh*, differing from Nah 1:5b only in the omission of the *kl*, is found in Ps 24:1. Thus, Albright alters an irreproachable MT in the interests of finding a rare verbal form. Such a procedure is not permissible.

C. And, finally, the last of his three proposals is quite plausible but cannot be wholeheartedly embraced. The MT of Nah 1:9b reads *l' tqwm pᶜmym ṣrh* "disaster will not arise twice." This line is syntactically impeccable, but does not make much sense in its present context. Thus many scholars have emended *tāqūm* to *yiqqōm* on the basis of the G *ekdikēsei*, and translate "he will not take vengeance on his foes twice." This rendering makes acceptable sense, but it does involve a consonantal change. Albright's suggestion, on the other hand, involves no alteration of the consonantal text. He reads *lō tāqūm paᶜᵃmayim ṣārēhū* "his enemies will not arise twice."[5] This makes acceptable sense, but necessitates postulating the use of a 3fs verb with a mpl subject designating persons. Which of these alternatives is superior is not easy to judge. Complicating the situation is the general disarray of the text, which makes confidence in any emendation difficult.

The preceding survey has uncovered no 3mpl *taqtulū*, but one *taqtul* form with a mpl subject designating persons in Group A (Ps 68:3) and one in Group C (Nah 1:9b). As was stated above, it is possible that both of these should be considered not *taqtul* but *taqtulū* forms.

C. *Verbal Forms with Infixed -t-.*

Verbal forms with an infixed *-t-* are now attested in Northwest Semitic dialects widely separated both in space and in time: in Byblian Canaanite, in Moabite and in Ugaritic. In light of this extensive diffusion over the Northwest Semitic area, it is altogether reasonable that traces of infixed *-t-* verbal forms should appear in Hebrew. But the Massoretes seemed to have recognized none, and scholars who have thought they have found some have had little success in converting their colleagues to their persuasion. In recent years under the impact of Ugaritic studies a renewed search for them has been led by Cross, Freedman and Dahood. In spite of their ingenuity, it is likely that their efforts will meet the same fate as those of their predecessors.

---

5. Albright, CBQ 7 (1945) 22-23.

1. *Context That Present Semantic Problems*

B. Syntactically speaking, the MT of Dt 33:27 *mᶜnh 'lhy qdm // wmtḥt zrᶜt ᶜwlm* is acceptable as it stands, and with one modification, "the arms of the Eternal One" for "everlasting arms," can be translated as has been the custom since the days of the King James version, "a refuge is the Ancient God // underneath are the arms of the Eternal One." The main problem is that the line does not quite harmonize with the context. Verse 26 speaks of the God of Jeshurun as a cloud-rider, a well known war figure, and v. 27b speaks of his enemies being dispossessed before him. Many commentators have noted the disharmony which v. 27a creates coming between these two lines.[6] Gaster attempts to eliminate this difficulty by emending v. 27a so that it too speaks of God not as a refuge but as a warrior. He repoints *mᶜnh* as *meᶜanneh* "he who humbles" and *mtḥt* as *meḥattēt* "he who shatters" and renders the line "who humbles the ancient gods // and shatters all time-honored might."[7]

Dahood builds upon Gaster's rendition. He accepts the latter's repointing of *mᶜnh*, but avoids any emendation of the consonantal text by taking *mtḥt* as a Dt participle of *nḥt* "descend," translating "the God of Old is a conqueror // one who lowers his arms, the Eternal."[8] He compares *mtḥt zrᶜt* as an expression of Yahweh clobbering his enemies with *naḥat zerōᶜō* "the descending blow of his arm" of Isa 30:30 and *kṯr ynḥt ṣmdm* "Kothar lowers the two clubs" of Ugaritic. The ingenuity of this reconstruction cannot be gainsaid, but it runs aground on the fact that a statement that God's might undergirds Israel is not out of place in the larger context, which is concerned with Israel's safety under his protection. Thus, any compelling force to emend the text at all is dissipated.

In two cases where the root *str* is read in the MT Dahood wants to read an infixed *-t-* form from the root *swr*.[9] These are Prv 22:3 = 27:12 *ᶜrwm r'h rᶜh wystr* "a wise man sees danger and hides" and Job 3:10 *ky l' sgr dlty btny // wystr ᶜml mᶜymy* "for he did not shut the doors of my womb // nor hid trouble from my eyes." In the former it is Dahood's contention that the reading "hide" implies that the wise man is a coward. Comparing this line with 14:16 *ḥkm yr' wsr mrᶜ* "the wise man is cautious and turns away from danger," he prefers to read the root *swr*. This suggestion is interesting and could be right, but reading a verbal form not once unambiguously attested in biblical Hebrew because one has qualms about the appropriateness of a particular word

---

6. Cf. SAYP p. 239 n. 83.

7. Gaster, JBL 66 (1947) 60-61.

8. Dahood, PNWSP, p. 45.

9. Ibid.

is dangerous business. The root *str* certainly makes good sense, and it may not have had overtones of cowardliness as it does in English. Again in Job 3:10 *str* fits the context superbly, and the only reason Dahood can find to read a form from *swr* is that the G *apēllaxen* seems to presuppose it. But the G is simply not sufficient justification for positing an infixed *-t-* form.

In Jer 1:13 ff Dahood's case is more plausible than in the above passages, but not so much so that his suggestion can be adopted. In this passage Jeremiah is granted a vision and an accompanying oracle. In the vision he sees a *syr npwḥ* "a fanned pot," that is, a pot whose fire has been made hot by blowing. In the oracle he is told to pronounce that *mṣpwn tptḥ hrʿh // ʿl kl yšby h'rṣ* "from the north disaster will.... // upon all the land's inhabitants." The vision and the oracle are connected by the catchwords *npwḥ* and *tptḥ*. Since *npḥ* "breathe, blow" is the root in the vision but *ptḥ* "open" in the oracle, many scholars have emended *tptḥ* in order to produce a verb from *npḥ*. The problem is that such a task necessitates alteration of the consonantal text because of the second *taw*. Dahood's suggestion to read an infixed *-t-* form from *pwḥ/npḥ* accomplishes this purpose and leaves the MT untampered with. He translates "evil shall blow down from the North."[1] This suggestion is quite cogent and must be taken seriously. But it is deprived of its urgency by the acceptibility of the MT. The root *ptḥ* often has the connotation of "loosen, release" and, hence, is a suitable root in speaking of the coming disaster from the north. Also, it is suitable as the correlative of the catchword *npwḥ*. In cases like this where a vision and an oracle are related by a pair of catchwords, the two words need not have identical meanings or identical vocalizations. The only essential requisite is that the two sound alike. *Nāpūaḥ* and *tippātaḥ* fulfill this requirement.

C. Cross and Freedman are responsible for the most ingenious reconstruction of an infixed *-t-* form. In their article on the Blessing of Moses they suggest that the MT of Dt 33:3 *hm tkw lrglk* "they....at thy feet" should be read *hmtkw lrglk* "they prostrate themselves at thy feet."[2] The evidence they adduce for their emendation is really quite substantial. The subject of the verb is *qdšyw* "his holy ones." From *lrglk* it is natural to suppose they are engaged in a gesture of worship. No one has yet succeeded in extrapolating a root with a suitable meaning from the consonants *tkw*. Cross and Freedman propose joining *hm* to *tkw*, taking the resulting verb as a 3mpl suff conj verb with an infixed *-t-* and a prefixed *h-* from the root *mwk/mkk* "to be low, humble." The prefixed

1. Ibid., p. 45 n. 5.

2. Cross and Freedman, JBL 67 (1948) 200 n. 16 (Cf. SAYP, p. 208 n. 16).

h- is to be expected on the analogy of the *h-* prefixed with infixed *-t-* forms in the Moabite Stone. The meaning of the root *mwk/mkk* is precisely the meaning required by the context, and this root is well known not only in Hebrew but in Aramaic, Arabic, and Ugaritic. Furthermore, a reflexive verb is needed and, as is well known, infixed *-t-* in all semitic languages has fundamentally a reflexive force. There can be little doubt that this is the most compelling reconstruction of this stichos proposed to date, and it has been accepted by J. T. Milik.[3] The only major reason not to accept it is the disquieting thought that Dt 33:2-3 is one of the most obscure passages in the Old Testament. This makes wholehearted embrace of any proposal difficult.

2. *Textual Corruption: Metathesis of* t̲ *and* š̲

B. Jer 18:14-15 has always presented a very difficult problem. Verse 14 reads as follows:

hyᶜzb mṣwr śdy // šlg lbnwn
'm yntšw mym zrym // qrym nwzlym

While many of the details are obscure, it is clear that line a deals with crags forsaking the steppe and snow Lebanon, and that line b concerns water and probably springs.[4] Practically all commentators claim that there has been metathesis of the *t* and *š* in *yntšw* and read *ynštw* from the root *nšt* "be dry, parched." This root is attested three times elsewhere in the Old Testament, Isa 41:17, Jer 51:30 and Isa 19:5, where its subject, as here, is water. This emendation is not a difficult one, for metathesis of letters is a quite common scribal error. And most important, the meaning attained thereby admirably fits the context. Crags do not leave the steppe, snow does not melt on Lebanon, nor do springs dry up.

Dahood, however, suggests reading an infixed *-t-* form from the root *nšh* "to forget."[5] This avoids any emendation of the consonantal text, but it raises formidable problems in the interpretation of the passage. *Mym* "water" must be the object, so Dahood is forced to understand the indefinite "men, people" as its subject, translating, "Or do men forget flowing waters, running springs?" This maneuver can be defended syntactically, but it destroys the very fine parallelism between the subjects of 14a,b and 15a. Crags and snow,

---

3. J. T. Milik, "Deux Documents inédits du Désert de Juda," *Biblica* 38 (1957) 252.

4. Cf. Dahood, ZAW 74 (1962) 207ff.; Albright, HUCA 23 (1950-51) 23; and S. Iwry, "Notes on Psalm 68," JBL 71 (1952) 164-65.

5. Dahood, ZAW 74 (1962) 207.

water and springs are dependable, but Yahweh's people forget their god. The contrast is between four natural phenomena on the one hand and human beings on the other.

3. *Textual Corruption: Metathesis of w and t*

B. The MT of Prv 27:15 reads *dlp ṭwrd bywm sgryr // w'št mdwnym nštwh* "constant dripping on a rainy day // and a contentious woman are alike." The verb quite obviously is from the root *šwh* "be alike." But according to the rules of Hebrew verbal morphology the form should be *nšwth*. Dahood avoids ascribing the transposition of the two consonants to scribal error or euphony[6] by suggesting that it is an infixed *-t-* form from *šwh*.[7] But there is a major problem which Dahood has overlooked. The verb is N stem. And, although in several semitic languages, an N stem and a T-prefix stem have combined to form an Nt stem (e.g. the NtD stem of Mishnaic Hebrew), as far as I can determine, an N stem with an infixed *-t-* is unattested.[8] Dahood's reading entails, therefore, positing not only the existence of an infixed *-t-* in Hebrew but an N infixed *-t-* verbal stem in Semitic. As a result, Dahood's proposal cannot be accepted.

In conclusion, there are no alleged examples of infixed *-t-* forms which fall into Group A, and only one (Dt 33:3) which falls into Group C.

D. *The Conjunction pa-*

Until only very recently it was assumed that the semitic conjunction *pa-* had disappeared not only in Hebrew but also in all of Northwest Semitic. The discovery of its existence in Ugaritic,[9] in Phoenician,[1] and in Old Aramaic,[2] however, showed that it was widespread throughout Northwest Semitic. And this demonstration has spawned an attempt to find it in Hebrew. To date, Dahood is responsible for all the suggested examples.

---

6. Cf. G-K-C 75x.

7. Dahood, PNWSP, p. 54.

8. Cf. C. Brockelmann, *Grundriss der vergleichenden Grammatik der semitischen Sprachen* (Hildesheim, 1961) p. 540ff.

9. Cf. UM p. 311 no. 1501.

1. Cf. J. Friedrich, *Phönizisch-Punische Grammatik* (Rome, 1951) p. 162.

2. Cf. G. Garbini, "La Congiunzione Semitica *pa-," *Biblica* 38 (1957) 422 and J. Fitzmeyer, "The Aramaic Inscriptions of Sefire I and II," JAOS 81 (1961) 212-13.

1. *Semantic Problems Created by the Presence of the Letter* pe

A. In Job 9:20 the MT reads *'m 'ṣdq py yršyᶜny* "though I am innocent, my mouth would declare me guilty." In a passage in which Job is bitterly complaining that, even if he were to get a court trial, God would pervert justice, it is passing strange to hear him admit that his words would condemn him. Ordinarily the expression "my mouth condemns me" would be tantamount to confession of guilt. It is possible, as Pope says,[3] to make sense of the MT by interpreting it to mean that God will, like a clever lawyer, twist Job's words of innocence so that they actually condemn him. But this interpretation is forced, to say the least. Most commentators avoid the difficulty by reading *pyw* "his mouth." But this reading has no MS or versional support and involves alteration of the consonantal text. Dahood takes the *pe* of *py* as a resumptive conjunction on *yršyᶜny*, and supposes that the *yodh*, being a vowel letter, could easily have been added when the scribes no longer understood the function of *pe*.[4] While some residue of doubt remains, it must be admitted that this last suggestion is the most facile way of handling the text.

B. The MT in Job 9:12 reads *hn yḥtp my yšybnw* "if he...., who can make him give it back?" Since the root *ḥtp* as a verb is a *hapax legomenon*, Dahood proposes that we read *hēn yaḥat pāmī yᵉšībēnnū* "if he should snatch away, who could resist him?"[5] He derives *yaḥat* from the root *ḥth* "remove, snatch away" as in Ps 52:7. Further, he argues that his reconstruction provides a resumptive conjunction before the apodosis beginning with *my* "who." The root *ḥtp* is, however, manifested by the noun *ḥeteḇ* one time in the Old Testament, and that one time is enough to establish with relative certainty the semantic range of the root. It occurs in Prv 23:28 *'p hy' kḥtp t'rb* "also, she lies in wait as for prey." When this verse is compared with Ps 10:9 *y'rb lḥṭwp ᶜny* "he lies in wait to snatch away the poor," it is apparent that *ḥtp* and *ḥṭp* have identical meanings, "to snatch away, prey on," or the like, and, in fact, may be variants of the same root. Since, therefore, we can arrive at a satisfactory meaning for *yḥtp* by associating it with the root *ḥṭp*, a motive for emending the text vanishes.

In Prv 10:6 *brkwt lr'š ṣdyq // wpy ršᶜym yksh ḥms* "blessing are (showered) upon the head of the righteous // but the mouth of the wicked conceals violence" Dahood wishes to delete the conjunction *w-* and read *py* as the conjunction *p-* in order to promote better parallelism.[6] He translates the

---

3. Pope, *Job*, *ad loc.*

4. Dahood, *Biblica* 38 (1957) 311-12.

5. Ibid., p. 310.

6. Ibid., p. 312 n. 1.

second stichos "violence shall cover the wicked." To be sure, better parallelism is hereby effected, but several problems arise. One, the *waw* must be deleted. Two, the word *ḥms* "violence" is never used in the sense of retributive punishment, but always of the harm done by the wicked to the righteous. It is harm wrongfully inflicted not just retribution. And three, the identity of v. 6b with v. 11b, where *py ršᶜym* must be original because of the parallel *py ṣdyq*, argues against any emendation of the former. Possibly, v. 11b has displaced the original v. 6b.

The MT of Prv 25:8 reads *'l tṣ' lrb mhr // pn mh tᶜśh b'ḥryth // bhklym 'tk rᶜk* "do not be quick to quarrel // lest, what will you do when it is over // when your neighbor shames you?" Practically all commentators remark about the awkwardness of *pen* "lest." Many suggest emendation to *ky* "for."[7] Dahood avoids any alteration by reading the *pe* as the conjunction *pa-* and the *nun* as an afformative often found attached to prepositions and conjunctions in West Semitic.[8] He translates "do not hasten forth to quarrel // for what will you do....?" This suggestion is ingenious, but certain considerations weigh heavily against it. On morphological grounds the difficulty in accepting it is compounded because not one but two particles not unambiguously attested in Hebrew must be read, *pa-* and the afformative *-n*. Furthermore, in no semitic language is *-n* attested on *pa-*.[9] On syntactical grounds, it is questionable whether *p-n* is any improvement on *pen*. One expects some subordinate conjunction here, but *pa-* seems to be exclusively a coordinate conjunction, meaning "and/but." And finally, even if *pa-* can mean "for, because," it is not easy to see how it would be an improvement on *pen*, especially since the construction "do not....lest" is a favorite one with the wise men.[1] In summary, then, in order to read *pn* as the conjunction *pa-* plus the afformative *-n* we suppose that three improbabilities (the use of *pa-*, the use of *-n*, and the use of *pa-* as a subordinate conjunction) were actualized in one and the same word. Such a happening is triply improbable.

The MT of Ct 3:10b *twkw rṣwp 'hbh mbnwt yrwšlm* is extremely difficult. Dahood's suggestion is to connect *mbnwt yrwšlm* "daughters of Jerusalem" with v. 11, and connect the final *pe* of *rṣwp* to *'hbh* as the conjunction *pa-*.[2] The

---

7. Cf. Toy, *Proverbs, ad loc.*

8. Dahood, PNWSP, p. 53.

9. To be sure, Dahood does have a point in comparing the pair *p-* and **pn* with *w-* and *wn* of Ugaritic. Analogically, it is true, one might expect **pn* to occur in Ugaritic, and the fact that it does not might be a result of the paucity of our sources.

1. Cf. Prv 5:9, 9:8, 20:13, etc.

2. Dahood, PNWSP, p. 53 n. 7.

remaining *rṣw* he interprets as the infinitive absolute of *rṣh* "take pleasure," translating "within it there is pleasure and love." The principal objection to Dahood's suggestion arises out of considerations of parallelism. Verse 9 states that Solomon has built himself a palanquin, and the first three stichoi of v. 10 describe its appearance. It is almost certain that the fourth, the one in dispute, does likewise. The best interpretation has been offered by Meek.[3] He, too, assigns *mbnwt yrwšlm* to v. 11. He then interprets *rṣwp* according to various cognates as "fitted" and *'hbh* according to an Arabic cognate as "leather" and renders "its interior fitted out with leather."

In Hos 7:1b *wgnb ybw' // pšṭ gdwd bḥwṣ* Dahood wishes to read *pᵉšāṭ* "and bands will roam in the streets" for MT *pāšaṭ* "bands will raid in the streets."[4] His reason--that *šāṭ* as a verb of motion nicely balances *ybw'*--is trivial. For *pšṭ* "make a raid" is also a verb of motion, and the connection of *pšṭ* with *gdwd* "marauding band" is too natural to permit emendation.

C. In Hos 4:2 there are five straight infinitive absolutes, each connected to the others by the conjunction *w- 'lh wkḥš wrṣḥ wgnb wn'p* "cursing and lying and murdering and stealing and committing adultery." Two verbal clauses follow: *prṣw wdmym bdmym ngᶜw* "they break forth (?) and touch blood to blood." Two problems arise. One concerns the meaning of *prṣw*. It could conceivably mean either "break in," that is, "steal," or "break out" in acts of violence. Against the former is that the prophet has already enumerated stealing. Against the latter is that *prṣ* in this sense is elsewhere always followed by a designation of the object of the violence. In addition, *prṣ* never elsewhere refers to physical acts of violence committed by men, but only of the judgment of Yahweh. The other problem concerns the poetic structure and the natural grouping of words. In vv. 1b and 3b there seems to be a 2-2 rhythm, so the question arises whether *prṣw* should not be joined with *wn'p* to form three pairs of infinitive absolutes. Also there is possibly a natural grouping of sins here, cursing and lying as sins of the mouth contrasting with murder and theft. Is it possible that adultery and "breaking out"(?) are meant to provide another contrasting pair?

Without postulating the existence of *pa-* in this verse, two textual changes would be necessary to effect the joining of *prṣw* to *wn'p*. A *waw* would need to be inserted between *wn'p* and *prṣw* and the final *waw* of *prṣw* would have to be deleted. Dahood avoids both of these changes by taking the initial *pe*

---

3. T. J. Meek, *The Song of Songs*, *The Interpreter's Bible* (12 vols. New York, 1951-57) 5, 120.

4. Dahood, PNWSP, p. 53 n. 7.

of *prṣw* as the conjunction *pa-* and its final *waw* as the vowel letter of *rāṣō* (an infinitive absolute of *rṣh*) which is then understood in the sense of wanton self indulgence, a meaning closely paralleled by the use of *rṣwn* in Gen 49:6.[5]

The problem is that none of the above arguments is really decisive. *Prṣ* can be taken in the sense of violent acts of destruction, and the meter of the entire passage is not at all clear. Nor is the contrast between the five infinitives so marked that we can easily assume that originally three pairs were grouped according to type of offense. The issue of the debate, therefore, must remain in doubt.

2. *A Numeral as the Free Noun in a Bound Phrase*

A. The phrase *bhrry 'lp* in Ps 50:10 is syntactically impossible. The bound form before a numeral is unparalleled. Dahood attaches the *pe* of *'lp* to the following verse as the conjunction *pa-*.[6] This leaves *bhrry 'l*, a phrase also found in Ps 36:7, which passes well in the context, "For all the field animals are mine // the cattle on the mighty mountains." This is such a happy solution to the difficulty of this verse that, provisionally at least, it must be accepted.

We have, then, in Group A Job 9:10 and Ps 50:10 and in Group C Hos 4:2.

---

5. Ibid.

6. Dahood, *Biblica* 38 (1957) 312.

CHAPTER FOUR
THE CUMULATIVE EVIDENCE

It is clear that the value of the grammatical forms analysed above for the dating of early Hebrew poetry, when assessed one by one, is limited. Verbal patterns that resemble those we can postulate for early poetic Hebrew appear in Ex 15, Jud 5, Hab 3, 2 S 22 = Ps 18, Dt 32 and Job, and nine examples of the 3mpl suffix *-mw* over against no examples of *-m* are found in Ex 15. Their presence in these poems is striking evidence for an early date.

In all other cases the grammatical forms discussed in the preceding chapters cannot legitimately be used as evidence of an early date. Admittedly, their presence in any given poem of unknown date may result from its genuinely early date rather than from archaizing. The point is that their presence cannot be entered as evidence of an early date. The reason is that, in the precise manner that they occur in poetry of unknown date, they also occur in standard poetry.

But, though these forms considered one at a time are rarely valuable for dating, an accumulation of several of them within one poem may be evidence of an early date. We are postulating that all were common features of early poetry. Therefore, one would expect that in genuinely early poems several would often occur together in one poem, in other words, that a clustering effect would result. But, on the other hand, since all are rare in standard poetic Hebrew, no clustering, rather an isolated form here and there, would be anticipated.

Concerning the latter, our expectations are confirmed, as no significant clustering is found in standard[1] poetry. Only twice do three forms occur together in the same poem, and in both instances two of the three are the two most commonly preserved archaic features, enclitic *-m* on the preposition *k-* (52 times in biblical poetry) and the 3mpl suffix *-mw* on the preposition *l-* (55 times in biblical poetry):

Isa 26:1-21	Lam 4:1-22
y/w opening syl 11	*-y* I 21
-mw on *l-* 14.16	*-mw* on *l-* 10.15
encl *-m* on *k-* 17.18	encl *-m* on *k-* 6

Twice more two forms are found in one poem, and in one of these one

1. In the following discussion no morphemes discussed in the *Excursus* are considered, because they appear to be archaisms already in early poetry. Therefore, the presence of the younger forms along side of them does not constitute evidence of archaizing. These morphemes will be discussed in chapter five.

of the forms is the suffix *-mw* on the preposition *l-*:

Isa 42:18-25
zū as rel 24
pref form 25

Lam 1:1-22
-y I 1.1.1
-mw on *l-* 19.22

In all other cases there is one form per poem.

Isa 1:21-26
-y I 21

Isa 9:8-10:4
encl *-m* (Gr.A) 10:1

Isa 15:1-16:11
-mw on *l-* 16:4

Isa 17:12-14
y/w opening syl 12

Isa 21:11-12
y/w opening syl 12.12

Isa 22:15-25
-y I 16.16

Isa 23:1-12
-mw on *l-* 1

Isa 30:1-5
-mw on *l-* 5

Isa 31:1-3
y/w opening syl 3

Isa 33:7-9
y/w opening syl 7

Isa 35:1-10
-mw on *l-* 8

Isa 40:18-20
y/w opening syl 18

Isa 40:25-26
y/w opening syl 25

Isa 41:21-29
encl *-m* on *k-* 25.25

Isa 43:1-7
encl *-m* on *b-* 2

Isa 43:8-13
-mw on *l-* 8

Isa 43:16-21
zū as rel 21

Isa 44:6-8
-mw on *l-* 7

Isa 46:5-11
y/w opening syl 5

Isa 48:20-21
-mw on *l-* 21

Isa 51:1-3
pref form 2

Isa 51:7-8
encl *-m* on *k-* 6

Isa 52:13-53:12
-mw on *l-* 53:8

Isa 56:9-12
-w 9.9

Jer 3:21-23
encl *-m* (Gr.C) 23

Jer 5:20-29
-anhū 22

Jer 10:17-18
-y I 17

Jer 13:20-27
encl *-m* on *k-* 21

Jer 15:15-21
encl *-m* on *k-* 18

Jer 18:13-17
encl *-m* (Gr.A) 14.15

Jer 22:20-23
-y I 23.23

Jer 49:14-16
-y I 16.16

Jer 50:21-27
encl *-m* on *k-* 26

Jer 51:12-14
-y I 13

Ezk 19:2-14
pref form 9

Ezk 27:3-9
-y I 3

Hosea 6:11b-7:7
encl *-m* on *k-* 7:4

Hosea 8:11-14
encl *-m* on *k-* 12

Hosea 10:11-15
-y I 11

Hosea 11:1-7
pref forms 4.4

Hosea 12:2-6
pref forms 5.5

Hosea 13:4-8
encl *-m* on *k-* 7

Obadiah
-y I 3

Micah 7:11-20
-y I 14

Hab 1:5-11
zū as rel 11

Hab 2:6-19
-mw on *l-* 7

Zeph 2:1-15
-w 14

Zech 9:9-17
encl *-m* on *k-* 15

Zech 10:1-2
encl *-m* on *k-* 2

Zech 10:6-12
encl *-m* on *k-* 7.8

Zech 11:17
-y I 17

All of these forms are, of course, archaisms, and we would expect to find evidence of this fact in the above poems. That is, we would anticipate finding the 3mpl suffix *-m* along side of *-mw*, the relative *'šr* along side of *zū/zō/ze*, verb forms from final y/w roots with a syllable-opening y/w lost along side of those with y/w retained, and verbal forms characteristic of standard poetic Hebrew along side of pref forms.[2] But occasionally, especially in the shorter poems, specimens of the forms characteristic of standard poetic Hebrew do not occur. In this situation, a poem datable during or after the eighth century manifests early forms without evidence of archaizing. An example is Isa 17:12-14:[3]

y/w opening syl	preserved: 12

Most poems written in standard poetic Hebrew, however, contain ample evidence of archaizing. Beside the one, two, or three early poetic forms, one or more standard poetic forms are present. Isa 26:1-21, Lam 4:1-22, and Isa 42:18-25 provide good illustrations:

	Isa 26:1-21	
a) y/w opening syl	preserved: 11.20	lost[4] 11
b) relative pron		*'šr* 9 (*k'šr*)
c) 3mpl suff on N/V		*-m* 11.14
on prep *l-*	vv. 14.16	
d) encl *-m* on prep *k-*	vv. 17.18	

	Lam 4:1-22	
a) y/w opening syl		lost 6.14.15.15.18
b) relative pron		*'šr* 20
c) 3mpl suff on N/V		*-m* 7.8.8.16.16.20
on prep *l-*	vv. 10.15	
d) encl *-m* on prep *k-*	v. 6	
e) *-y* I	v. 21	

	Isa 42:18-25	
a) verb in past narr	pref 25	w-pref 25.25.25 (2 initial)
b) y/w opening syl		lost 24
c) relative pron	*zū* 24	
d) 3mpl suff on N/V		*-m* 19.22

---

2. The prepositions *k-* and *b-* without enclitic *-m* along side of examples of it with enclitic *-m*, *lhm* beside *lmw*, and *annū* beside *anhū* are not evidence of archaizing, since both members of the respective pairs are present in early poetic Hebrew. And the absence of *-y* I, *-y* II, *-w*, or enclitic *-m* is irrelevant for the detection of archaizing, since these forms are optional even in early poetry.

3. Under each of the passages in the lists to follow are three columns. In the left one are the grammatical features being considered. The middle one contains any early poetic forms found in the poem and the right one any standard poetic forms. No forms common to both early and standard poetic Hebrew are listed.

4. No examples of the loss of the final *y* in verbs that are also medial *y* (e.g. *hyh*) are considered.

Poems that Resemble Early Poetry

For the language of a poem to resemble early poetic Hebrew, the poem must not only exhibit a goodly number of forms characteristic of early poetry but fail to exhibit forms characteristic of standard poetic Hebrew. In other words, one must find clustering without evidence of archaizing. One undatable poem only meets both of these requisites, Ex 15:

a) verb in past narr	pref (7)[5] pref // suff (3) pref // w-pref (1)
b) y/w opening syl	preserved 5
c) relative pron	*zū* 13.16
d) *-an-* plus *-hū*	*anhū* 2
e) 3mpl suff on N/V	*-m* (9)
f) *-y* I	v. 6
g) encl *-m* on prep *k-*	vv. 5.8

Poems that Resemble Standard Poetry

The vast majority of the undatable poems resemble standard poetry in that they contain no more than two early forms, exclusive of the suffix *-mw* and the enclitic *-m* on prepositions, and in addition exhibit one or more standard forms:

Gen 49

a) verb in past narr		w-pref (7, 4 initial)
b) y/w opening syl		lost 8.8
c) 3mpl suff on N/V		*-m* 6.6.6.6.7.7
d) *-y* I	v. 11a	
e) *-y* II	v. 11b	

Dt 33

a) verb in past narr		w-pref (5, 4 initial)
b) y/w opening syl		lost 10
c) relative pron		*'šr* 8.29 (textually dubious)
d) 3mpl suff on prep *l-*	v. 2.2	
e) *-y* II	v. 16	
f) encl *-m*	v. 11 (Gr.A)	

Jud 5

a) verb in past	pref (6) w-suff (3) pref // suff (2) suff // w-suff (1)	suff // w-pref (1)
b) relative pron	*ze* 5	*'šr* 27 (textually dubious)
c) 3mpl suff on N/V		*-m* 20.21

2 S 1:19-27

a) verb in past narr	pref 22	suff // w-pref 27
b) 3mpl suff on N/V		*-m* 23

---

5. For convenience, in certain cases only totals will be given. Such figures are enclosed in parentheses. Numerals without parentheses refer to verses.

2 S 22 = Ps 18

a) verb in past narr	pref (18) pref // suff (2) pref // w-pref (3)	**w-pref initial (7)**
b) y/w opening syl		**lost 16**
c) 3mpl suff on N/V		-*m* (12)

Hab 3

a) verb in past narr	pref (9) pref // suff (2)	suff // w-pref (3)
b) y/w opening syl		lost 10
c) 3mpl suff on N/V		-*m* 14
d) encl -*m* on prep *k*-	v. 14	

Ps 2

a) y/w opening syl		lost 1
b) 3mpl suff on N/V	-*mw* 3.3.5	-*m* 9.9
on prep *l*-	v. 4	
on prep *'l*	v. 5	

Ps 5

a) y/w opening syl		lost 11
b) 3mpl suff on N/V	-*mw* 11	-*m* 10.10.10.11
on *ʿl*	v. 12	

Ps 9-10

a) y/w opening syl		lost 9:16
b) relative pron	*zū* 9:16, 10:2	*'šr* 10:6
c) 3mpl suff on N/V		-*m* 9:6.7.16, 10:17

Ps 11

a) y/w opening syl		lost 4.7
b) 3mpl suff on N/V	-*mw* 7	-*m* 2.6
c) encl -*m* on prep *b*-	v. 2	

Ps 17

a) relative pron	*zū* 9	
b) 3mpl suff on N/V	-*mw* 10.10	-*m* 14.14.14

Ps 21

a) y/w opening syl		lost 12
b) 3mpl suff on N/V	-*mw* 10.11.13	-*m* 10.10.11

Ps 22

a) verb in past narr	w-suff (1)	w-pref (1, plus 6 suff)
b) y/w opening syl		lost 14.18.28.30
c) 3mpl suff on N/V	-*mw* 5	
d) encl -*m*	v. 16 (Gr.C)	

Ps 24

a) verb in past narr	pref (2)	
b) relative pron		*'šr* 4

Ps 28

a) 3mpl suff on N/V		-*m* 3.4.4.5.5.9.9
on prep *l*-	v. 8	

Ps 29

a) y/w opening syl		lost 2
b) encl *-m*	v. 6 (Gr.A)	
on prep *k-*	v. 6.6	

Ps 30

a) verb in past narr	pref 9.9	suff // w-pref 3.12 (plus 9 suff)
b) y/w opening syl		lost 5
c) *-y* II	v. 8	

Ps 31

a) y/w opening syl		lost 11.18
b) relative pron	*zū* 5	*'šr* 8.20
c) 3mpl suff on N/V		*-m* 21.21
d) encl *-m*	v. 12 (Gr.C)	

Ps 32

a) verb in past narr	pref 5 pref // suff 5	(5 suff)
b) y/w opening syl		lost 3
c) relative pron	*zū* 8	

Ps 35

a) relative pron		*'šr* 8.11
b) 3mpl suff on N/V	*-mw* 16	*-m* 6.6.7.13.25

Ps 36

a) y/w opening syl	preserved 8.9	lost 13
b) 3mpl suff on N/V		*-m* 9

Ps 39

a) y/w opening syl	preserved 7	*-m* 7
b) 3mpl suff on N/V		

Ps 44

a) verb in past narr	pref 3 pref//w-pref//suff 3	w-pref 3.3 w-pref//suff (//pref) 3
b) y/w opening syl		lost 11
c) 3mpl suff on N/V		*-m* 3.3.4.4.4
on prep *l-*	vv. 4.11	

Ps 45

a) y/w opening syl		lost 18
b) 3mpl suff on N/V	*-mw* 17	

Ps 49

a) y/w opening syl		lost 13.14.15.19.20.21
b) 3mpl suff on N/V	*-mw* 12	*-m* (10)
on prep *l-*	v. 14	

Ps 55

a) y/w opening syl		lost 24
b) relative pron		*'šr* 15.20
c) 3mpl suff on N/V		*-m* 10.16.16.20.24
on prep *l-*	v. 20	
on prep *ᶜl*	v. 16	

Ps 56

a) y/w opening syl		lost 7
b) relative pron		*'šr* 7 (*k'šr*)
c) 3mpl suff on N/V		*-m* 6
on prep *l-*	v. 8	

Ps 57

a) y/w opening syl	preserved 2	lost 7
b) 3mpl suff on N/V		*-m* 5

Ps 58

a) y/w opening syl		lost 4.9
b) relative pron		*'šr* 6
c) 3mpl suff on N/V	*-mw* 7.7	
on prep *l-*	vv. 5.8	
d) encl *-m* on prep *k-*	vv. 5.8.8.9.10.10	

Ps 59

a) y/w opening syl		lost 7.15
b) 3mpl suff on N/V	*-mw* 12.12.13.13.14	*-m* 12.13
on prep *l-*	v. 9	

Ps 62

a) y/w opening syl		lost 5
b) relative pron	*zū* 12	
c) 3mpl suff on N/V		*-m* 5

Ps 64

a) y/w opening syl		lost 5
b) relative pron		*'šr* 4
c) 3mpl suff on N/V		*-m* 4.4.8.8.9
on prep *l-*	v. 6.6	
on prep *ʿl*	v. 9	

Ps 65

a) 3mpl suff on N/V		*-m* 4.10 (encl *-m*?)
b) encl *-m*	v. 10 (Gr.C)	

Ps 66

a) verb in past narr	pref 6.6	
	w-suff 17	
	pref // suff 6	
	w-suff // suff 17	
b) y/w opening syl		lost 4.5.14
c) relative pron		*'šr* 14.16.20
d) 3mpl suff on prep *l-*	v. 7	

Ps 68

a) y/w opening syl		lost 25
b) relative pron	*zū* 29	
	ze 9	
c) 3mpl suff on N/V		*-m* 28.28

Ps 72

a) y/w opening syl		lost 11
b) *-an-* plus *-hū*	*anhū* 15	
c) 3mpl suff on N/V		*-m* 14.14

Ps 73

a) y/w opening syl		lost 10.12.19
b) 3mpl suff on N/V	-*mw* 5.6.7	-*m* 4.9.17.18.20
on prep *l*-	vv. 6.10.18	
c) encl -*m* on prep *k*-	v. 15	

Ps 74

a) verb in past narr	pref 14	(8 suff)
	pref // suff 14	
b) relative pron	*ze* 2	
c) 3mpl suff on N/V		-*m* 4.8.17

Ps 77

a) verb in past narr	pref 17.17.18	suff // w-pref 19 (plus 8 suff)
	pref // suff 17.18	
b) y/w opening syl	preserved 4	lost 17.17

Ps 79

a) relative pron		'*šr* 6.6.12
b) 3mpl suff on N/V		-*m* 3.12.12
c) -*w*	v. 2	
d) encl -*m* on prep *k*-	v. 5	

Ps 80

a) verb in past narr	pref 9.9.12	w-pref // suff 10
	pref // w-pref 9	
b) y/w opening syl		lost 11
c) relative pron		'*šr* 16
d) 3mpl suff on N/V	-*mw* 6	-*m* 6
on prep *l*-	v. 7	

Ps 81

a) verb in past narr	pref 7.8.8.13	
	pref // suff 7.8	
	pref // w-pref 8.13	
b) 3mpl suff on N/V		-*m* 13.16

Ps 83

a) y/w opening syl	preserved 3	
b) relative pron		'*šr* 13
c) 3mpl suff on N/V	-*mw* 12.12.12	-*m* 5.9.16.16

Ps 88

a) y/w opening syl		lost 11
b) relative pron		'*šr* 6
c) 3mpl suff on N/V		-*m* 6
on prep *l*-	v. 9	
d) encl -*m* on prep *k*-	v. 6	

Ps 89

a) verb in past narr		(4 suff)
b) y/w opening syl		lost 6
c) relative pron		'*šr* 22.52.52
d) 3mpl suff on N/V	-*mw* 18	-*m* 10.12.13.33
e) encl -*m*	v. 51 (Gr.A)	
on prep *k*-	v. 47	

Ps 90

a) y/w opening syl		lost 9
b) 3mpl suff on N/V		*-m* 5.10
c) encl *-m* on prep *k-*	v. 9	

Ps 92

a) 3mpl suff on N/V		*-m* 8
b) encl *-m* on prep *k-*	v. 8	

Ps 95

a) verb in past narr	pref 10	w-pref initial 10
b) y/w opening syl		lost 8.9.9
c) relative pron		*'šr* 4 (textually dubious) 5 (" ") 9.11

Ps 99

a) verb in past narr	pref 6.7	
b) y/w opening syl		lost 3.5.9
c) 3mpl suff on N/V		*-m* 6.8.8
on prep *l-*	v. 7	

Ps 105

a) verb in past narr	pref (1) pref // w-pref (1)	w-pref (22, 10 initial) w-pref // suff (4)
b) y/w opening syl		lost 18.28
c) relative pron		*'šr* 5.9.26
d) 3mpl suff on N/V		*-m* 12.14.25 plus very often

Ps 106

a) verb in past narr	pref (6) pref // w-pref (6)	w-pref (54, 30 initial) w-pref // suff (4)
b) y/w opening syl		lost (9)
c) relative pron		*'šr* 34.38
d) 3mpl suff on N/V		*-m* 8.9.10 plus very often

Ps 119

a) y/w opening syl		lost 73.74.82 plus often
b) relative pron		*'šr* 38.39.47.48.49.63
c) 3mpl suff on N/V		*-m* 70.118.129 plus often
on prep *l-*	v. 165	

Ps 132

a) relative pron	*zō* 12	*'šr* 2
b) 3mpl suff on N/V		*-m* 12

Ps 138

a) verb in past narr	pref 3 pref // w-pref 3	
b) y/w opening syl		lost 4

Ps 139

a) verb in past narr	pref 13.16 pref // suff 13.16	
b) y/w opening syl		lost 16.18
c) relative pron		*'šr* 15.20
d) 3mpl suff on N/V		*-m* 16.18

Ps 140

a) y/w opening syl		lost 10(K). 14
b) relative pron		*'šr* 3.5
c) 3mpl suff on N/V	*-mw* 4.10.10	*-m* 11
d) encl *-m* on prep *k-*	v. 4	

Prv 8

a) verb in past narr	pref 29	w-pref initial 30 (plus 4 suff)
b) y/w opening syl		lost 11
c) 3mpl suff on N/V		*-m* 9

Prv 22:17-24:34

a) y/w opening syl		lost 22:28, 23:33, 24:31
b) relative pron	*ze* 23:22	*'šr* 22:28, 23:1, 24:29
c) 3mpl suff on N/V		*-m* 22:18.23, 23:11.11, 24:2.22
on prep *l-*	23:20	
d) encl *-m* on prep *k-*	23:7	

Prv 25-29

a) y/w opening syl	preserved 26:7	lost 25:7, 28:1.28, 29:16
b) relative pron		*'šr* 25:7.28
c) 3mpl suff on N/V		*-m* 28:28, 29:16

Canticles

a) verb in past narr		(25 suff)
b) y/w opening syl		lost 1:6, 2:12 plus often
c) 3mpl suff on N/V		*-m* 5:3, 6:6, etc.
d) encl *-m* on prep *k-*	6:10, 7:2	

Poems Whose Relationship to Early and Standard Poetry is Equivocal

These poems fall into two categories. First, many undatable poems contain a single early poetic form and no evidence of archaizing. While it is theoretically possible that they are early, the one early form cannot be admitted as evidence of their antiquity, because a similar distribution of forms is present in standard poetry. The poems in this category are:

Gen 9:26-27

a) 3mpl suff on prep *l-*	v. 26.26

Ps 50

a) *-w*	v. 10

Ps 61

a) encl *-m* on prep *k-*	v. 7

Ps 63

a) encl *-m* on prep *k-*	v. 6

Ps 101

a) *-y* I	v. 5

Ps 110

a) *-y* II	v. 4

	Ps 113
a) -*y* I	vv. 5.6.7.9

	Ps 116
a) verb in past narr	pref 3.4 pref // suff 3

	Ps 123
a) -*y* I	v. 1

	Ps 141
a) encl -*m* on prep *k*-	v. 7

	Ps 142
a) relative pron	*zū* 4

	Ps 143
a) relative pron	*zū* 8

Second, a limited number of poems resemble early poetry in that they manifest more early forms than any standard poems, but resemble standard poetry in that they contain evidence of archaizing. Four poems within this group contain three early forms, exclusive of -*mw* and enclitic -*m* on prepositions:

	Balaam Oracles	
a) y/w opening	preserved 24.6	
b) relative pron		(*'šr* 24:4, but must be deleted)
c) 3mpl suff on N/V		-*m* 23:22
d) -*w*	vv. 23:18, 24:3.15	
e) encl -*m*	24:19 (Gr.A)	

	Ps 78	
a) verb in past narr	pref (17) pref // suff (3) pref // w-pref (9)	w-pref (56, 37 initial) w-pref // suff (15)
b) y/w opening syl	preserved 44	lost (9)
c) relative pron	*ze* 54	*'šr* (7)
d) 3mpl suff on N/V on prep *l*-	vv. 24.66	-*m* 3.5.7.8 plus often

	Ps 104	
a) verb in past narr	pref (4) pref // suff (1)	
b) y/w opening syl		lost 8.11
c) relative pron	*ze* 8.26	*'šr* 16.17 (textually dubious)
d) 3mpl suff on N/V		-*m* 11.21.22.24.27.27.29.35
e) -*w*	vv. 11.20	

	Ps 114	
a) verb in past narr	pref 3 pref // w-pref // suff 3	w-pref // suff (// pref) 3
b) -*y* I	v. 8	
c) -*w*	v. 8	

Two others have more than three early forms, exclusive of *-mw* and enclitic *-m* on prepositions:

Dt 32

a)	verb in past narr	pref (19) pref // w-pref (1)	w-pref (7, 4 initial) w-pref // suff (1)
b)	y/w opening syl	preserved 37	lost 38.39
c)	relative pron		'šr 38 (textually dubious)
d)	*-an-* plus *-hū*	*-anhū* 10.10.10	
e)	3mpl suff on N/V	*-mw* (4)	*-m* (11)
	on prep *l-*	vv. 32.35	
	on prep *ᶜl*	v. 23	

Job

a)	verb in past narr	pref (25) pref // suff (2) pref // w-pref (3) w-suff (3) suff // w-suff (3)	w-pref (14, 5 initial) w-pref // suff (3)
b)	y/w opening syl	preserved 19:2, 21:38	lost 3:16 plus very often
c)	relative pron	*ze* 15:17, 19:19	'šr 3:23, 4:8.19 plus very often
d)	3mpl suff on N/V	*-mw* 27:23	*-m* 4:19.19, 5:5 plus very often
	on prep *l-*	(10)	
	on prep *ᶜl*	(8)	
e)	encl *-m*	4:20, 15:18, 31:11 (Gr.A) 7:15, 8:18 (Gr.C)	
	on prep *k-*	(11)	
	on prep *b-*	(5)	
	on prep *l-*	(4)	

CHAPTER FIVE
EVALUATION

Evaluation of the Method

A. *Evidence of Archaizing*

In the last three chapters the results of an application of linguistic methodology to the problem of dating early Hebrew poetry have been described. Before evaluating these results in detail it is necessary to confront two methodological problems. The first concerns the use of *'šr*, the 3mpl suffix *-m*, the loss of y/w opening a syllable, and the verbal patterns of standard poetic Hebrew as evidence of archaizing. Already the difficulties involved in the use of *'šr* and *-m* have been commented upon. And we must confess that we do not know when a syllable-opening y/w began to be elided, nor when the verbal forms of standard poetic Hebrew began to supplant the early forms. We must reckon with the possibility that both of these processes began very early, so that not only *'šr* and *-m* but an elided y/w and the verbal forms of standard poetic Hebrew might have been present in the earliest Israelite poetry.

To be sure, we do have one poem which manifests an extraordinary concentration of early forms without simultaneously exhibiting any later forms: Ex 15. And there is ample opportunity in this poem for later forms to crop up. Virtually the entire poem is past narrative, no less than nine verbs or nouns receive the 3mpl pronominal suffix, and the relative pronoun occurs twice, albeit in similar phrases. Thus, Ex 15 tends to support the proposition that at the beginning of the historical period the forms of standard poetic Hebrew were absent from Hebrew poetry. But despite the strength of this evidence, it cannot prove that they were not existent already in the early period. So it is necessary to evaluate the data described in chapters two through four under the assumption that the presence of standard poetic forms does not constitute evidence for archaizing.

In this re-evaluation, the rationale for using the presence of early forms as evidence of an early date is somewhat modified. Heretofore, our argument has been that a poem should be dated early if it contains forms in common use in the early period. But if the forms of standard poetic Hebrew are present in early poetry, then already in early poetry what we have been calling early poetic forms are archaisms or in the process of becoming so. Hence, this argument becomes inapplicable. We would, however, still expect early poems to contain a far greater concentration of archaic forms than poems of a much later date. And that a concentration of archaic forms is absent from standard poetry confirms our expectation. When, therefore, a concentration of them does occur, it is likely to be evidence of an early date. So, on the need for a clustering effect our present argument does not differ from our former one, though the justification for entering this clustering as evidence is not the same for the two. But the major difference between them lies elsewhere. If standard poetic forms are present already in early poetic Hebrew, then their occurrence in a poem cannot count against an early date. We are left without a test for archaizing.

Now for the re-evaluation. Concerning individual forms, we found that only two occur with sufficient density in any one poem to be significant for dating: verbal patterns in past narrative and the 3mpl suffix *-mw*. Verbal patterns of early poetry occur extensively in Ex 15, Jud 5, Hab 3, 2 S 22 = Ps 18, Dt 32 and Job. Only in Job are the patterns of standard poetic Hebrew at all distinctly discernible. According to the present argument, this fact need not deter us from using the presence of the early patterns as evidence of an early date. Numerous instances of the 3mpl suffix *-mw* occur in Ex 15, Dt 32, Ps 2, Ps 59, Ps 73 and Job. Assuming that the presence of *-m* is evidence of archaizing, only its concentration in Ex 15 is of value for dating. Assuming the contrary, its concentration in the other poems is also of value.

Turning to a consideration of the clustering of individual forms, it is at this point that the forms listed in the *Excursus* at the end of chapter three are relevant. It is virtually certain that they are already archaic in the earliest Hebrew poetry. We are here assessing the case for an early date on the assumption that all the other early forms are also archaic in early poetry. Thus, in evaluating the cumulative evidence the two groups can be merged. When this is done, no alterations in the picture presented by standard poetry result, for all of the forms listed in the *Excursus* occur in poems otherwise having none or only one archaism:

Isa 28:1-4
-an(na) 3 (Gr.A)

Hos 4:1-10
conj *p-* 2 (Gr.C)

Obadiah
-y I 3
-an(na) 13 (Gr.A)

Nah 2:1-22
-ahū 4

But the total number of early forms in two undatable poems, Dt 33 and Jud 5, is raised above the total found in any standard poem, exclusive of enclitic *-m* or *-mw* on prepositions:

Dt 33
-y II 16
encl *-m* 11 (Gr.A)
encl *-m* on *l-* 22
-an(na) 7 (Gr.A)
infixed *-t-* 3 (Gr.C)

Jud 5
Verb pref (6)
w-suff (3)
pref // suff (2)
suff // w-suff (1)
ze 5
-an(na) 26 (Gr.C)

Admittedly, however, since the third form in Jud 5 is a questionable reconstruction of the energetic ending, the total there cannot be taken very seriously. Otherwise in undatable poetry forms from the Excursus occur in poems containing either an insignificant number of early forms:

    Gen 49
    -*y* I 11a
    -*y* II 11b
    -*an(na)* 19 (Gr.C)

    Nah 1:1-10
    -*ahū* 8.9
    -*taqtulu(ū)* 9b (Gr.C)

    Ps 28
    -*mw* on *l*- 8
    lost of *he* in H stem 7

    Ps 45
    -*mw* 17
    lost of *he* of H stem 18

    Ps 50
    -*w* 10
    p- 10 (Gr.A)

    Hab 3:10
    verb pref (9)
        pref // suff (2)
    encl -*m* on *k*- 14
    -*ahū* 10

    Ps 68
    zū 29
    ze 9

    Ps 116
    verb pref (2)
        pref // suff (1)
    lost of *he* of H stem 6

    Prv 1:20-33
    -*an(na)* 20 (Gr.A)

    Prv 8
    verb pref 29
    -*an(na)* 3 (Gr.A)

    Prv 25-29
    y/w opening syl 26:7
    -*ahū* 29:18

or a large number of forms:

    Dt 32
    verb pref (19)
        pref // w-pref (1)
    y/w opening syl 37
    -*anhu* 10.10.10
    -*mw* (4)
    -*mw* on *l*- 32.35
    -*mw* on ^c*l* 23
    3fs suff conj ending -*t* 36

    Job
    verb pref (25)
        pref // suff (2)
        pref // w-pref (3)
        w-suff (3)
        w-suff // suff (3)
    y/w opening syl 19:2, 31:38
    ze 15:17, 19:19
    -*mw* 27:23
    -*mw* on *l*- (10)
    -*mw* on ^c*l* (8)
    encl -*m* 4:20, 15:18, 31:11 (Gr.A)
                7:15, 8:18 (Gr.C)
    encl -*m* on *k*- (11)
    encl -*m* on *b*- (5)
    encl -*m* on *l*- (4)
    -*ahū* 24:23
    -*an(na)* 39:23 (Gr.A)
    p- 9:10 (Gr.A)

Even after the addition of these forms what is unquestionably significant clustering still occurs only in Ex 15, Dt 32 and Job. Assuming that the presence of standard poetic forms is evidence of archaizing, this clustering is evidence of an early date only for Ex 15. Assuming the contrary, it is evidence of an early date also for Dt 32 and Job. Clustering of a lower order occurs in the Balaam Oracles, Dt 33, Jud 5, and Pss 78, 104, and 114. Under the former assumption the value of even this moderate clustering is cancelled by the presence of standard forms within these same poems. Under the latter assumption this negative evidence is ruled out of court.

B. *Prophetic Versus Psalmodic Types*

The second methodological problem arises out of the fact that most of the poetry datable to the eighth century or thereafter--and all of it coming from the eighth century itself--is prophetic, whereas most of the poetry exhibiting evidence of an early date is psalmodic. Therefore, that the latter manifests a substantially greater number of early forms than the former may be a function, not of date, but of a difference in type. It may be that psalmodic types, originating in the midst of a conservatively oriented cult, preserved ancient grammatical forms far longer than did other poetic traditions in Israel, so that by the eighth century prophetic types had shed archaic forms but psalmodic types had not. A psalm might look old, but not be old.[1a]

This consideration means that the results described in the preceding pages cannot be accepted until we find reasonable reassurance that by the eighth century psalmodic types as well as prophetic types retained only vestiges of early forms. A demonstration that certain psalms written in standard poetic Hebrew must surely be dated in or around the eighth century would go a long way toward reassuring us. But this is a well-nigh impossible task. The dating of individual psalms is a most precarious undertaking. Usually all that can be said is that nothing absolutely prohibits a dating in such and such a time; positive evidence favoring such a date is seldom forthcoming.

Positive clues suggesting a date between 930 and 721 can be detected, however, in at least one psalm. This is Ps 78. The forms of standard poetic Hebrew are overwhelmingly predominant in it. And yet it manifests more pref forms referring to simple events in the past and a more extensive clustering than do other poems written in standard poetic Hebrew. This suggests that it may come from a period in which standard forms have only recently replaced the early ones. Such an explanation accounts both for the predominance of the former and the abnormally high incidence of the latter. Thus, fixing the probable date of this psalm between 930 and 721 would be doubly important. Not only would it show that the forms of standard poetic Hebrew were predominant in psalmodic types as well as prophetic types by this date, but also would hint that they gained ascendency not too long before this.

1a. Cf. M. Tsevat, *A Study of the Language of the Biblical Psalms*, JBL Monograph Series (Philadelphia, 1955).

The reason for dating Ps 78 between 930 and 721 is the polemic against the northern kingdom which is evident at three places in the psalm. In vv. 9-10 the Ephraimites are accused of retreating on the day of battle, thus breaking their covenant with Yahweh. In vv. 56-64 the defeat at Shiloh is said to be the result of God's rejection of Israel because of her idolatry. And, finally, in vv. 65-72 the rejection of the northern kingdom in favor of Judah and the house of David is narrated. Simply put, the contention here is that this polemic can best be understood by dating Ps 78 in the period of the divided monarchy. Its *raison d'etre* would be the legitimation of Judah as the Yahweh-chosen successor to the empire of David and Solomon in a period when the two kingdoms were battling ideologically as well as politically and militarily.

Amazingly enough, however, none of the three dates most commonly assigned to Ps 78 fall within this period. Eissfeldt defends a united monarchy date.[1] The psalm, he says, presents an explanation of why the seat of political and cultic authority passed from Shiloh to Jerusalem. The reason is found in the idolatry of the Ephraimites in the time of Eli, when the ark resided at Shiloh. This idolatry occasioned the defeat of the middle Palestinian tribes by the Philistines and loss of the ark. As a result Yahweh rejected the tribes of Joseph and chose David, a Judean, to rule in Jerusalem.

The principal difficulty with this interpretation is that, for two reasons, David's choice of Jerusalem for the seat of his kingdom cannot easily be interpreted as a rejection of Ephraim in favor of Judah: one, Jerusalem, though within the territorial boundaries of Judah, did not belong to the tribe of Judah, but to the Jebusites; two, the choice of the neutral site was one of the factors that helped to conciliate the northern tribes for the loss of their political autonomy. It is, therefore, highly doubtful whether an Ephraimite or a Judean would have viewed such a choice as a rejection by Yahweh of the former. It is much more likely that Yahweh's choice of Judah, Zion, and David mentioned in vv. 67-72 refers to the southern kingdom of Judah after the division of the united monarchy.

Many scholars, on the other extreme, defend a post-exilic date.[2] They refer the controversy between Ephraim and Judah to the Samaritan schism. While a conceivable interpretation, it is most unlikely, since the poem contains no hint that it should be interpreted allegorically.

Most assign Ps 78 to the time of the deuteronomistic reforms under Josiah or perhaps a little later.[3] But, since the northern kingdom has long

---

1. Otto Eissfeldt, *Das Lied Moses Deuteronomium 32:1-43 und Das Lehrgedicht Asaphs Psalm 78 samt einer Analyse der Umgebung des Mose-Liedes* (Berlin, 1958).

2. H. J. Kraus, *Psalmen* (Neukirchen, 1960) pp. 535ff.

3. See the discussion in Kraus.

since met disaster by this time, they are hard put to explain the polemic against it. And it is now generally agreed that the sources of Deuteronomy, both as to its phraseology and its theology of history, were not innovations of the seventh century, but extend far back into Israel's history. Just because a psalm has a distinctly Deuteronomistic flavor does not mean that it should be dated in or around Josiah's time.[4]

It is likely, then, that Ps 78 should be dated in the period of the divided monarchy. But the probability of error in this type of dating is very high. Hence, the attempt to demonstrate by means of dating individual psalms that by the eighth century psalmodic traditions of poetic composition were no more archaizing than prophetic traditions must be judged inconclusive, though suggestive. All is not lost, however, for two arguments of a more general nature can be brought into play at this point.

First, in spite of our inability to date specific psalms incontrovertibly to the pre-exilic period, it is virtually certain that a very large number of them do derive from this period.[5] We now know that most of the psalms are not the outpouring of individual piety, but were composed in intimate connection with the ongoing celebration of the cult. And the most extensive creative flowering of the cult in ancient Israel was in the first Solomonic temple. These two considerations lead inexorably to the conclusion that most of the psalms were composed during the lifetime of this temple. Not that no psalms were composed in the second temple! Some undoubtedly were, but, notwithstanding its many innovations, the second temple was essentially a derivative of the first. Thus, it is only reasonable to expect that its hymnody was likewise derived. Now, if most of the psalms were composed in the pre-exilic period, it is also likely that a substantial number were composed in the first half of this period. For example, we can be quite sure that many of the so-called royal and Zion psalms were composed before the career of Isaiah, for the motifs and the theology found in them are determinative of much of his message.

When the above facts are correlated with the fact that all but a mere handful of psalms, when considered one by one, do not more significantly

---

4. Eissfeldt points out, in regard to the Deuteronomistic theology of history exhibited by Ps 78, that this same understanding of history is explicitly stated in the Mesha Stone, c.850. Mesha states that the displeasure of Chemosh with his people was responsible for Moab's past defeats by Israel and that his renewed approbation has led to Mesha's victories over Israel celebrated on the stone. In regard to the reference to "high places" in v. 58, he points out that already in Jud 6 Gideon tears down a high place dedicated to Baal.

5. Cf. the statement by Otto Eissfeldt, *The Old Testament an Introduction*, trans. P. R. Ackroyd (New York, 1965), "In recent Psalm study, there is a tendency, unlike that of Psalm study at about the turn of the last century, to ascribe at least a substantial number of psalms to the pre-exilic period, even to the early pre-exilic period," p. 448.

resemble early poetic Hebrew than do prophetic poems of the eighth century and after, the inevitable conclusion is that psalmodic composition is no more archaistic than prophetic composition in the pre-exilic period. The argument can be stated succinctly as follows: most of the psalms are pre-exilic; also, most of the psalms resemble pre-exilic prophetic poems in the use of archaic forms; thus the probability is very high that many of the psalms that resemble prophetic poetry are at the same time pre-exilic. Therefore, psalmodic poetic composition probably resembles prophetic poetic composition in the pre-exilic period.

A second argument of a more general nature reinforces the conclusions arrived at by the first. It has become increasingly clear in recent years that the prophetic class stands in a much more integral relationship with the cult than was ever suspected in the past, even performing certain cultic functions. Whether any of the writing prophets are cult prophets in the technical sense is open to dispute, but it is generally conceded that cultic types and phraseology have influenced prophetic diction.[6] Given this state of affairs, one would have to expect that the prophets borrowed from the cultic diction in common use in their day. Therefore, prophetic speech can be used as a mirror by which to learn of cultic speech. If, then, prophetic diction of the eighth century does not resemble early poetic Hebrew, neither should psalmodic diction.

In conclusion, while no psalm datable on non-linguistic criteria to the early pre-exilic period can be found, it is possible to determine by indirect routes that psalmodic composition in this period was no more archaic than prophetic composition of the same period.

Evaluation of the Results

A clustering of the linguistic forms studied in the preceding chapters is a precondition for their use as evidence of an early date. The clustering may be one of two kinds. Either a sizable number of examples of one form must occur in a given poem, or a sizable number of different forms, each of which may occur only once. Given this prerequisite only a very small number of poems contain linguistic evidence of an early date: Ex 15, Dt 32, Jud 5, 2 S 22 = Ps 18, Hab 3 and Job. Of these Ex 15, Dt 32 and Job contain both kinds of clustering. Jud 5, 2 S 22 = Ps 18 and Hab 3 manifest only the first type.

If the presence of forms characteristic of standard poetic Hebrew is not an indication of archaizing, then, the early forms in these poems can be used as evidence of an early date without qualification. Under this condition we cannot specify more precisely the date of any of these poems, except to say that they belong in the early period. The time span we are dealing with, from

---

6. Cf. Eissfeldt, *The Old Testament An Introduction*, pp. 80f.

the 13th century (the date of our reconstructed early poetic Hebrew) to the eighth century (the date we know positively that standard poetic Hebrew is in common use) is far too extensive to permit even guesses as to absolute dates. Nor can we establish even a relative chronology.

If, however, the presence of forms characteristic of standard poetic Hebrew is indicative of archaizing, then, only the forms in Ex 15 can be used without qualification as evidence of an early date, for it lacks standard forms. The use of early forms in Dt 32, Jud 5, 2 S 22 = Ps 18, Hab 3 and Job must be qualified, for each one contains standard forms. None of them, with the possible exception of Job, exhibit any significant number of verbal forms characteristic of standard poetic Hebrew. But they do have other standard forms: Dt 32, 2 S 22 = Ps 18, Hab 3 and Job a considerable number, Jud 5 a very few, most of which are textually suspect.

The precise nature of this qualification is unclear, however. It may be that the presence of standard forms renders utterly useless the evidential value of the early forms. In other words, perhaps we should take the presence of standard forms as indicative of conscious archaizing and altogether disregard the presence of early forms. On the other hand, it may be that the presence of standard forms along with a clustering of early ones indicates an origin in the period of transition from early to standard poetic Hebrew. In such a period one would expect the older forms to maintain much of their old vitality, and so to occur frequently, not merely vestigially. Also, one would expect the younger forms to be growing in popularity, and so also to occur frequently.

It is not possible to opt confidently for either of these alternatives. The presence of standard forms cannot but pose conscious archaizing as a viable alternative. But, then, in no poem datable to the eighth century or afterwards is there a clustering of early forms. Possibly we are faced with a both-and alternative. Some may have been composed in the transition period and others much later by archaizing authors.

If some were composed in the period of transition, then, we can tentatively propose the following relative chronology: oldest is Ex 15, which contains no standard forms; possibly next, at the beginning of the transition period, should come Jud 5, which manifests numerous early forms, a very few standard ones; next, in the transition period, come Dt 32, 2 S 22 = Ps 18, Hab 3 and Job, all of which contain numerous examples of both; then, shortly after this period, when the forms of standard poetic Hebrew have become firmly rooted, comes Ps 78, where standard forms are overwhelmingly predominant, but where early ones are more numerous than in standard poetry; and, finally, comes all undatable poetry that resembles standard poetry, in which only traces of early forms are visible.

Any attempt to anchor this relative chronology in time is most precarious. Only very indefinite guidelines can be sighted. We know that standard poetic Hebrew has altogether supplanted early poetic Hebrew by the eighth century. For how many years previous this situation obtained is unknown. We have proposed that our reconstructed early poetic Hebrew was current in the thirteenth century. How much longer it continued in common use is unknown. In the stretch of time between the thirteenth and eighth centuries, the single most momentous political and cultural event in Israel was the rise of the monarchy under David and Solomon. If this event had a leveling effect on the language, thereby promoting the exclusive use of standard poetic Hebrew, then, we can set the period of transition as roughly contemporaneous with the United Kingdom.

Within these guidelines we can propose as a working hypothesis the following absolute chronology: Ex 15 should be dated in the twelfth century; Jud 5 possibly at the end of that century; Dt 32, 2 S 22 = Ps 18, Hab 3 and Job in the eleventh-tenth centuries; Ps 78 in the late tenth or early ninth; and poems resembling standard poetry in the ninth or thereafter.

It is crucial to keep distinctly in mind the extremely tenuous nature of the relative and absolute chronologies just described. They are constructions whose girders are "ifs." They are working hypotheses, nothing more. Even without impugning the soundness of the methodology employed in this study, not only the leveling effect imputed to the united monarchy, but also the legitimacy of using the presence of early forms in Dt 32, Jud 5, 2 S 22 = Ps 18, Hab 3, Job and Ps 78 as a clue to their date can be seriously challenged. But what cannot be challenged without first exposing the inadequacies of the methodology is the use of linguistic evidence as a very strong argument for dating Ex 15 early. This is the one unequivocal, firmly grounded conclusion of this study.

Many poems alleged to be early by scholars do not yield, according to this study, positive linguistic evidence of their antiquity. It is well to reflect briefly on this state of affairs. Some of them exhibit numerous forms of standard poetic Hebrew (e.g. Gen 49 and Dt 33). If the presence of these forms is indicative of archaizing, then, a revision of currently held opinion is in order.[7] If not, then, no evidence has been uncovered by this study which would count against their being early. Many other allegedly early poems exhibit no evidence of archaizing, but neither do they manifest a clustering of early forms. As for these, this study occasions no suspicion of their antiquity. But it does prohibit the use of what early forms they do contain as evidence of this fact.

---

7. It must be remembered, however, that both of these poems are collections of smaller independent units. Thus, the dating of one unit says nothing about the date of the others.

The results of this study harmonize nicely with the results of many previous essays, linguistic and otherwise, to date Hebrew poetry, but are discordant with others. For example, the studies of Cross and Freedman, using almost exclusively morphological, lexical and prosodic evidence, concur in dating Ex 15, Jud 5 and 2 S 22 = Ps 18 early.[8] Eissfeldt, using non-linguistic evidence exclusively, agrees in dating Dt 32 early.[9] But, on the other hand, Noth, using primarily form critical methodology, dates Ex 15 late.[1] And rare indeed is a man who would date Job early. It is pointless to extend the list. These examples are sufficient to set the problem. Hopefully, the present study will contribute significantly to the ongoing discussion.

---

8. The relevant essays of Cross and Freedman are collected in SAYP.

9. Eissfeldt, *Das Lied Moses*.

1. Martin Noth, *Exodus*, trans. J. S. Bowden (Philadelphia, 1962).

B I B L I O G R A P H Y

Albright, W. F., "The Oracles of Balaam," JBL 63 (1944) 207-33.

__________, "The Old Testament and Canaanite Language and Literature," CBQ 7 (1945) 5-31.

__________, "The Psalm of Habakkuk," *Studies in Old Testament Prophecy* (ed. H. H. Rowley, Edinburgh, T & T Clark, 1950) pp. 1-18.

__________, "A Catalogue of Early Hebrew Lyric Poems (Psalm 68)," HUCA 23 (1950-51) 1-39.

__________, "Some Canaanite-Phoenician Sources of Hebrew Wisdom," *Wisdom in Israel and in the Ancient Near East, Supplements to Vetus Testamentum* 3 (Leiden, 1955) 1-15.

__________ and W. L. Moran, "A Re-interpretation of an Amarna Letter from Byblos (EA 82)," JCS 2 (1948) 239-48.

Allegro, J. M., "Uses of the Semitic Demonstrative Element *z* in Hebrew," VT 5 (1955) 309-12.

Barth, J., "Die Casusreste im Hebräischen," ZDMG 53 (1899) 593-99.

Calderone, P. J., "The Rivers of *Maṣor*," *Biblica* 42 (1961) 423-32.

Cross, F. M. Jr., *Studies in Ancient Yahwistic Poetry*, Dissertation, Johns Hopkins University, Baltimore, 1950.

__________, and D. N. Freedman, "The Blessing of Moses," JBL 67 (1948) 191-210.

__________, and __________, *Early Hebrew Orthography: A Study of the Epigraphic Evidence*, American Oriental Series 36, New Haven, Yale University Press, 1952.

__________, and __________, "A Royal Song of Thanksgiving - II Samuel 22 = Ps 18," JBL 72 (1953) 15-34.

__________, and __________, "The Song of Miriam," JNES 14 (1955) 237-50.

Dahood, M., "Canaanite-Phoenician Influences in Qoheleth," *Biblica* 33 (1952) 30-52, 191-221.

__________, "Some Northwest Semitic Words in Job," *Biblica* 38 (1957) 306-20.

__________, "Some Ambiguous Texts in Isaias," CBQ 20 (1958) 41-49.

__________, *Northwest Semitic Philology and Job, The Bible in Current Catholic Thought*, ed. J. L. McKenzie (New York, Herder and Herder, 1962) pp. 55-74.

__________, "Philological Notes on Jer 18:14-15," ZAW 74 (1962) 207-09.

__________, *Proverbs and Northwest Semitic Philology*, Rome, Pontifical Biblical Institute, 1963.

Driver, G. R., "Hebrew Notes on Prophets and Proverbs," JTS 41 (1940) 162-75.

__________, "Hebrew Studies," JRAS (1948) 164-65.

Eissfeldt, O., *Das Lied Moses Deuteronomium 32:1-43 und Das Lehrgedicht Asaphs Psalm 78; samt einer Analyse der Umgebung des Mose-Liedes*. Berichte über die Verhandlungen der Sächsischen Akademie der Wissenschaften zu Leipzig, philologisch-historische Klasse, Band 104, Heft 5, Berlin, Akademie-Verlag, 1958.

Freedman, D. N., "Notes on Genesis," ZAW 64 (1952) 190-94.

__________, "Archaic Forms in Early Hebrew Poetry," ZAW 72 (1960) 101-07.

Garbini, G., "La Congiunzione Semitica **pa-*," *Biblica* 38 (1957) 419-27.

Gaster, T. H., "Psalm 29," JQR 37 (1946) 55-65.

__________, "An Ancient Eulogy on Israel: Deuteronomy 33:3-5, 26-29," JBL 66 (1947) 53-62.

Ginsberg, H. L., *Kitvê Ugarit*, Jerusalem, 1936.

__________, "Some Emendations in Isaiah," JBL 69 (1950) 51-60.

Goetze, A., "The Tenses of Ugaritic," JAOS 58 (1939) 266-309.

Harris, Z. S., *The Development of the Canaanite Dialects*, New Haven, American Oriental Society, 1939.

Held, M., "The YQTL-QTL (QTL-YQTL) Sequence of Identical Verbs in Biblical Hebrew and in Ugaritic," *Studies and Essays in Honor of Abraham A. Neuman*, ed. by Meir ben-Horin *et al* (Brill, Leiden for Dropsie College, Philadelphia, 1962) pp. 281-90.

Hummel, H. D., "Enclitic *Mem* in Early Northwest Semitic, especially Hebrew," JBL 76 (1957) 85-107.

Iwry, S., "Notes on Psalm 68," JBL 71 (1952) 161-65.

Jirku, A., "Eine Renaissance des Hebräischen," FF 32 (1958) 211-12.

Milik, J. T., "Deux Documents inédits du Désert de Juda," *Biblica* 38 (1957) 245-68.

Moran, W. L., "The Putative Root *ᶜtm* in Isa 9:18," CBQ 12 (1950) 153-54.

__________, "The Use of the Canaanite Infinitive Absolute as a Finite Verb in the Amarna Letters from Byblos," JCS 4 (1950) 169-72.

__________, "New Evidence on Canaanite *taqtulū(na)*," JCS 5 (1951) 33-35.

__________, "'Does Amarna Bear on Karatepe?'--An Answer," JCS 6 (1952) 76-80.

__________, "The Hebrew Language in its Northwest Semitic Background," *The Bible and the Ancient Near East*, ed. G. E. Wright (Garden City, New York, Doubleday, 1961) pp. 54-72.

Obermann, J., "Does Amarna Bear on Karatepe?" JCS 5 (1951) 58-61.

O'Callaghan, R. T., "Echoes of Canaanite Literature in the Psalms," VT 4 (1954) 164-76.

Patton, J. H., *Canaanite Parallels in the Book of Psalms*, Baltimore, The Johns Hopkins Press, 1944.

Pope, M. H., "Ugaritic Enclitic *-m*," JCS 5 (1951) 123-28.

__________, *El in the Ugaritic Texts*, *Supplements to Vetus Testamentum* 2, Leiden, Brill, 1955.

__________, *Job*, New York, Doubleday, 1965.

Sarna, N. M., "Some Instances of the enclitic *-m* in Job," JJS 6 (1955) 108-10.

Saydon, P. P., "The Use of Tenses in Deutero-Isaiah," *Biblica* 40 (1959) 290-301.

Singer, A. D., "The Vocative in Ugaritic," JCS 2 (1948) 1-10.

Tsevat, M., *A Study of the Language of the Biblical Psalms*, JBL Monograph Series 9, Philadelphia, Society of Biblical Literature, 1955.

Weiss, R., "On Ligatures in the Hebrew Bible (*m*=*nw*)," JBL 83 (1963) 188-94.

www.ingramcontent.com/pod-product-compliance
Lightning Source LLC
Chambersburg PA
CBHW022104160426
43198CB00008B/351
9781628372458